BUYING A HOME IN GREECE AND CYPRUS

by

Joanna Styles

SURVIVAL BOOKS • LONDON • ENGLAND

First published 2000
Second edition 2001

Survival Books Limited, 1st Floor, 60 St. James's Street,
London SW1A 1ZN, United Kingdom
☎ +44 (0)207-493 4244, 📧 +44 (0)207-491 0605
✉ info@survivalbooks.net
💻 www.survivalbooks.net

British Library Cataloguing in Publication Data.
A CIP record for this book is available from the British Library.
ISBN 1 901130 47 9

Printed and bound in Italy by LegoPrint

ACKNOWLEDGEMENTS

My sincere thanks to all those who contributed to the successful publication of this book, in particular the many people who took the time and trouble to read and comment on the draft versions. I would especially like to thank David Hampshire (editor), Joanna Styles (regions, research, re-writing and updating), Athina Tsakirakis (for her excellent research on Greece), Joe & Kerry Laredo (proof-reading and formatting), Graham Cockroft (Cymply Cyprus), Fivos Hadjigeorgiou (Tritonia Developers), Karen Verheul, Veronica Orchard and Ron & Pat Scarborough for their help and everyone else who contributed in any way whom I have omitted to mention. Also a special thank-you to Jim Watson for the superb illustrations, cartoons, maps and cover.

By the same publisher:

The Alien's Guide to Britain
The Alien's Guide to France
Buying a Home Abroad
Buying a Home in Britain
Buying a Home in Florida
Buying a Home in France
Buying a Home in Ireland
Buying a Home in Italy
Buying a Home in Portugal
Buying a Home in Spain
Living and Working Abroad
Living and Working in America
Living and Working in Australia
Living and Working in Britain
Living and Working in Canada
Living and Working in France
Living and Working in Germany
**Living and Working in Holland, Belgium
  and Luxembourg**
Living and Working in Ireland
Living and Working in Italy
Living and Working in London
Living and Working in New Zealand
Living and Working in Spain
Living and Working in Switzerland
Rioja and its Wines
The Wines of Spain

What Readers and Reviewers

When you buy a model plane for your child, a video recorder, or some new computer gizmo, you get with it a leaflet or booklet pleading 'Read Me First', or bearing large friendly letters or bold type saying 'IMPORTANT – follow the instructions carefully'. This book should be similarly supplied to all those entering France with anything more durable than a 5-day return ticket. It is worth reading even if you are just visiting briefly, or if you have lived here for years and feel totally knowledgeable and secure. But if you need to find out how France works then it is indispensable. Native French people probably have a less thorough understanding of how their country functions. – Where it is most essential, the book is most up to the minute.

Living France

We would like to congratulate you on this work: it is really super! We hand it out to our expatriates and they read it with great interest and pleasure.

ICI (Switzerland) AG

Rarely has a 'survival guide' contained such useful advice This book dispels doubts for first-time travellers, yet is also useful for seasoned globetrotters – In a word, if you're planning to move to the USA or go there for a long-term stay, then buy this book both for general reading and as a ready-reference.

American Citizens Abroad

It is everything you always wanted to ask but didn't for fear of the contemptuous put down – The best English-language guide – Its pages are stuffed with practical information on everyday subjects and are designed to complement the traditional guidebook.

Swiss News

A complete revelation to me – I found it both enlightening and interesting, not to mention amusing.

Carole Clark

Let's say it at once. David Hampshire's Living and Working in France is the best handbook ever produced for visitors and foreign residents in this country; indeed, my discussion with locals showed that it has much to teach even those born and bred in l'Hexagone – It is Hampshire's meticulous detail which lifts his work way beyond the range of other books with similar titles. Often you think of a supplementary question and search for the answer in vain. With Hampshire this is rarely the case – He writes with great clarity (and gives French equivalents of all key terms), a touch of humour and a ready eye for the odd (and often illuminating) fact – This book is absolutely indispensable.

The Riviera Reporter

The ultimate reference book – Every conceivable subject imaginable is exhaustively explained in simple terms – An excellent introduction to fully enjoy all that this fine country has to offer and save time and money in the process.

American Club of Zurich

Have Said About Survival Books

What a great work, wealth of useful information, well-balanced wording and accuracy in details. My compliments!

Thomas Müller

This handbook has all the practical information one needs to set up home in the UK – The sheer volume of information is almost daunting – Highly recommended for anyone moving to the UK.

American Citizens Abroad

A very good book which has answered so many questions and even some I hadn't thought of – I would certainly recommend it.

Brian Fairman

A mine of information – I may have avoided some embarrassments and frights if I had read it prior to my first Swiss encounters – Deserves an honoured place on any newcomer's bookshelf.

English Teachers Association, Switzerland

Covers just about all the things you want to know on the subject – In answer to the desert island question about the one how-to book on France, this book would be it – Almost 500 pages of solid accurate reading – This book is about enjoyment as much as survival.

The Recorder

It's so funny – I love it and definitely need a copy of my own – Thanks very much for having written such a humorous and helpful book.

Heidi Guiliani

A must for all foreigners coming to Switzerland.

Antoinette O'Donoghue

A comprehensive guide to all things French, written in a highly readable and amusing style, for anyone planning to live, work or retire in France.

The Times

A concise, thorough account of the DOs and DON'Ts for a foreigner in Switzerland – Crammed with useful information and lightened with humorous quips which make the facts more readable.

American Citizens Abroad

Covers every conceivable question that may be asked concerning everyday life – I know of no other book that could take the place of this one.

France in Print

Hats off to Living and Working in Switzerland!

Ronnie Almeida

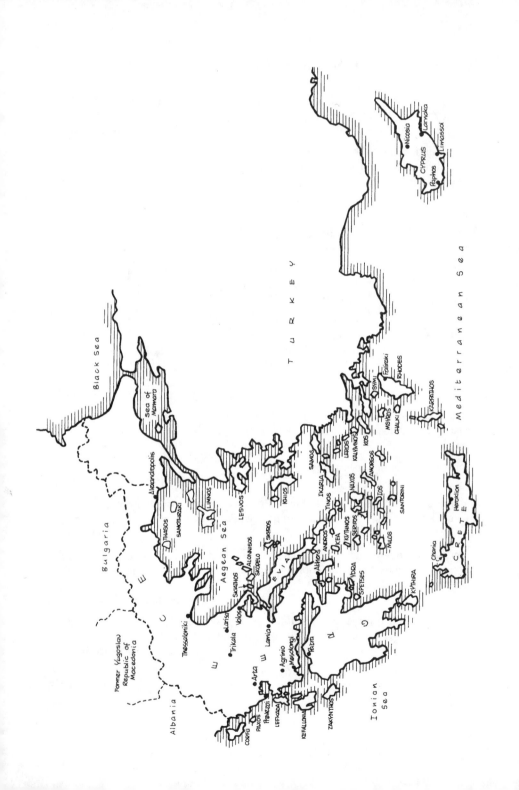

CONTENTS

IMPORTANT NOTE

Readers should note that the laws and regulations concerning buying property in Greece and Cyprus aren't the same as in other countries and are liable to change periodically. **I cannot recommend too strongly that you always check with an official and reliable source (not necessarily the same) and take expert legal advice before paying any money or signing any legal documents. Don't, however, believe everything you're told or read – even, dare I say it, herein!**

To help you obtain further information and verify data with official sources, useful addresses and references to other sources of information have been included in all chapters and in **Appendices A** and **B**. Important points have been emphasised throughout the book **in bold print**, some of which it would be expensive or foolish to disregard. **Ignore them at your peril or cost.** Unless specifically stated, the reference to any company, organisation, product or publication in this book *doesn't* constitute an endorsement or recommendation.

AUTHOR'S NOTES

- Note that, unless otherwise indicated, the information contained in this book applies only to the Republic of Cyprus and not to the self-proclaimed Turkish Republic of Northern Cyprus (covering 37 per cent of the island), occupied and recognised only by Turkey.

- Names of towns can be a problem, particularly in Greece, where various names are often used for the same town or region. This book generally gives the most common name used internationally.

- **Prices quoted should be taken as estimates only**, although they were mostly correct when going to print and fortunately don't usually change overnight in Greece and Cyprus. Prices in this book include value added tax (unless otherwise indicated), although prices in Greece and Cyprus are sometimes quoted exclusive of tax.

- His/he/him (etc.) also mean her/she/her (no offence ladies!). This is done simply to make life easier for both the reader and, in particular, the author, and *isn't* intended to be sexist.

- Warnings and important points are shown in **bold** type.

- All spelling is (or should be) English and not American.

- All times are shown using am (ante meridiem) for before noon and pm (post meridiem) for after noon. All times are local, so check the time difference when making international telephone calls (see page 70).

- The following symbols are used in this book: ☎ (telephone), 🖷 (fax), 🖥 (Internet) and ✉ (e-mail).

- Frequent references are made throughout this book to the European Union (EU), which comprises Austria, Belgium, Denmark, Finland, France, Germany, Greece, Ireland, Italy, Luxembourg, the Netherlands, Portugal, Spain, Sweden and the United Kingdom, and the European Economic Area (EEA), which comprises the EU countries plus Iceland, Liechtenstein and Norway.

- Lists of **Useful Addresses** and **Further Reading** are contained in **Appendices A** and **B** respectively.

- For those who are unfamiliar with the metric system of **Weights & Measures**, conversion tables are included in **Appendix C**.

- Maps of Greece and Cyprus showing the regions are included in **Appendix D** and a map of the eastern Mediterranean is on page 6.

INTRODUCTION

If you're planning to buy a home in Greece or Cyprus or even just thinking about it – this is **THE BOOK** for you! Whether you want a villa, farmhouse, townhouse or an apartment, a holiday or a permanent home, this book will help make your dreams come true. The purpose of *Buying a Home in Greece and Cyprus* is to provide you with the information necessary to help you choose the most favourable location and the most appropriate home **to satisfy your individual requirements.** Most importantly, it will help you avoid the pitfalls and risks associated with buying a home abroad, as homebuying for most people is one of the largest financial transactions they will undertake during their lifetimes.

You may already own property in your home country; however, buying a home in Greece or Cyprus (or in any foreign country) is a different matter altogether. One of the most common mistakes many people make when buying a home abroad is to assume that the laws and purchase procedures are the same as in their home country. **This is almost certainly not the case!** Buying property in Greece and Cyprus is generally safe, although if you don't obtain legal advice and follow the rules provided for your protection, a purchase can result in a serious financial loss – as many people have discovered to their cost.

Before buying a home in Greece or Cyprus you need to ask yourself *exactly* why you want to buy a home there? Do you 'simply' want a holiday home, is your primary concern a long-term investment, or do you wish to work or retire there? Where and what can you afford to buy? Do you plan to let your home to offset the running costs? How will local taxes affect your investment? *Buying a Home in Greece and Cyprus* will help you answer these and many other questions. It won't, however, tell you where to live, what to buy, or, having made your decision, whether you'll be happy – that part is up to you!

For many people, buying a home in Greece and Cyprus was previously a case of pot luck. However, with a copy of *Buying a Home in Greece and Cyprus* to hand you'll have a wealth of priceless information at your fingertips – information derived from a variety of sources, both official and unofficial, not least the hard won personal experiences of the authors, their friends, colleagues and acquaintances. Furthermore, this book will reduce the risk of making an expensive mistake that you may bitterly regret later and will help you make informed decisions and calculated judgements instead of uneducated guesses and rash assumptions (forewarned is forearmed!). **Most important of all, it will help you save money and will repay your investment many times over.**

The world-wide recession in the early '90s caused an upheaval in world property markets, during which many so-called 'gilt-edged' property investments went to the wall. However, property remains one of the best long-term investments and it's certainly one of the most pleasurable. Buying a home in Greece or Cyprus is a wonderful way to make new friends, broaden your horizons and revitalise your life – and it provides a welcome bolt-hole to recuperate from the stresses and strains of modern life. I trust this book will help you avoid pitfalls and smooth your way to many happy years in your new home, secure in the knowledge that you have made the right decision.

Good luck!

David Hampshire (Editor)
October 2001

1.

WHY GREECE OR CYPRUS?

Greece – land of the Gods and the ancient cradle of modern civilisation – is a country rich in culture, history and tradition. The country evokes images of glorious summer sunshine and cobalt blue skies, endless white sandy beaches, picturesque whitewashed villages and deserted islands, sleepy harbours and colourful fishing boats, friendly people (the Greek work for 'foreigner' is the same as 'guest'), and a simple, relaxed way of life. Greece is largely unspoilt with little industry and few high-rise buildings outside the major cities – the islands in particular have escaped the scourge of indiscriminate development common in many other Mediterranean countries. The country also enjoys one of the healthiest diets in Europe, consisting largely of fish, fresh fruit and vegetables, olive oil and wine. Greece is one of the most beautiful countries in the world and a holiday paradise with more than 1,400 islands (relatively few of which are inhabited), over 15,000km (9,320mi) of coastline and some of the finest beaches in the world. It's also one of Europe's last 'undiscovered' paradises for holiday homeowners and retirees.

Cyprus – legendary birthplace of Aphrodite, the goddess of love – is the third-largest island in the Mediterranean (after Sicily and Sardinia) with a fascinating history, during which it has been home to (or ruled by) Assyrians, Egyptians, Persians, Alexander the Great, Romans, Byzantines, Crusaders, Lusignans, Venetians and the British. Today it has a distinctly Greek feel, with which it has much more in common than simply its language. Cyprus is noted for its reliable sunshine, blue skies, excellent beaches, pine-clad mountains, wealth of archaeological sites, timeless villages, modern cosmopolitan towns, unspoilt countryside, interesting wildlife and rich cultural heritage. The island is a botanist's dream with an abundance of wild flowers – almost 2,000 different species of plants flourish there, over 100 of which are found nowhere else. Cyprus benefited hugely from the legacy of its last rulers, the British, who were largely responsible for the island's excellent communications, its legal system and public services, good health system and schools, low crime rate, efficient road system (where traffic drives on the left) and, not least, the English language, which is spoken by some 90 per cent of the population. Today, Cyprus enjoys relatively low unemployment, a low cost of living (including very low taxation for retirees), a healthy economy and a high standard of living (higher than Greece, Portugal and Spain).

As a location for a holiday, retirement or permanent home, Greece and Cyprus have much to offer, and in addition to a wide choice of properties and good value for money, both enjoy mild climates with over 300 days of sunshine a year. There are many excellent reasons for buying a home in Greece or Cyprus, although it's important not to be under any illusions about what you can expect from a home there. The first and most important question you need to ask yourself is *exactly* why you want to buy a home in Greece or Cyprus? For example, are you seeking a holiday or a retirement home? If you're seeking a second home, will it be mainly used for short holidays ,e.g. one or two weeks, or for lengthier stays? Do you plan to let it to offset the mortgage and running costs? If so, how important is the property income? Are you primarily looking for a sound investment or do you plan to work or start a business?

Often buyers have a variety of reasons for buying a home abroad; for example, many people buy a holiday home with a view to living abroad permanently or semi-permanently when they retire. If this is the case, there are many more factors to take into account than if you're 'simply' buying a holiday home that you will occupy for just a few weeks a year, when it's usually wiser not to buy at all! If, on the other hand, you plan to work or start a business in Greece or Cyprus, you will be faced with a completely different set of criteria.

Can you really afford to buy a home in Greece or Cyprus? What of the future? Is your income secure and protected against inflation and currency fluctuations? In the '80s, many foreigners purchased holiday homes abroad by taking out second mortgages on their principal homes and stretching their financial resources to the limit. Not surprisingly, when the recession struck in the early '90s many people lost their homes or were forced to sell at a huge loss when they were unable to keep up their mortgage payments. Buying a home abroad can be a good, long-term investment, although it's possible to get your fingers burnt in the occasionally volatile property market in many countries, including Greece and Cyprus.

Property values in Greece and Cyprus generally increase at an average of less than 5 per cent a year or in line with inflation (with no increase or very little in real terms), although in some fashionable resorts and developments prices rise faster than average, which is usually reflected in higher purchase prices. There's a stable property market in most of Greece and Cyprus (barring recessions), which acts as a discouragement to speculators wishing to make a fast buck. You also need to recover the costs associated with buying a home when you sell. **You shouldn't expect to make a quick profit when buying property in Greece or Cyprus, but should look upon it as an investment in your family's future happiness, rather than merely in financial terms.**

There are both advantages and disadvantages to buying a home in Greece or Cyprus, although for most people the benefits far outweigh any drawbacks. Among the many advantages are guaranteed sunshine and high temperatures (year round in many areas); one of the least polluted regions in the world; good value for money; easy and relatively inexpensive to get to (particularly for most Europeans); good rental possibilities in most areas (although letting a holiday home is officially prohibited in Cyprus); good local tradesmen and services (particularly in resort areas); a healthy diet and good food and wine at reasonable prices; relatively low cost of living (25 to 50 per cent lower than in many northern European and North American cities) and low taxes for retirees in Cyprus; a slow, relaxed pace of life typified by *avro* – it can wait until tomorrow; the friendliness and hospitality of the local people; the dramatic beauty of the Mediterranean on your doorstep; and, last but not least, an unsurpassed quality of life.

Naturally, there are also a few disadvantages, not least the relatively high purchase costs associated with buying property in Greece; unexpected renovation and restoration costs (if you don't do your homework); the dangers of buying a property with debts and other problems (if you don't take legal advice); overcrowding in popular tourist areas during the peak summer season; traffic congestion and pollution in many towns and cities; severe water shortages in some regions (particularly during the summer); homes can be difficult to sell (particularly in Cyprus); and the expense of getting to and from a holiday home if you don't live in Europe or in a country with good connections (flights to Cyprus can be expensive and direct flights aren't available from many countries).

Unless you know exactly what you're looking for and where, it's wise to rent for a period until you're more familiar with an area. As when making any major financial decision, you should never be too hasty. Many people make expensive (even catastrophic) errors when buying a home abroad, usually because they do insufficient research and are in too much of a hurry, often setting themselves impossible deadlines. Not surprisingly, most people wouldn't dream of acting so rashly when buying property in their home countries. It isn't uncommon for buyers to regret their decision after some time and wish they had purchased a different property in a different region – or even in a different country!

Before deciding to buy a home in Greece or Cyprus, you should to do extensive research and read a number of books especially written for those planning to live or work there. It also helps to study specialist property magazines such as *World of Property* and *International Property* (see **Appendix A** for a list), and to visit property exhibitions such as those organised by Outbound Publishing (1 Commercial Road, Eastbourne, East Sussex BN21 3XQ, UK, (☎ 01323-726040; 💻 www.outbound-newspapers.com). **Bear in mind that the cost of investing in a few books or magazines (and other research) is tiny compared with the expense of making a big mistake – however, don't believe everything you read or are told!**

This chapter provides information about permits and visas, retirement, working, starting a business, communications, getting to Greece and Cyprus, and getting around (particularly regarding driving).

DO YOU NEED A PERMIT OR VISA?

Before making any plans to buy a home in Greece or Cyprus, you must check whether you will need a visa or residence permit and ensure that you will be permitted to use a property when you wish and for whatever purpose you've in mind. If there's a possibility that you or a family member will wish to live or work permanently in Greece or Cyprus, you should enquire whether it will be possible before making any plans to buy a home there.

While those from European Union (EU) countries are free to buy property in Greece and Cyprus, most aren't permitted to remain longer than three months a year without applying for a temporary residence permit (*Ipiresía Allodhapón*). Application for permits must be made to the local police (*Astynomia*) or in larger cities such as Athens, Patra, Rhodes and Thessalonika, at the Aliens Bureau (*Grafio Tmimatos Allodapon*). Note that offices aren't common in small towns and in many areas you will need to travel to a regional capital or large city to apply. Allow plenty of time when making applications, as Greek bureaucracy grinds slowly. Usually residence and work permits are valid for one year and may be renewed for up to five years, after which an application to extend a permit is necessary.

Greece: Citizens of certain EU countries, including Belgium, Germany, Italy, Luxembourg, the Netherlands and Spain can visit Greece with a national identity card, while others require a full passport. A non-EU national usually requires a visa to work, study or live in Greece. All foreigners need a residence permit to live permanently in Greece and non-EU nationals may need a visa to enter Greece, either as visitors or for any other purpose. EU nationals and visitors from a number of other countries don't require a visa (see below). Non-EU nationals wishing to remain in Greece for longer than three months must obtain a long-stay visa and apply for a residence permit within one week of their arrival.

Cyprus: Cyprus has associate member status of the EU and is expected to become a full member by around 2004. EU nationals and those of many other countries don't need a visa to enter the country, only a valid passport. Applications for residence permits must be made to the Migration Department in Nicosia and are usually valid for two years.

When in Greece or Cyprus, you must always carry your passport or residence permit (if you have one), which serves as an identity card, a document all local nationals must carry by law. You can be asked to produce your identification papers at any time by the police and other officials and if you don't have them you can be taken to a police station and interrogated. **Note that permit infringements are taken very seriously by the authorities and there are penalties for breaches of regulations, including fines and even deportation for flagrant abuses.**

Visitors

Visitors can remain in Greece or Cyprus for a maximum of 90 days at a time.

Greece: Visitors to Greece from EU countries plus Andorra, Australia, Canada, Cyprus, the Czech Republic, Hungary, Iceland, Japan, Malta, Monaco, New Zealand, Norway, Singapore, Slovakia, South Korea, Switzerland and the USA *don't* require a visa for stays of up to 90 days. All other nationalities require a visa to visit Greece, although the list of countries requiring visas is liable to change at short notice and therefore you should check with the Greek embassy in your home country. A three-month visa costs around US$20. Greek immigration authorities may require non-EU visitors to produce a return ticket and proof of accommodation, health insurance and financial resources. **Note that Greece will refuse entry to any foreigners, whatever their nationality, whose passport indicates that they've visited Northern Cyprus since November 1993.**

If you're a non-EU national, it isn't possible to enter Greece as a tourist and change your status to that of an employee, student or resident. You must return to your country of residence and apply for a long-stay visa. However, if you wish to prove you've left, you must have your passport stamped. This is legal, although your total stay mustn't exceed six months (180 days) in a calendar year. At present, non-EU nationals are allowed only one visa extension of six months. Note that the Greek immigration authorities are strict regarding visas and if you haven't applied for one and have remained in the country for six months, you may find that you're fined on the spot upon your departure.

Cyprus: Visas aren't required by EU nationals and those from Australia, Canada, New Zealand and the USA for stays of less than three months. For stays of longer than three months a permit must be obtained from the Migration Department of the Ministry of the Interior in Nicosia. If you're visiting Cyprus to seek employment or study, you will need a visa. EU nationals can apply for this once they're in Cyprus, but non-EU nationals must apply for a visa before their arrival. Foreigners wishing to work in Cyprus need a Temporary Work and Residence Permit, which is usually valid for two years.

RETIREMENT

Greece: Retired and non-active EU nationals don't require a long-stay visa before moving to Greece, but a residence permit is necessary and an application should be made within one week of your arrival. Non-EU nationals require a visa to live in Greece for longer than three months and should make an application to their local Greek consulate well before their planned departure date. Non-employed residents must provide proof (on request) that they've an adequate income or financial resources to live in Greece without working.

Cyprus: Retired and non-active nationals from most countries don't require a long-stay visa before moving to Cyprus, but a residence permit is necessary and an application should be made on arrival in Cyprus to the Migration Department in Nicosia. Non-employed residents must provide proof that they've an adequate income or financial resources to live in Cyprus. In 2001, the annual income requirement was CY£7,000 for a single person and CY£10,000 for a married couple (excluding mortgage or rental payments). There are substantial tax benefits for retirees in Cyprus, which has double-taxation treaties with many countries under which retirees' pensions aren't subject to withholding tax at source. Foreign retirees living in Cyprus are taxed at a lower rate and pay income tax on imported pensions at the rate of only 5 per cent, with the first CY£5,000 exempt. Some countries ,e.g. Canada and the UK, have an agreement with Cyprus that allows state pensions to remain index-linked when pensioners are resident in Cyprus. There are also a number of duty-free privileges for retirees, including the importation of a duty-free car (a duty-free, medium-size saloon car costs just over half the average EU price) and personal effects.

WORKING

If there's a possibility that you or any family members will wish to work in Greece or Cyprus, you must ensure that it will be possible before buying a home there. If you don't qualify to live and work in Greece or Cyprus by birthright, family relationship or, in the case of Greece, as a national of a European Union (EU) or European Economic Area (EEA) country, obtaining a work permit may be difficult or impossible. Greek employers must apply for a work permit on behalf of a non-EU national whom they wish to employ. If you're a national of an EU country you don't require official approval to live or work in Greece, although you still require a temporary residence permit. If you visit Greece or Cyprus to look for a job, you've three months to find employment or set up in business and once employment has been found you must apply for a residence permit within one week.

Before moving to Greece or Cyprus to work, you should dispassionately examine your motives and credentials. What kind of work can you realistically expect to do there? What are your qualifications and experience? Are they recognised? How good is your Greek? Unless your Greek is fluent, you won't be competing on equal terms with the local workforce (you won't anyway, but that's a different matter!). Most Greek employers aren't interested in employing anyone without, at the very least, a working knowledge of Greek, unless it's in the tourist industry dealing exclusively with foreigners. Are there any jobs in your profession or trade in the area where you plan to live? The answers to these and many other questions can be quite disheartening, but it's better to ask them *before* moving to Greece or Cyprus, rather than afterwards.

Greece: The Greek equivalent of the English Job Centre is the OAED (*Organismos Apasholisseos Ergatikou Dynamikou*), which has a special department for European job-seekers. You should also bear in mind that unemployment is a major problem in Greece and you shouldn't expect to find work there easily. Work permits are usually only granted if you've qualifications or expertise not easily found in the Greek labour market. Note that nationals of African, Asian and Central American countries are not granted work permits unless they're employed as corporate managers, technical experts or are employees of an offshore company.

Cyprus: In Cyprus, you will be competing with well qualified Cypriots for jobs and a work permit is usually granted only when a Cypriot cannot be found to fill a position. There are strict regulations regarding work permits for non-Cypriots and if you're going to Cyprus to work (or study) you will need a visa available *only* from the Migration Department, Ministry of the Interior, Nicosia. EU nationals can apply for a permit after they've arrived, but non-EU nationals must obtain a visa *before* arriving in Cyprus. A work permit is usually granted on an annual basis or from three months upwards for jobs associated with the tourist industry.

Many people turn to self-employment (see below) or start a business to make a living, although this path is strewn with pitfalls for the newcomer. **Many foreigners don't do sufficient homework before moving to Greece or Cyprus.** While hoping for the best, you should plan for the 'worst-case scenario' and have a contingency plan and sufficient funds to last until you're established (this also applies to employees). If you're planning to start a business in Greece, you must also do battle with the notoriously obstructive and slow local bureaucracy.

SELF-EMPLOYMENT

If you're an EU national you can work as a self-employed person in Greece, although it's very difficult in Cyprus (particularly if you will be competing with Cypriots) unless you're creating jobs or trading only in foreign currency. If you want to be self-employed in a profession or start a freelance business in Greece, you must meet certain legal requirements and register with the appropriate organisations, e.g. the Ministry of Labour (*Ypourgio Ergassias*), within 15 days of starting a business. The head office of their International Relations Service is at Ypourgio Ergassias, Tmima Diethnon Scheseon, 40 Piracus Street, Athens 101-82 (☎ 01-522 9140).

Under Greek law, a self-employed person must have an official status and it's illegal simply to hang up a sign and start business. Members of some professions and trades must have certain qualifications and certificates recognised in Greece. You can obtain a direct comparison between foreign qualifications and those recognised in Greece from the Inter-University Centre for the recognition of Foreign Educational Qualifications (*Diapanepistimiako Kentro Anagnorisis Titlon Spoudon tis Allodapis/DIKATSA*, 112 Sygrou Avenue, Athens 117-41, ☎ 01-922 2533). Don't be in too much of a hurry to register, as from the date of registration you must pay hefty social security, pension and health insurance payments, and are also liable for income tax and VAT (*Foros Prostithemis Aksias/FPA*).

As a self-employed person, you don't have the protection of a limited company should your business fail and there are few tax advantages. It may be advantageous to operate as a limited company, e.g. an *eteria periorismenis efthynis* (EPE), which is a limited-liability company employing at least two people. An EPE must have a minimum share capital of €17,500 divided into share certificates held by the partners (yes, they're called partners!), each of whom is liable for the debts of the company up to the amount of his share certificates. Alternatively, if you find a partner with whom you wish to do business, then a partnership (*omorythmos eteria/OE*) can be formed.

Always obtain professional advice before deciding whether to operate as self-employed, a partner or a limited company in Greece, as there are far-reaching social security, tax and other implications. If you're self-employed you may be exempt from paying Greek social security contributions for up to 12 months, provided you continue to pay social security contributions in your home country and hold an exemption certificate (E1O1). Cyprus has recently concluded agreements with Greece and the UK whereby the self-employed are exempt from social security contributions from one to three years. In the UK, the exemption certificate is issued by the Overseas Branch of the Department of Social Security, Newcastle-upon-Tyne, NE98 1YX.

There are many drawbacks to being self-employed in Greece and Cyprus, which may outweigh any advantages. Social security contributions for the self-employed are much higher than for salaried employees and they receive fewer benefits. As a self-employed person, you aren't entitled to unemployment benefit should your business fail and there are no benefits for accidents at work.

STARTING A BUSINESS

The associated with starting a business in Greece or Cyprus is considerable and among the worst in the western world. For foreigners the red tape is almost impenetrable, especially if you don't speak Greek, and you will be inundated with official documents and must be able to understand them. It's only when you come up against the full force of local bureaucracy that you understand what it *really* means to be a foreigner! However, despite the red tape, Greece and Cyprus are traditionally countries of small companies and individual traders, where the economic philosophy actually encourages and even nurtures the creation of small businesses. **Note, however, that it's extremely difficult to obtain a permit to start a business in Cyprus if you will be competing with Cypriots and won't be creating jobs, and therefore most of the following information applies only to Greece.**

Before undertaking any business transactions it's important to obtain legal advice to ensure that you're operating within the law. There are severe penalties for anyone who ignores the regulations and legal requirements. It's also important to obtain legal advice before establishing a limited company. All businesses must register for value-added tax in Greece, while in Cyprus you must register when your gross annual turnover exceeds CY£12,000. Non-EU nationals require a special licence to start a business in Greece and no commitments should be made until this has been granted. Among the best sources of help and information are local chambers of commerce and town halls.

Generally speaking, you shouldn't consider running a business abroad in a field in which you don't have previous experience, and it's often wise to work for someone else in the same line of business in order to gain experience, rather than jump in at the deep end. Always thoroughly investigate an existing or proposed business before investing any money. **As any expert can tell you, Greece and Cyprus aren't countries for amateur entrepreneurs, particularly amateurs who don't speak fluent Greek!** Many small businesses in Greece and Cyprus exist on a shoe string and certainly aren't what would be considered thriving enterprises. As in many countries, most people are self-employed for the lifestyle and freedom it affords (no clocks or bosses!), rather than the financial rewards. It's important to keep your plans small and manageable and work well within your budget, rather than undertaking some grandiose scheme.

A useful guide for anyone starting a business in Greece is **Barclays Business Guide to Greece** published by Barclays Bank plc in the UK. International accountants such as Price Waterhouse have offices throughout Greece and are an invaluable source of information (in English) on subjects such as forming a company, company law, taxation and social security. In Cyprus, business information is provided by international banking groups such as the Central Bank of Cyprus (💻 www.central bank.gov.cy) or Hellenic Bank. Many countries maintain chambers of commerce in Greece, which are another good source of information and assistance. The Cyprus Chamber of Commerce and Industry (PO Box 21455, 1509 Nicosia, ☎ 357-266 9500) provides extensive information as well as annual membership.

Buying an Existing Business: It's much easier to buy an existing business than to start a new one, and it's less of a risk. The paperwork for taking over an existing business is also simpler, although still complex. Note, however, that buying a business that's a going concern is difficult as the locals aren't in a habit of buying and selling businesses, which are usually passed down from generation to generation. If you plan to buy a business, always obtain an independent valuation (or two) and employ an accountant to audit the books. **Never sign anything you don't understand completely even if you think you understand it, you should still obtain unbiased professional advice, from local experts such as banks and accountants, before buying a business.** In fact, it's best not to start a business until you've established the infrastructure, including an accountant, lawyer and banking facilities. There are various ways to set up a small business and it's essential to obtain professional advice regarding the best method of establishing and registering a business, which can significantly influence your tax position. It's important to employ an accountant to do your books.

Starting a New Business: Most people are far too optimistic about the prospects for a new business and over-estimate income levels (it often takes years to make a profit) and under-estimate costs. You must be realistic or even pessimistic when calculating your income and over-estimate the costs and under-estimate the revenue (then reduce it by 50 per cent!). While hoping for the best, you should plan for the worst and have sufficient funds to last until you're established (under-funding is the major cause of business failures). New projects are rarely, if ever, completed within budget, and you need to ensure that you've sufficient working capital and can survive until a business takes off. Greek and Cypriot banks are extremely wary of lending to new businesses, especially businesses run by foreigners. If you wish to borrow money to buy property or for a business venture, you should also carefully consider where and in what currency to raise the necessary finance.

Location: Choosing the location for a business is even more important than the location for a home. Depending on the type of business, you may need access to motorways and rail or air links, or to be located in a popular tourist area or near local attractions. Local plans regarding communications, industry and major building developments, e.g. housing developments and new shopping centres, may also be important. Plans regarding new motorways and main roads as well as rail links are available from local town halls.

Employees: Hiring employees shouldn't be taken lightly in Greece or Cyprus and must be taken into account *before* starting a business. You must enter into a contract and employees enjoy extensive rights. It's also *very* expensive to hire employees, as in addition to salaries you must pay social security contributions (up to €174.70 or CY£1,495 monthly), 14 months' salary (in Greece), and pay for annual and public holidays. Should you wish to dismiss an employee, severance payments are also high, particularly in Greece.

Offshore Companies: There are tax incentives for offshore companies registered in both Greece and Cyprus. Greece permits the establishment of an offshore company if the enterprise operates legally and deals exclusively with commercial business outside Greece. The company is totally exempt from income tax, its foreign personnel enjoy tax advantages, and cars and personal effects can be imported and retained free of duty and taxes. There's no legal minimum investment, although in practice registration isn't approved if the annual foreign exchange imported is less than US$50,000. An offshore company in Greece may employ up to four employees.

Cyprus: With some 40,000 registered offshore companies Cyprus describes itself as a tax-incentive country rather than a tax haven, and it offers many tax benefits to offshore companies registered there. Offshore companies must be approved by the Central Bank of Cyprus and, while there's no minimum investment requirement, the recommended minimum is CY£10,000 and a company must have a minimum of two shareholders. Tax benefits include income tax at 4.25 per cent of annual net profits, duty-free cars and personal effects, and employees who live and work in Cyprus are taxed at half the normal rate.

Type of Business: The most common businesses operated by foreigners in Greece and Cyprus include holiday accommodation, e.g. bed & breakfast, villas, apartments and cottages, catering, e.g. bars, cafés and restaurants, shops, property agencies, translation bureaux, language schools, and holiday and sports centres, e.g. tennis, golf and water sports). The majority of businesses established by foreigners are linked to the leisure and catering industries, followed by property investment and development. Note that in Cyprus certain businesses are termed 'saturated activities' and applications for investment in such businesses are rejected outright. In 2001 'saturated activities' were real estate development, tertiary education and public utility services. Check with the Central Bank of Cyprus for up to date information.

Companies: Companies cannot be purchased 'off the shelf' in Greece or Cyprus and it usually takes a number of months to establish one. Incorporating a company takes longer and is more expensive and more complicated than in many other European countries. There are a number of types of 'limited companies' or business entities and choosing the right one can be difficult. The most common form of company created by foreigners in Greece is an *eteria periorismenis efthynis* (EPE), a private limited company with a minimum share capital of €17,500 (part of which can be fixed assets) and at least two shareholders. **Always obtain professional legal advice regarding the advantages and disadvantages of different limited companies.**

KEEPING IN TOUCH

In recent years there has been extensive investment in communications services in both Greece and Cyprus, including telephones (fixed and mobile), fax, mail and courier services, and both countries now enjoy a comparatively high standard of communications.

Telephone

The Greek telephone service is run by the *Organismós Telepikononion Elládos* (OTE), originally a state-owned monopoly but recently partly privatised (some 49 per cent). The company has made modernisation of its system one of its priorities and has installed integrated services digital network (ISDN) lines throughout most of the country. DSL is also widely available. The OTE has offices in most towns, from where long-distance calls can be made and telegrams and faxes can be sent (larger offices only). There is also the facility where you can plug your laptop computer into a telephone line, for this you a normal telephone rate will be charged. Note that calls are expensive in Greece, where the OTE has a monopoly on all calls other than those made from mobile phones (although competition is planned). If you use public telephone booths to make calls, bear in mind that there are different types: blue and silver booths are for local calls, orange and silver ones are for long-distance calls. A new telephone card system has recently been introduced, for which cards can be purchased at OTE offices and from kiosks in most towns. When making a call from an OTE office, you're assigned a booth and pay for calls afterwards. Greece also has a mobile telephone service, encompassing the most populous regions. **Emergency telephone numbers are listed at the front of telephone directories.**

The telephone system in Cyprus is operated exclusively by the Cyprus Telecommunications Authority (CTA) and telecommunications are excellent, which has been an important factor in establishing the island as an international offshore business centre. ISDN lines have recently been installed and hi-tech submarine cables link Cyprus with the neighbouring continents. Cyprus has a reliable telephone service and public call boxes are located in the centre of towns and villages as well as other locations (hotels and restaurants also have public phones). Public phones accept 2¢, 5¢, 10¢ and 20¢ coins and Telecards, which are available for CY£3, CY£5 and CY£10 from banks, post offices, souvenir shops and kiosks. Most telephone operators in Cyprus speak English. For directory enquiries, dial 192 for domestic numbers and 194 for international numbers. Cyprus also has a mobile phone service run by CYTA and imported phones operating on the GSM system can be used in Cyprus.

Installation: When moving into a new home in Greece or Cyprus with a telephone line, you must open an account in your name. If you're planning to move into a property without an existing telephone line, you will need to have one installed.

Bear in mind that you may be charged for telephone poles as well as the line. The installation of telephone poles is notoriously slow, as telephone pole workers may only service certain areas once or twice a year! To have a telephone installed or reconnected, contact the local telephone company agent, a list of which is included in telephone directories. Expect to pay at least €40 in Greece for the installation of a telephone in a private home. If you're taking over a property from the previous occupants, you should arrange for the account to be transferred to your name from the day you take possession. **However, before you can do this, the previous occupant must have already closed his account, so check in advance that this has been done.** If you move into a property where the telephone hasn't been disconnected or transferred to your name, you should ask for a special reading. To have a telephone connected or installed, you must prove that you're the owner or tenant of the property, e.g. with an electricity bill, confirmation of purchase or a lease, and the transfer will cost around €30. You will also require your passport or residence permit.

International Calls: It's possible to make direct International Direct Dialling (IDD) calls to most countries from both private and public telephones. A full list of country codes is shown in the information pages of telephone directories, plus area codes for main cities and tariffs. To make an international call you dial 00, the country code, the area code (without the first zero) and the subscriber's number. There's a flat rate of €0.34 per minute for calls to Zone E countries, which includes all EU countries, plus Australia, Canada, Cyprus and the USA. An increasing number of expatriates make use of call-back or 'indirect access' services whereby you call a number abroad or a special access number and can make international calls over leased lines at much lower rates than OTE's.

Internet 'Telephone' Services: The success of the Internet is built on the ability to view and collect information from computers around the world by connecting to a nearby service for the cost of a local phone call. If you have correspondents or friends who are connected to the Internet, you can make long-distance and international 'calls' for the price of a local phone call. Internet users can buy software or use Internet services such as IDT Net2Phone (🖳 www.net2phone.com) and Creative WebPhone (🖳 www.netspeak.com) that effectively turn your personal computer into a voice-based telephone. All you need is a sound card, a microphone, a modem and access to an Internet provider. The Internet is also useful for sending e-mail.

Greece isn't particularly well catered for when it comes to Internet facilities, although it's improving rapidly and many large organisations now list their e-mail and Internet addresses. Notes, however, that websites are usually in Greek only or 'under construction'. The lack of facilities stems from a shortage of lines available from Internet providers, which is improving. Internet cafés are becoming commonplace in large towns and cities. Cyprus is well provided with Internet services and CTA has recently made a huge investment in Internet facilities.

Mobile Phones: In common with most western countries, mobile phones are becoming increasingly popular in Greece and Cyprus. There are several mobile phone companies in Greece such as Mobitel, Panafon and Telestet providing competitive prices and services (shop around and compare prices before buying a phone or signing a service contract). If you take a mobile phone to Greece or Cyprus, it will work only if it operates on the GSM system.

Fax: There has been a huge increase in the use of fax machines in the last decade in Greece and Cyprus, helped by lower prices, the introduction of cheaper call rates and, in Greece, the failings of the post office (a fax is handy for sending letters, order forms, etc.). Fax machines can be purchased from telephone companies and stores. Shop around for the best price. Before taking a fax machine abroad, check that it will work there (i.e. is compatible) or that it can be modified. Note, however, that getting a fax machine repaired abroad may be impossible unless the same machine is sold there. There are no public fax facilities in Cyprus, although there are private business offices providing fax services in resorts and major towns.

Mail Services

There's a post office (*tachidromío*), depicted by a yellow sign, in most towns and villages in Greece and Cyprus, where in addition to the usual post office services a range of others are provided. These include telephone calls, telegrams, fax and telex transmissions, domestic and international cash transfers, and currency exchange. Note that in Cyprus, telegrams must be handed in to CTA offices or relayed by phone (dial 196 between 7am and 7pm). A *poste restante* service is provided in both countries and mail can be collected for up to a month from main post offices (for which your passport is necessary).

Business hours for main post offices in towns and cities in Greece and Cyprus are usually from 7.30am to 2pm. In larger towns they usually stay open until around 7pm, Mondays to Fridays and also open from 8 or 9am to noon on Saturdays. Main post offices in major towns don't close for lunch and may also provide limited services outside normal business hours. In small towns and villages, post offices may close for lunch and may be also closed one day a week. You shouldn't expect post office staff to speak English or other languages in Greece, although in resort areas some English may be spoken.

The Greek mail delivery service has a reputation as one of the slowest in Europe, although services have improved in recent years and aren't as bad as they're sometimes portrayed. The Cypriot mail service is generally very efficient. Delivery times vary according to where letters are posted, e.g. around three to eight days to European countries and five to eleven days to North America. Bear in mind that mail to and from Greek islands without an airport takes considerably longer to arrive at its destination. For important documents you should use the registered (*sistiméno*) service, although this is slow unless you send it via the express (*katepígonda*) service. Airmail letters up to 20g cost €0.35 or CY£0.35 to EU countries and €0.60 or CY£0.36 to North America. Stamps can be purchased from small kiosks (*períptero*) located on street corners (which levy a 10 per cent surcharge in Greece), as well as from post offices. Stamps can also be purchased from hotels and news-stands in Cyprus.

Standard post boxes in Greece are small, square yellow containers usually mounted on a post, possibly with two slots: one for local mail (*esorikó*) and the other for overseas mail (*exoterikó*). Red post boxes are for the rapid mail service. The international postal identification, written before the four-digit postal code, is 'G' for Greece and 'C' for Cyprus.

Courier Services: The only guaranteed way to send something urgently is by courier or to 'send' letters by fax or e-mail. Express mail and courier services are provided by the post office, airlines, and international courier companies such as DHL, Federal Express and UPS. One of the most economical ways to send urgent international letters or parcels is via the post office's EMS express mail service, serving around 160 countries.

GETTING THERE

This isn't so important if you're planning to live permanently in Greece or Cyprus and will be spending most of your time there. One of the major considerations when buying a holiday home abroad is the cost of getting there. How long will it take to get to a home abroad, taking into account journeys to and from airports, ports and railway stations? How frequent are flights, ferries or trains at the time(s) of year when you plan to travel? Are direct flights or trains available? What is the cost of travel from your home country to the region where you're planning to buy a home? Are off-season discounts or inexpensive charter flights available? If a long journey is involved, you should bear in mind that it may take you a day or two to recover, e.g. from jet-lag after a long flight. Obviously the travelling time and cost of travel to a home abroad will be more critical if you're planning to spend frequent weekends there, rather than a few long visits.

Airline Services: All major international airlines provide scheduled services to Athens, where a much needed new international airport opened in 2001 (🖥 www.aia.gr), and many also fly to other Greek destinations such as Thessalonika, Heráklion (Crete), Prévesa, Rhodes and Corfu. The Greek national airline, Olympic Air, is Greece's principal international carrier, which shares major routes to the UK with British Airways and Virgin. Cyprus is served by some 35 international and 85 charter airlines, including Cyprus Airways (the national carrier), which links it with all corners of the world via international airports at Larnaca and Paphos.

Train Services: It's possible to travel to Greece by rail from northern Europe via Italy, although it's necessary to take a ferry from Brindisi to Patra in the Peloponnese. Bear in mind that it takes over 17 hours to get to Athens from the UK! Athens, Thessalonika and Larissa are connected by rail to most European cities.

Ferry Services: There are regular sailings to Greece from several countries, including Ancona and Brindisi in Italy, Limassol in Cyprus and Haifa in Israel. The main ports for passenger ferries in Cyprus are Limassol and Larnaca. Note that ferry travel schedules can be erratic or cancelled in bad weather and reservations are essential in high season.

Always allow plenty of time to get to and from airports, ports and railway stations, particularly when travelling during peak hours, when traffic congestion at times can be dreadful.

GETTING AROUND BY PUBLIC TRANSPORT

Public transport services in Greece and Cyprus vary considerably according to where you live, although there have been improvements in recent years. Public transport is good (if chaotic) in Athens and in most towns in Cyprus. There's a metro system in

Athens (currently with two lines in operation) and an 18km (11mi) extension is being built for the 2004 Olympic Games. However, outside the main towns and cities public transport can be sparse and most people find it necessary to have their own transport; many Greek island airports are served only by taxis. Taxis are common in resort areas (in Cyprus they operate like buses and are shared by passengers) and are relatively inexpensive by European. Information about public transport can be obtained from local tourist offices in Greece and Cyprus and from national tourist offices abroad.

Bus: The standard means of land transport in both Greece and Cyprus is the bus. There's an extensive network of routes covering nearly every point on the Greek mainland and buses also provide connections between the ports and major towns on the islands. Services on major routes, both on the mainland and on the islands, are frequent and efficient. Buses in Greece are generally punctual, particularly on the major routes, and prices reasonable, e.g. Athens to Thessalonika costs around €20 one way. Services are less frequent off the major routes, although even the remotest villages are connected by bus to the provincial capital at least once a week. On the Greek islands there are usually buses connecting the main towns and ports but bear in mind that buses may not run to and from the airport.

The bus network throughout Greece is run by *Kratikó Tamío Ellinikón Leoforión* (KTEL), an association of regional bus companies. KTEL provides an extensive service and details are available from the Greek Tourist Organisation. Buses that operate between major towns and cities are air-conditioned and can be booked through travel agents. Smoking is prohibited on these buses, although as with many rules in Greece this is often ignored. Note that not all buses are air-conditioned and the quality of service varies between the many companies involved. The OSE, the State Railway Organisation, also operates express buses on a few long-distance routes, which depart from train stations.

In Cyprus, buses are essentially the only public transport and the island is generally well-served, although some services may run only once a day. Scheduled services operate between towns and villages and between major towns and beaches. Most bus services are run by one of four main companies: EMAN, Costas, Kallenos, and Kemek. Timetables are only a rough guide – some would say just a suggestion of when a bus *may* arrive!

Another common means of transport in Cyprus is the 'service taxi', which is a Mercedes taxi shared by up to seven people, where each passenger's fare depends on the distance travelled – prices are fixed irrespective of the number of passengers. Fares are reasonable and journeys fast. They operate at half-hour intervals on fixed routes and mainly run between the larger towns during peak times. Service taxis pick up and drop off passengers at any point along their route.

Rail: The Greek railway organisation, *Organismos Sidirodromon Ellados* (OSE), operates ancient trains, which are gradually being replaced by newer rolling stock. However, rail travel isn't the best way of getting around Greece (although it can be pleasant) and there are few lines. The main routes are Athens to Thessalonika and Thessalonika to Alexandroupolis. Trains are fast and efficient in the cities but very slow in rural areas, stopping at every station. However, despite the slow pace of travel it's usually reliable and the fares are low (around half the standard bus fare). Rail services in Greece are limited to the mainland. An excellent book for rail buffs is *Greece by Rail* by Zane Katsikis (Bradt). **There are no rail services in Cyprus.**

Air: Greece's major domestic airline is Olympic Air, although Air Greece, a relatively new airline, offers discounted fares on the major routes. Most routes involve travelling to or from Athens or Thessalonika. The domestic network is adequate and useful, particularly for inter-island travel. Fares aren't refundable and at peak times (especially to the islands) flights must be booked well in advance. Air travel is easily the most expensive means of getting around Greece and discounts are virtually unknown.

Ferries and Hydrofoils: Island-hopping is one of the delights of Greece for the independent traveller and one of the last public transport 'adventures' in western Europe. However, bear in mind that ferry services can be erratic with sailings greatly reduced out of season and often cancelled altogether in bad weather. There are three different kinds of boat: ordinary ferries that operate the main services; hydrofoils and local boats (*kaïkia*), which do short trips and excursions during the summer. It's worth noting that outside the summer season most Greek ferries operate primarily for the benefit of Greeks, most of whom travel from their island to the mainland (Athens) and back, and not between islands.

Costs are reasonable for long journeys, although shorter inter-island hops are more expensive. Routes and journey times vary enormously and before you purchase a ticket it's wise to check the exact route and the estimated duration. Ferry companies should charge the same fare for the same route, although the larger ferries have three classes. It's best to buy your ticket on the day of departure (arrive early in high season) unless you need to reserve a cabin or a car space. On most services, fares for cars are high, which you should bear in mind when travelling by car as it may be cheaper to rent a car at your destination. It's usually sensible to buy single tickets, as you may wish to return by a different route or with a different ferry company. Hydrofoils (*dhelfínia*) are twice as fast and expensive as conventional ferries, and increasingly serve more routes, although they operate mainly between the Cyclades, Dodecanese and Sporades island groups.

Note that in recent months strong safety fears have been voiced over Greek ferries, especially the older boats, some of which may be more than 30 years old and are best avoided (it's easy to tell which they are – the new boats are always very crowded!), and when you board a ferry or hydrofoil you should locate at least two exits and the life jackets. For travel on new vessels you will probably have to book at least 24 hours in advance even in low season.

Athens has two ferry ports: Piraeus and Rafina. Piraeus is the principal gateway to most islands, although some island groups (such as the Ionian and Sporades) aren't served. Piraeus is one of the most confusing ports in the world and becomes a 'circus' in summer, when it's virtually impossible to make sense of the timetables. Rafina is Athens' back door to Andros, Tinos, Mykonos, Paros and Naxos and is much nearer to the new international airport than Piraeus. Paros is the main hub of inter-island ferries within the Cyclades and to other island groups.

Ferry information is available from the local police (*limenarkhio*) at most harbours on the islands. Smaller islands may have only a marine post, but the officer will have a list of schedules. Hydrofoil information can also be obtained from Ceres' offices in main towns and from travel agents. The National Tourist Office of Greece (NTOG) publishes a comprehensive summer ferry schedule and there's a useful book entitled ***Greek Island Hopping*** by Frwein Poffley (Thomas Cook).

DRIVING

Greece: Greece has some of the worst traffic problems in Europe. Traffic jams and pollution are part of daily life in Athens, where some 1.5 million cars pack the streets, and the country has the highest accident rate in Europe after Portugal. In central Athens, cars are banned in an attempt to reduce the smog (*néfos*) that envelops one of the world's most polluted cities. It's best to use public transport in Athens and leave your car at home. Road conditions are often perilous, road surfaces changing without warning and rights of way apparently decided on a whim by drivers. Petrol and diesel in Greece are the cheapest in the EU and even cheaper in Cyprus. You should also bear in mind that some islands, such as Hydra, are completely car-free.

Like motorists in all countries, Greeks have their own idiosyncrasies and customs, many of which are peculiar to a particular city or region. The personalities of most Greeks change the moment they get behind the wheel of a car, when even the most placid person can become an aggressive, impatient and intolerant homicidal maniac with a unshakeable conviction in his own immortality. The average Greek driver aspires to be a racing driver, as is evident on most country roads where many accidents are due to dangerous overtaking – stricter controls introduced in 1992 haven't had much impact on the death toll. When driving in Greece you should regard all drivers as totally unpredictable and drive defensively. On motorways and main roads you must keep a safe distance from the vehicle in front and can be fined for not doing so. **As a general rule, the closer the car is behind you, the further you should be from the vehicle in front.** Greeks have little respect for traffic rules and many believe that many rules are merely recommendations, particularly those regarding parking (in Athens, a car is a device used to create parking spaces).

Greece's major road network covers around 40,000km (25,000mi), 9,000km (5,600mi) of which are national roads. Road improvements are one of the government's priorities and there's a major programme under way to convert many national roads into motorways including an ambitious project to complete a 680km (425mi) east-west corridor along the north of the country by 2006. A north-south axis motorway (1,000km/620mi) has recently been completed and there are other good fast roads between Patra, Athens, Corinth, Vólos and Thessalonika, although these are toll roads costing between €1 and 2.50 per section. However, tolls are more than compensated for by the speed and safety of these roads. Note that some toll booths are unmanned and are equipped only with a net into which you deposit the correct change. Greek motorways are generally good, although the quality of other roads is extremely variable and in some areas even fairly major roads are full of potholes and in a dreadful state. You should therefore exercise extreme caution when driving, as an apparently good road can rapidly turn into a bumpy track without warning. Speed limits in Greece are 50kph (31mph) in built up areas, 90kph (56mph) on main roads and 120kph (75mph) on motorways.

Cyprus: After Greece, you'll find driving in Cyprus generally relaxing, where, with the exception of taxis, most traffic circulates according to internationally-recognised road rules. Roads are generally good and major towns are linked by a network of modern roads. Driving is probably the best means of getting around on the island and decidedly quicker than using buses. The island has good driving conditions and there are excellent dual carriageways linking Nicosia with the main towns of

Limassol and Paphos. However, off the main routes roads may be single-lane only with poor surfaces. **Driving is on the left** and distances are given in kilometres on both maps and road signs, which are often in Greek and English, although this cannot be relied on throughout the island. The speed limit is 40kph (24mph) in built-up areas, 75kph (46mph) on main roads and 100kph (62mph) on motorways, where there's also a minimum speed limit of 65kph (40mph). Petrol in Cyprus is slightly cheaper than in most European countries, although considerably more expensive than in North America. The typical cost for driving 18,000km (around 11,000mi) a year is some CY£1,000, including insurance, petrol, servicing and road tax.

If you exceed the speed limit in Greece or Cyprus, you're liable for a large fine depending on your speed and the prevailing limit. Police are empowered to issue traffic on-the-spot fines, although if you cannot pay there and then you will be given a specific place to pay within a given time. Legally, helmets must be worn on motorcycles, although you'll see many bare-headed motorcyclists (fines of up to €30 can be imposed on offenders). First-aid kits, fire extinguishers and warning triangles should be carried in cars, but petrol cans are prohibited. Railway crossings often don't have protective barriers and caution must be used when approaching them.

Importing a Car

Before planning to import a car into Greece or Cyprus you should check the latest regulations. In Greece, EU nationals can import and use an EU-registered car for up to six months, after which you must officially import it and pay Greek road tax and customs duties (or remove it from the country). Note that if you take your car to Greece, it's important to be able to prove when it was imported and therefore you should have your papers stamped at customs when entering the country. There are heavy fines for unregistered cars and those without their papers stamped. If you wish to import a vehicle from within the EU, no tax is payable providing VAT was paid when it was purchased and you've owned it for at least six months. The associated paperwork can be completed by a customs agent and is well worth the fee. Once you obtain a Greek residence card you aren't permitted to drive a vehicle with foreign registration, although a period of grace is allowed (six months) while awaiting your Greek registration papers. Non-residents may keep and use a foreign registered car in Greece for up to six months a year, providing they pay Greek road tax. Vehicles imported from outside the EU require an exhaust emissions certificate. Full information regarding the importation of vehicles is available from the Ministry of Transport and Communications, Directorate General for Transport, Xenofondos 13, TK 101 91 Athens (☎ 01-325 4515).

In Cyprus, foreign residents can buy a car duty-free and change it at stated intervals – an attractive incentive and one worth investigating as considerable savings can be made. Cars imported into Cyprus are allowed to remain for three months, but may not be taken across the 'Green Line' into northern Cyprus. Once you've become a resident of Cyprus you must register an imported car with the authorities. Bear in mind that the Cypriot car market is dominated by Japanese manufacturers and although many European models are sold, spare parts aren't always readily available and obtaining them from abroad can take some time.

Driving Licences

It's no longer necessary for EU residents to exchange their pink EU licence for a Greek licence. Non-EU nationals must apply for a Greek driving licence as soon as they become residents. Non-residents don't require a Greek driving licence to buy or operate a Greek-registered car and may drive in Greece for a maximum of six months a year with a foreign or international driving permit (IDP). Note that for your licence to be recognised by the Greek authorities it must be at least six months old. Your licence must be carried when driving in Greece, along with your vehicle's registration papers (proof of ownership) and insurance certificate. The minimum age for driving in Greece is 18 for a motor car or motorcycle over 125cc, 16 for a motorcycle between 50 and 125cc, and 14 for a motorcycle (moped) up to 50cc. In Cyprus a foreign or international driving licence is valid for six months, but residents must apply for a Cypriot licence before the six-month period has expired.

Car Insurance

Under Greek law, motor vehicles, trailers and semi-trailers must be insured when entering the country. However, it isn't mandatory for cars insured in most European countries to have an international insurance 'green' card. Motorists insured in an EU country, the Czech Republic, Hungary, Liechtenstein, Norway, Slovakia and Switzerland are automatically covered for third party liability in Greece. The categories of car insurance available in Greece include third party, which is the minimum required by law, third party fire and theft (called part comprehensive in some countries) and fully comprehensive (total loss).

In Cyprus, you need to check with your insurance company before arriving on the island whether your car will be insured during your stay. Green Cards for foreign insurance aren't valid and when you arrive you will be insured on the spot for a fee covering the intended length of your stay. If you plan to remain on the island for a long period (or indefinitely) you should insure your car with a local insurance company.

Car Crime

Most European countries have a problem with car crime, i.e. thefts of and from cars, and Greece and Cyprus are no exception. Foreign registered vehicles are popular targets. If you drive anything other than a worthless heap you should have theft insurance, which includes your car stereo and your personal belongings. If you drive a new or valuable car, it's wise to have it fitted with an alarm, an engine immobiliser (the best system) or another anti-theft device, plus a visible deterrent, such as a steering or gear stick lock. It's particularly important to protect your car if you own a model that's desirable to car thieves, e.g. most new sports and executive cars, which are often stolen by professional crooks to order.

A good security system won't stop someone breaking into your car (which usually takes most thieves a matter of seconds) and may not prevent your car being stolen, but it will at least make it more difficult and may persuade a thief to look for an easier target. Radios, tape and CD players attract a lot of the wrong attention in some towns and coastal resorts. If you buy an expensive stereo system, you should buy one with a removable unit or with a removable (face-off) control panel that you can pop in a pocket or bag. However, never forget to remove it, even when stopping for a few minutes. Some manufacturers provide stereo systems that won't work when they're removed from their original vehicles or are inoperable without a security code.

When leaving your car unattended, store any valuables (including clothes) in the boot or out of sight. If you leave your car papers in your car, make sure that you have a copy. If possible, avoid parking in long-term car parks as they are favourite hunting grounds for car thieves. Foreign-registered cars, particularly camper vans and mobile homes, are popular targets in Greece. When parking overnight or when it's dark, parking in a well-lit area may help deter car thieves. If your car is stolen or anything is stolen from it, report it to the police in the area where it was stolen. You can report it by telephone, but must go to the station to complete a report. Don't, however, expect the police to find it or even take any interest in your loss. Report a theft to your insurance company as soon as possible.

General Road Rules

The following general road rules may help you adjust to driving in Greece and Cyprus. Don't, however, expect other motorists to adhere to them (many local drivers invent their own 'rules').

● You may have already noticed that the Greeks drive on the right-hand side of the road. It saves confusion if you do likewise! If you aren't used to driving on the right, take it easy until you're accustomed to it. Be particularly alert when leaving lay-bys, T-junctions, one-way streets, petrol stations and car parks, as it's easy to lapse into driving on the left. It's helpful to display a reminder, e.g. 'Think Right!', on your car's dashboard. Note, however, that Cypriots drive on the left and if you come from a country that drives on the right, the above comments apply equally in 'reverse'!

● Alcohol is a major factor in many road accidents and drink-driving laws are strict in Greece, where the permitted blood-alcohol concentration is 50mg of alcohol per 100ml of blood, as in most other EU countries. In Cyprus, the permitted blood alcohol concentration is 90mg of alcohol per 100ml of blood, which isn't as strict as in the UK or the USA.

● All motorists must carry a red breakdown triangle and a full set of spare bulbs and fuses. It's mandatory in Greece (and recommended everywhere) to carry a fire extinguisher and a first-aid kit. The Greek national motoring organisation (ELPA) is on hand in main towns and on major roads to help motorists who break down and has centres in Athens, Ioannína, Corfu, Crete, Larissa, Patra, Trípolis and Vólos. Dial 174 for information and 104 in an emergency.

● Main roads in Greece are designated priority roads, shown by signs. On secondary roads *without* priority signs and in built-up areas, you must give way to vehicles coming from your RIGHT. **Failure to observe this rule is the cause of many accidents.** The priority rule was fine when there was little traffic, but nowadays most countries (Greece included) realise the necessity of having 'stop' or 'give way' signs at junctions. Most Greek motorists no longer treat passage as a

God-given right, although some still pull out without looking. The priority to the right rule usually also applies in car parks, but never when exiting *from* car parks or dirt tracks. If you're ever in doubt about who has the right of way, it's wise to give way (particularly to large trucks!). In Cyprus, there are 'stop' or give way' signs at junctions and the give way to the right (or left) rule doesn't apply.

- The wearing of seat belts is *compulsory* in both Greece and Cyprus, and includes passengers in rear seats when seat belts are fitted. Children under the age of 12 in Greece and under five in Cyprus aren't permitted to ride in the front of a vehicle. A baby under nine months of age must be strapped into a cot on a rear seat and an infant aged from nine months to three years must have an approved child safety seat. You can be fined for not wearing a seat belt. Note that if you have an accident and weren't wearing a seat belt, your insurance company can refuse to pay a personal injury claim.

- Jumping a red light in Greece can result in a fine of around €150 and even for not dipping your headlights in town you can be fined €30. **Be warned!**

- Horns should only be used in emergencies, particularly in towns at night, when lights should usually be flashed to warn other motorists or pedestrians.

- Always come to a complete stop when required at intersections and ensure that you stop behind the white line. Intersections are a favourite spot for police patrols waiting for motorists to put a wheel a few centimetres over the line.

- White or yellow lines mark the separation of traffic lanes. A solid single line or two solid lines means no overtaking in either direction. A solid line on your side of the road, means that overtaking is prohibited in your direction. You may overtake only when there's a single broken line in the middle of the road or double lines with a broken line on your side of the road. No overtaking may also be shown by the international road sign of two cars side by side (one red and one black).

- Always check your rear view and wing mirrors carefully before overtaking, as motorists often seem to appear from nowhere and zoom past at a 'zillion' miles an hour, especially on country roads. If you drive a right-hand drive (RHD) car in Greece you should take extra care when overtaking – the most dangerous manoeuvre in motoring.

- Many motorists seem to have an aversion to driving in the inside lane on a three-lane motorway, in effect reducing it to two lanes. It's illegal to overtake on an inside lane unless traffic is being channelled in a different direction. Motorists must indicate before overtaking and when moving back into an inside lane after overtaking, e.g. on a motorway.

- Be particularly wary of moped riders and cyclists. It isn't always easy to see them, particularly when they're hidden by the blind spots of a car or are riding at night without lights. Many young moped riders seem to have a death wish and tragically hundreds of them lose their lives each year. They are constantly pulling out into traffic or turning without looking or signalling. **Follow the example set by other motorists, who, when overtaking mopeds and cyclists, usually give them a wide . . . . WIDE berth.** If you knock them off their bikes you may have a difficult time convincing the police that it wasn't your fault; far better to avoid them (and the police).

- Cars mustn't be overloaded, particularly roof-racks, and luggage weight shouldn't exceed that recommended in manufacturers' handbooks. Greek police make spot checks and fine offenders around €30 on the spot for overloaded cars.

- Be careful where you park, particularly in cities where your car can be clamped or towed away in a flash. *Never* park across entrances, at bus stops or taxi ranks, in front of fire and ambulance stations and schools (which may be indicated by coloured kerbstones) or near pedestrian crossings. Always check parking signs carefully and look for kerb markings (ask someone if you aren't sure whether parking is permitted).

- All motorists in Greece and Cyprus must be familiar with the local highway code, available from book shops.

Car Rental

Multinational car rental companies such as Alamo, Avis, Europcar, Hertz, National and Thrifty have offices in most large towns and major airports in Greece and Cyprus. If you're visiting in high season, you should reserve a rental car before arriving. Car rental in Greece is *very* expensive, particularly for short periods, and includes VAT at 18 per cent (13 per cent in the Dodecanese, north-eastern Aegean and the Sporades). There are also optional extras such as a collision damage waiver (CDW) of around €10 daily, without which you're liable for the first €4,500 of damage. High season weekly rates with unlimited mileage start at around €30 for a small model such as an Opel Corsa. Rates reduce considerably for longer rental periods, e.g. a month or longer. Local rental companies are usually cheaper than the nationals, although cars must be returned to the pick-up point. Older cars can also be hired from many garages at lower rates than those charged by the national car-hire companies, although they aren't always in good condition.

To hire a car in Greece you must be aged at least 21, although a few companies have a higher age of 23, and for certain categories of vehicles the age limit is 25. Drivers must have held a full licence for a minimum of one year and most companies have an upper age limit of 60 or 65. If a credit card isn't used, there's usually a cash deposit of €60 per day. If you wish to take your hire car on a ferry or to another country, you must have written authorisation from the rental company. Note that rental mopeds or motorcycles cannot be taken on ferries in Greece.

Car rental in Cyprus is quite reasonable by international standards, although the condition of rental cars often leaves much to be desired. Be particularly wary of bad brakes and if possible, test drive a car before you rent it. High-season rates start at CY£11 a day for small cars (usually Japanese), including unlimited mileage and most insurance (but excluding VAT). You must also pay a collision damage waiver of CY£3 per day. In high-season you should book well in advance, although it's worth checking out fly-drive deals which can reduce the cost of car hire considerably. Rental cars in Cyprus are fitted with distinctive red plates with numbers prefixed with a 'Z' and police are usually fairly tolerant of foreign motorists. Note that you aren't permitted to cross the Green Line into northern Cyprus in a rental car. To hire a car in Cyprus you must be aged at least 21 and for certain categories of vehicles the age limit is 25. Drivers must have held a full licence for a minimum of one year and most companies have an upper age limit of 60 or 65. If a credit card isn't used, there's usually a daily cash deposit.

Note that many car rental contracts state in the small print that you're not permitted to use normal cars on dirt tracks, which are commonly found on many Greek islands and in the countryside. If any damage is done to the undercarriage, you will liable for this. Rental cars can be ordered with a luggage rack and child seats can be fitted for an extra charge. You can also hire a 4-wheel-drive vehicle (handy for country roads), station wagon, minibus, prestige luxury car, armoured limousine or a convertible, possibly with a choice of manual or automatic gearbox. Minibuses accessible to wheelchairs can also be hired. Vans and pick-ups are available from the major rental companies by the hour, half-day or day, or from smaller local companies (which are cheaper).

Cars can also be rented for use in Greece and Cyprus through the US offices of major international rental companies such as Alamo (☎ 800-327 9633), Avis (☎ 800-331 1212), Budget (☎ 800-527 0700) and Hertz (☎ 800-654 3131) by booking a car through the hire companies' American offices and paying by credit card. This is a legitimate practice and you can save 50 per cent or more on local hire rates. The car hire companies have no way of knowing where the calls were made and therefore cannot prevent it. Toll-free (800) numbers of other US-based rental companies can be obtained from international directory enquiries, but note that you will pay international rates when phoning from abroad.

2.

FURTHER CONSIDERATIONS

This chapter contains important considerations for most people planning to buy a home in Greece or Cyprus, particularly those planning to live there permanently or semi-permanently. It contains information about the climate, geography, health, insurance, shopping, pets, television and radio, learning Greek, crime, public holidays and time difference.

CLIMATE

In general, Greece enjoys a typical Mediterranean climate with hot, dry summers and cool, wet winters. However, the Greek climate differs considerably depending on the location, elevation and distance from the coast, and it isn't possible to generalise. Many regions and areas are influenced by the surrounding mountains, islands and other geographical features, and some even have their own micro-climates. If you're planning to live in Greece and don't know whether the climate in a particular region will suit you, you should rent accommodation until you're sure, as the extremes of hot and cold in some areas are too much for some people. However, you can be sure of sunshine throughout most of the country from spring to autumn and Greece boasts over 3,000 hours of sunshine a year.

Greece can be divided into several main climatic regions. Northern Macedonia and northern Epiros have a climate similar to the Balkans, with freezing winters and very hot, humid summers. In the mountains in this part of Greece, summers can also be very short and during the winter the mountains are covered in snow from November to May. Temperatures in Thessalonika average 5°C (40°F) in winter and 25°C (70°F) in summer, although high humidity can make it appear much hotter. The area experiences rain most of the year and the average rainfall is around 50mm (2in) per month.

The Attica peninsula, the Cyclades, the Dodecanese, Crete and the central and eastern Peloponnese enjoy a typically Mediterranean climate. Winters are generally mild (particularly by northern European standards) with daytime temperatures averaging around 14°C (58°F). Snow is extremely rare in the Cyclades but the high mountains of Crete and the Peloponnese are snow-covered throughout the winter and it has been known to snow in Athens. Summers are very hot with average daytime temperatures of 32°C (94°F), although some respite is provided by the northern *meltémi* winds in July and August. However, although the *meltémi* lowers the temperature and reduces humidity, the strong wind often causes havoc with ferry schedules and sends everything flying. Summer evenings are usually pleasantly cool on the islands.

The western Peloponnese, Stereá Ellhada, Epiros and the Ionian islands escape the *meltémi* winds and have less severe winters than northern Greece, but have the highest rainfall, with an average of around 270mm (11in) a month during the winter in Crete. Crete is, however, the warmest place in Greece and you can swim in the warm waters off its southern coast from mid-April to November. The North-eastern Aegean islands, Halkidiki and the Pelion peninsula have a climate that's mid-way between that of the harsher Balkans to the north and the southern Mediterranean.

The best time to make a house-hunting visit to Greece is the spring (or autumn), when it's pleasantly warm but not usually too hot, the countryside is a mass of flowers and the hordes of tourists have yet to arrive. However, note that outside the high season not all services will be operating or offering the quality of service they provide in the summer, and some islands may be virtually at a standstill.

Winters can be harsh in most of Greece, but the most dependable winter weather can be found in the Dodecanese especially Rhodes and in southern parts of Crete, although winters in most islands are generally mild and a blessed relief from frozen northern Europe. In summer, hot and dry conditions are common everywhere except from some higher altitudes, which should be borne in mind when buying a home in Greece. The average sea-level temperature in July is around 27°C (81°F). Most islands have little rainfall in summer and parts of the country frequently suffer drought conditions.

Approximate average maximum/minimum temperatures for selected towns are shown below in Centigrade and Fahrenheit (in brackets):

Location	Spring	Summer	Autumn	Winter
Athens	20/11 (70/52)	33/23 (96/76)	24/15 (78/60)	13/6 (56/42)
Corfu	22/14 (74/58)	29/20 (88/70)	26/17 (82/64)	13/7 (56/44)
Heráklion	20/12 (70/54)	29/22 (88/72)	24/17 (78/64)	16/9 (61/48)
Rhodes	22/14 (74/58)	28/20 (86/70)	26/22 (82/72)	14/10 (58/50)
Halkidiki	24/14 (77/58)	30/20 (90/70)	26/17 (82/64)	10/3 (50/36)

Cyprus: Hardly surprisingly, the overwhelming attraction of Cyprus (apart from the tax incentives) for most foreigners is its excellent climate with an average of 340 days sunshine per year, and it is, along with Portugal's southern Algarve coast and Spain's Costa del Sol, the warmest area in Europe in winter. Cyprus is noted for its moderate climate with short, mild winters, when temperatures rarely fall below 16°C (62°F), with the exception of the Troodos mountains, where snow falls in winter and skiing is popular. Summers are long, hot and dry everywhere except in the Troodos, which becomes a veritable haven in summer, and some parts of the island can get extremely hot in the months of July and August, despite the sea breezes. As in all southern European countries, spring and autumn are the most pleasant seasons, when it's warm and sunny but rarely too hot. The light rainy season falls in the winter months from December to February, with an average of 14 days rain in January.

Most of Cyprus has a climate classed as 'arid Mediterranean' and it's the hottest, driest island in the Mediterranean. Summers are generally very hot and last from May to late September, when temperatures average 30°C (90°F) on the coast and 38°C (100°F) inland. Nicosia is the driest and hottest part of the island. There's no rain during the summer months and relatively little falls in May and October. The Troodos mountains are the wettest part of the south of the island and have an average of around 200mm (49in) of rain annually, although from January to March rain falls as snow. In common with many southern European countries, Cyprus periodically suffers from lack of rainfall leading to droughts and water shortages.

Spring and autumn are short compared with northern European seasons and April is the height of spring when the landscape is covered in flowers, before becoming dry and dusty until winter. Winters in Cyprus can hardly be classed as such (at least not by northern European standards), although the Troodos mountains are cold and in some areas the temperature may drop suddenly. The sea is generally warm most of the year in Cyprus, which enjoys average temperatures of 19°C (68°F) in winter and 28°C (86°F) in the summer months.

Approximate average maximum/minimum temperatures for Cyprus' main towns are shown below in Centigrade and Fahrenheit (in brackets):

Location	Spring	Summer	Autumn	Winter
Nicosia	36/10 (96/50)	40/17 (103/63)	28/6 (82/42)	22/2 (71/34)
Larnaca	32/12 (70/38)	32/12 (90/53)	27/8 (80/47)	21/3 (70/38)
Paphos	30/12 (86/54)	33/19 (91/65)	26/10 (79/50)	22/5 (71/41)

Frequent weather forecasts are broadcast on TV and radio and published in daily newspapers in both Greece and Cyprus. A quick way to make a *rough* conversion from Centigrade to Fahrenheit is to multiply by two and add 30.

GEOGRAPHY

Greece: Greece is situated at the southern tip of the Balkan peninsula and is the only member of the European Union (EU) without a land frontier with another member. To the north, Greece borders Albania, the former Yugoslav Republic of Macedonia, and Bulgaria, while to the east lies Turkey whilst the south the country is surrounded by the Ionian and Aegean seas. Greece consists of a peninsula and almost 10,000 islands (although only around 115 are inhabited) some 3,000 of which make up around 20 per cent of the country's landmass. Around 80 per cent of the mainland is mountainous, with ranges extending into the sea as peninsulas or chains of islands. Greece is a mountainous, stony country with a highly indented and rugged coast, dotted with ancient fortifications. According to Greek mythology, when making the world the Gods distributed the available soil to each country after sieving it and tossed the rejected stones over their shoulders – to make Greece! The Pindos range of mountains almost divides the country in two from north-west to south-east.

The capital of Greece is Athens, the country's largest city with a population of over 4 million and home to the country's principal port, Piraeus. The second-largest city is Thessalonika, the capital of Macedonia, which has a population of around 1 million and is itself an important seaport, providing a gateway to the Balkans. Greece is divided into ten regions or prefectures of which Macedonia is the largest. The mainland regions are Central Greece, Epiros, Macedonia, Peloponnese, Thessaly and Thrace, while the island groups are the Cyclades, Dodecanese, Ionian, North-eastern Aegean, Saronic Gulf and Sporades. Crete and Elvia don't belong to any group and for administrative purposes are divided into prefectures or nomes (*nomoi*). The regions of Greece are shown on the map in **Appendix D** and a map of the eastern Mediterranean showing Greece and Cyprus is on page 6.

Cyprus: Cyprus is Europe's southernmost point and the Mediterranean's third-largest island after Sardinia and Sicily, being 240km (150mi) long and 100km (62mi) wide. The island, although politically part of Europe, is actually geographically nearer the Middle East, with Turkey to the north (a mere 69km/43mi away) and Israel, Lebanon and Syria to the east. Because of its geographical position, the island has been of huge strategic importance to invaders from Europe and Asia throughout its history. Cyprus has two mountain ranges: the Troodos in the west of the island crowned by Mount Olympus (2,000m/6,600ft), the island's highest peak and snow-covered for much of the winter, and the Keryneia chain stretching along the northern part of the island. The Troodos have been extensively reforested in recent years and pine and oak forests now cover the western slopes, which are home to an interesting and unique range of flora and fauna. It's in these mountains that most of Cyprus' rivers emerge in the rainy season and several dams have been constructed in the area.

Cyprus has some 768km (480mi) of extremely varied coastline, ranging from spectacular white cliffs and rocky coves to long sandy beaches. There are two natural harbours at Limassol and Famagusta, and Larnaca has a man-made port. In the centre of the island is the central plain known as the Mesaoria Plain, home to the capital Nicosia and where much of the island's agricultural activity takes place. The plain is relatively fertile, although farming takes place only in winter and spring, as it receives no water outside these seasons.

Apart from Nicosia (pop. c. 200,000), all the major cities are situated on the coast. Limassol is the second-largest city and the island's biggest port, and Larnaca and Paphos, both important holiday resorts, are the third and fourth-largest respectively. Cyprus can roughly be divided into the regions shown on the map in **Appendix D** and the island is also shown on the map of the eastern Mediterranean on page 6.

HEALTH

One of the most important aspects of living in Greece or Cyprus (or anywhere else for that matter) is maintaining good health. The quality of health care and health care facilities in Greece leaves much to be desired, although they're improving. In 1983, a national health-service was introduced in common with many other countries of southern Europe. However, although medical training is of a high standard, the health service is one of the worst in Europe, largely because of under-funding, with overcrowded hospitals and standards of hygiene well below northern Europe. If you're hospitalised in Greece, your relatives are expected to provide your food and often your bedding! Not surprisingly, health care costs per head in Greece are the lowest in the European Union and the country spends a relatively small percentage of its GDP on health. Public and private medicine operate alongside each other in Greece and complement one another, although public health facilities are limited in some areas.

Greece's public health system provides free or low cost health care for those who contribute to Greek social security, plus their families and retirees (including those from other EU countries). Members are charged 25 per cent of the actual cost of prescriptions, although there are higher charges for non-essential medicines plus substantial contributions for many services, including spectacles, dentures, dental and other treatment. If you don't qualify for health care under the public health system, it's essential to have private health insurance. This is recommended in any case if you can afford it, owing to the inadequacy of public health services and long waiting lists for specialist appointments and non-urgent operations. Visitors to Greece should have holiday health insurance (see page 55) if they aren't covered by a reciprocal arrangement.

Emergency treatment is free to all nationalities in public hospitals and there are outpatient clinics (*yatría*) attached to hospitals and in rural areas. They're typically open from 8am to noon and treat minor health problems and it's often easier to obtain prompt emergency treatment here than at a public hospital. There are 24-hour emergency hospitals in major towns and on the large islands, and private hospitals and clinics in major towns and resort areas. English-speaking Greek doctors and foreign doctors practise in resort areas and major cities, and advertise in the local expatriate press. Pharmacists are highly qualified in Greece and you can obtain treatment for minor ailments at chemists (farmakío) as well as medical advice. In larger towns and resort areas, pharmacists often speak English. Pharmacies aren't usually open in the afternoon or at weekends, but a duty-chemist roster is posted in pharmacy windows and published in the local press. In a medical emergency you should phone 166 for an ambulance. Homeopathic remedies are widespread and there are homeopathic pharmacies in most large towns.

Greeks are among the world's healthiest people and have one of the highest life expectancies in the EU. The incidence of heart disease is among the lowest in the world, which is attributed in large part to their diet (which includes lots of garlic, olive oil and red wine), as is that of cancers. However, the country has a high rate of smoking-related health problems and the proportion of smokers is one of the highest in the EU.

In Cyprus, since independence from Britain, one of the government's main priorities has been health, and nowadays the quality of health care in Cyprus is high and life expectancy and child mortality statistics compare favourably with other western countries. Many doctors are trained in Britain and people living in many Middle Eastern countries choose to visit Cyprus for medical treatment. The country has a public health service funded through social security payments paid by Cypriot residents. **However, this service isn't available to visitors, who require private health insurance, although emergency treatment is free to anyone regardless of nationality.** Public and private medicine operate alongside one another in Cyprus and complement each other.

The public health system provides free or low cost health care for those who contribute to social security, plus their families and retirees. If you don't qualify for health care under the public health system (and you won't unless you contribute to the social security system), it's essential to have private health insurance unless you wish to pay by high medical bills. Private doctors abound in Cyprus and clinics are usually open from 9am to 1pm and from 4 to 7pm, Mondays to Fridays. Doctors charge around CY£10 for a consultation and the cost of most treatment is around half that of northern European countries.

Pharmacists are highly qualified (and usually speak English) and provide medical advice and treatment for minor ailments. They don't generally open at weekends, although a duty roster is posted in windows of chemists and published in the local press (or you can also phone 192 for information). In a medical emergency you should phone 199.

General: Among expatriates, common health problems include sunburn and sunstroke, stomach and bowel problems (due to the change of diet and more often, water, but also poor hygiene), and various problems caused by excess alcohol. Other health problems are caused by the high level of airborne pollen in spring (note that spring comes earlier to Greece and Cyprus than northern European countries), which particularly affects asthma and hay fever sufferers. If you aren't used to the very hot sun, you should limit your exposure and avoid it altogether during the hottest part of the day, wear protective clothing (including a hat) and use a sun block. Too much sun and too little protection will dry your skin and cause premature ageing, to say nothing of the risks of skin cancer. Care should also be taken to replace the natural oils lost from too many hours in the sun and the elderly should take particular care not to exert themselves during hot weather.

The mild climates of Greece and Cyprus are therapeutic, especially for sufferers of rheumatism and arthritis and those who are prone to bronchitis, colds and pneumonia. The slower pace of life is also beneficial for those who are prone to stress (it's difficult to remain up-tight while napping in the sun), although it takes some foreigners time to adjust. The climate and lifestyle in any country has a noticeable affect on mental health and people who live in hot climates are generally happier and more relaxed than those who live in cold, wet climates (such as northern Europe).

Health (and health insurance) is an important issue for anyone retiring abroad. Many people are ill-prepared for old age and the possibility of health problems, and foreigners who can no longer care for themselves are often forced to return to their home countries. There are few state residential nursing homes in Greece or Cyprus, or hospices for the terminally ill. Provision for handicapped travellers is also poor and wheelchair access to buildings and public transport is well below the average for Western Europe.

Pre-Departure Check: If you're planning to take up residence in Greece or Cyprus, even for only part of the year, it's wise to have a health check before your arrival, particularly if you've got a record of poor health or are elderly. If you're already taking regular medication, you should note that the brand names of drugs and medicines vary from country to country, and you should ask your doctor for the generic name. If you wish to match medication prescribed abroad, you will need a current prescription with the medication's trade name, the manufacturer's name, the chemical name and the dosage. Most drugs have an equivalent in other countries, although particular brands may be difficult or impossible to obtain abroad.

It's possible to have medication sent from another country and usually no import duty or value added tax is payable. If you're visiting a holiday home in Greece or Cyprus for a limited period, you should take sufficient medication with you to cover your stay, although in an emergency, a local doctor will write a prescription that can be taken to a local pharmacy. You should also take some of your favourite non-prescription drugs, e.g. cold and flu remedies, creams, etc., with you, as they may be difficult or impossible to obtain locally or may be much more expensive. If applicable, also take a spare pair of spectacles, contact lenses, dentures or hearing aid.

There are no immunisation requirements for Greece or Cyprus, although you may be advised to consider having certain vaccinations as a precaution if you're going to live there permanently. Domestic tap water is safe to drink, but you should be wary of drinking from public fountains, as not all of them provide drinking water (some have signs). Many people prefer the taste of bottled water, particularly in periods of drought when the quality of tap water sometimes deteriorates.

INSURANCE

An important aspect of owning a home in Greece or Cyprus is insurance, not only for your home and its contents, but also for your family or friends when visiting the country. If you live in Greece or Cyprus permanently you will require additional insurance. It's unnecessary to spend half your income insuring yourself against every eventuality, but it's important to insure against an event that could precipitate a major financial disaster, such as a serious accident or your house being demolished by a storm or earthquake. The cost of being uninsured or under-insured can be astronomical.

As with anything connected with finance, it's important to shop around when buying insurance, when simply collecting a few brochures from insurance agents or making a few telephone calls could save you a lot of money. Note, however, that not all insurance companies are equally reliable or have the same financial stability, and it may be better to insure with a large international company with a good reputation than with a small local company, even if this means paying a higher premium. Read insurance contracts carefully and make sure that you understand the terms and the cover provided before signing them. Some insurance companies will do almost anything to avoid paying claims and will use any available legal loophole, therefore it pays to deal only with reputable companies (not that this provides a foolproof guarantee). Policies often contain traps and legal loopholes in the small print and it's sometimes wise to obtain legal advice before signing a contract.

In all matters regarding insurance, you're responsible for ensuring that you and your family are legally insured in Greece or Cyprus. Regrettably you cannot insure yourself against being uninsured or sue your insurance agent for giving you bad advice! Bear in mind, that if you wish to make a claim on an insurance policy, you may be required to report an incident to the police within 24 hours (this may also be a legal requirement). The law in Greece and Cyprus may differ considerably from your home country or your previous country of residence, and you should *never* assume that it's the same. If you're uncertain of your rights, you should obtain legal advice for anything other than a minor claim.

The following section contains information about health insurance, household insurance (building, contents and third party liability), and holiday and travel insurance. See also **Car Insurance** on page 34.

Health Insurance

If you're visiting, living or working in Greece or Cyprus, it's extremely risky not to have health insurance for your family, as if you're uninsured or under-insured you could be faced with some very high medical bills. When deciding on the type and extent of health insurance, make sure that it covers *all* your family's present and future health requirements *before* you receive a large bill. A health insurance policy should cover you for *all* essential health care whatever the reason, including accidents, e.g. sports accidents, and injuries, whether they occur in your home, at your place of work or while travelling. Don't take anything for granted, but check in advance.

Greece: If you're planning to take up residence in Greece and will be contributing to Greek social security, you and your family will be entitled to subsidised or (in certain cases) free medical and dental treatment. The Greek national health system is operated by the *Idrima Kinonikon Asfalisseon* (IKA). When you start work you must obtain a medical booklet (*iatrico vivliario*) from your local IKA office, which must be presented each time you visit a doctor or hospital. Doctor and hospital treatment within the Greek system is free, but you will be charged 25 per cent of the cost of prescriptions. Most foreign residents also subscribe to a complementary health insurance fund, which pays the portion of medical bills that isn't paid by social security. Residents who don't contribute to social security should have private health insurance, which is mandatory for non-EU residents when applying for a visa or residence permit.

Note that some foreign insurance companies don't provide sufficient cover to satisfy Greek regulations, therefore you should check the minimum cover necessary with a Greek consulate in your country of residence. For further information, contact the International Relations office (IKA, Tmima Diethon Scheseon, 178 Kifissias Avenue, Athens 15231, ☎ 01-647 1140). The IKA deals with health, sickness, maternity and old age benefits, whereas the local OAED handle unemployment and family benefits, and can advise on claiming benefits covered by their department.

If you live in a remote area of Greece that isn't covered by a local IKA office, you'll have to pay the cost of any medical treatment in advance and re-claim it from the IKA office in Athens. However, the refund will be only a proportion of the cost and you will be responsible for the balance. If you receive treatment under these circumstances, it's necessary to obtain receipts and documentation in order to make a claim.

Cyprus: It's important to note that *only* Cypriot nationals and residents who contribute to social security payments are entitled to treatment under the public health system and there are *no* reciprocal agreements with EU nationals. If you contribute to Cypriot social security, you and your family are entitled to free or subsidised medical treatment. Otherwise you must make sure that your family is fully covered by private health insurance.

Private Insurance: If you aren't covered by Greek or Cypriot social security you should take out private health insurance. It's advantageous to be insured with a company that will pay large medical bills directly. Most private health insurance policies don't pay family doctors' fees or pay for medication that isn't provided in a hospital or there's an 'excess' payment that often exceeds the cost of treatment. Most will, however, pay for 100 per cent of specialists' fees and hospital treatment in the best hospitals. Generally, the higher the premium, the more choice you have regarding doctors, specialists and hospitals. You should avoid a company that reserves the right to cancel a policy when you reach a certain age, e.g. 65 or 70, or which increases premiums sharply as you get older, as trying to take out a new policy at the age of 65 or older at a reasonable premium is difficult. If you already have private health insurance in another country, you may be able to extend it to cover you in Greece or Cyprus.

Changing Employers or Insurance Companies: When changing employers or leaving Greece or Cyprus, you should ensure that you have continuous health insurance. If you and your family are covered by a company health plan, your insurance will probably cease after your last day of employment. If you're planning to change your health insurance company, you should ensure that important benefits aren't lost, e.g. existing medical conditions won't usually be covered by a new insurer. When changing medical insurance companies, you should inform your old company if you have any outstanding bills for which they're liable.

Health Insurance for Visitors

Visitors spending short periods in Greece or Cyprus, e.g. up to a month, should have a travel health insurance policy (see page 55), particularly if they aren't covered by an international health policy. If you plan to spend up to six months in Greece or Cyprus you should either take out a travel policy, a special long-stay policy or an international health policy, which should cover you in your home country and when travelling in other countries. Note that premiums vary considerably and it's important to shop around. Most international health policies include repatriation or evacuation (these may be optional), which may also include shipment (by air) of the body of a person who has died abroad to his home country for burial. Note that an international policy also allows you to choose which country you want to have treatment in.

Most international insurance companies offer health policies for different areas, e.g. Europe, world-wide excluding North America, and world-wide including North America. Most companies offer different levels of cover, for example, basic, standard, comprehensive and prestige levels of cover. There's always an limit on the total annual medical costs and some companies also limit the fees for specific treatment or care, such as specialists, operations and hospital accommodation. A medical examination isn't usually required for international health policies, although pre-existing health problems are excluded for a period, e.g. one or two years.

Claims are usually settled in major currencies and large claims are usually settled directly by insurance companies (although your choice of hospitals may be limited). Always check whether an insurance company will settle large medical bills directly, as if you're required to pay bills and claim reimbursement from an insurance company, it can take several months before you receive your money (some companies are slow to pay). It isn't usually necessary to translate bills into English or another language, although you should check a company's policy. Most international health insurance companies provide emergency telephone assistance.

The cost of international health insurance varies considerably depending on your age and the extent of cover. Note that with most international insurance policies, you must enrol before you reach a certain age, e.g. between 60 and 80, to be guaranteed continuous cover in your old age. Premiums can sometimes be paid monthly, quarterly or annually, although some companies insist on payment annually in advance. When comparing policies, carefully check the extent of cover and exactly what is included and excluded from a policy (often this is indicated only in the *very* small print), apart from premiums and excess charges. In some countries, premium increases are limited by law, although this may apply only to residents of the country where a company is registered, and not to overseas policyholders. Although there may be significant differences in premiums, generally you get what you pay for and can tailor premiums to your requirements. The most important questions to ask yourself are: does the policy provide the cover required and is it good value for money? If you're in good health and are able to pay for your own out-patient treatment, such as visits to your family doctor and prescriptions, then the best value may be a policy covering specialist and hospital treatment only.

Reciprocal Health Agreements (Greece): If you're entitled to social security health benefits in another EU country or in a country with a reciprocal health agreement with Greece, you will receive free or reduced cost medical treatment there. If you live in the EU, you should apply for a certificate of entitlement to treatment (form E111) from your local social security office at least three weeks before you plan to travel to Greece. An E111 is open-ended and valid for life. However, you must continue to make social security contributions in the country where it was issued and if you become a resident in another country, e.g. in Greece, it becomes invalid. It covers emergency hospital treatment but doesn't include prescribed medicines, special examinations, X-rays, laboratory tests, physiotherapy or dental treatment. If you use the E111 in Greece, you must sometimes pay in advance and apply for a reimbursement from Greek social security (instructions are provided with the form), which can take months. **Note, however, that you can still receive a large bill from a Greek hospital, as your local health authority assumes only a percentage of the cost!**

Participating countries include EU member states and most other European countries, **excluding** Albania, Cyprus, Switzerland and Turkey. The USA doesn't have a reciprocal health agreement with Greece and therefore American students and other Americans who aren't covered by Greek social security *must* have private health insurance in Greece. British visitors or Britons planning to live in Greece can obtain information about reciprocal health treatment from the Department of Social Security, Overseas Branch, Newcastle-upon-Tyne, NE98 1YX, UK.

Household Insurance

Household insurance in Greece and Cyprus generally includes the building, its contents and third party liability, all of which are contained in a multi-risk household insurance policy. Policies are offered by both local and international insurance companies, whose premiums are similar, although foreign companies may provide wider cover.

Building: Although it isn't compulsory if you don't have a mortgage, it's wise for owners to take out building insurance that covers damage to their home due to fire, smoke, water, explosion, storm, freezing, snow, theft, vandalism, malicious damage, acts of terrorism, impact, broken windows and other natural catastrophes (such as falling trees). Insurance should include glass, external buildings, aerials and satellite dishes, gardens and garden ornaments. Bear in mind that most of Greece lies in an earthquake zone (most buildings on the island of Kefallonia were destroyed in an earthquake in 1953) and Cyprus is also affected by earthquakes from time to time, therefore you should ensure that damage caused by earthquakes is included. Cover for earthquakes, lightning damage and subsidence usually aren't included in a standard policy, so check exactly what's excluded and what it will cost to include extra risks.

Note that if a claim is the result of a defect in design or construction, the insurance company won't pay up – another reason why you should have a survey before buying.

Property insurance is based on the cost of rebuilding your home and should be increased each year in line with inflation. **Make sure that you insure your property for the true cost of rebuilding.** It's important to have insurance for storm damage, which can be severe in some areas. If floods are one of your concerns (flash floods aren't uncommon), make sure that you're covered for water coming in from ground level, not just for water seeping in through the roof. Always read the small print of contracts. If you own a home in an area that has been hit by a succession of natural disasters (such as floods), your insurance premiums may be increased dramatically or your policy may even be cancelled.

Contents: Contents are usually insured for the same risks as a building (see above) and are usually insured for their replacement value (new for old), with a reduction for wear and tear for clothes and linen. Valuable objects are covered for their actual declared and authenticated value. Most policies include automatic indexation of the insured sum in line with inflation. Contents insurance may include accidental damage to sanitary installations, theft, money, replacement of locks following damage or loss of keys, frozen food, alternative accommodation cover, and property belonging to third parties stored in your home. Some items, however, are usually optional, including credit cards, frozen foods, emergency assistance (plumber, glazier, electrician, etc.), redecoration, garaged cars, replacement pipes, loss of rent, and the cost of travel to Greece or Cyprus for holiday homeowners. Many policies include personal third party or legal liability, although this may be an option.

Items of high value must usually be itemised and photographs and documentation, e.g. a valuation, should be provided. Some companies recommend or insist on a video film of belongings. When claiming for contents you should produce the original bills (always keep bills for expensive items), if possible, and should bear in mind that replacing imported items may be much more expensive if you need to buy them locally. Note that contents' policies usually contain security clauses and if you don't adhere to them a claim won't be considered. If you're planning to let a property, you may be required to inform your insurer. A building must be secure with good locks and many companies offer a discount if properties have steel reinforced doors, high security locks and alarms (particularly alarms connected to a monitoring station). An insurance company may send someone to inspect your property and advise on security measures. Policies pay out for theft only when there are signs of forcible entry and you aren't usually covered for thefts by a guest or tenant (but you may be covered for thefts by domestic personnel). All-risks policies offering a world-wide extension to a household policy covering jewellery, cameras and other items aren't usually available from Greek or Cypriot companies, but are available from a number of foreign companies.

Community Properties: If you own a property that's part of a community development (see page 138), building insurance is included in your service charges, although you should check exactly what's covered. You must, however, still be insured for third party risks in the event that you cause damage to neighbouring apartments or buildings, e.g. through flood or fire.

Holiday Homes: Premiums are generally higher for holiday homes because of their high vulnerability (particularly to burglaries) and are often based on the number of days a year a property is inhabited and the interval between periods of occupancy.

Cover for theft, storm, flood and malicious damage may be suspended when a property is left empty for more than three weeks at a time. It's possible to negotiate cover for periods of absence for a hefty surcharge, although valuable items are usually excluded. If you're absent from your property for long periods, e.g. more than 60 days a year, you may also be required to pay an excess on a claim arising from an occurrence that takes place during your absence (and theft may be excluded). You should read all small print in policies. **Note that, where applicable, it's important to ensure that a policy specifies a holiday home and *not* a principal home.**

In areas with a high risk of theft, e.g. major cities and most resort areas, an insurance company may insist that you fit extra locks, e.g. two locks on external doors, including a mortise deadlock, internal locking shutters and security bars or metal grilles on windows. A policy may specify that all forms of protection on doors must be used whenever a property is unoccupied, and that all other forms, e.g. shutters, must also be used when a property is left empty for more than a few days. Some companies may not insure holiday homes in high risk areas. It's unwise to leave valuable or irreplaceable items in a holiday home or a home that will be vacant for long periods. **Note that some insurance companies will do their utmost to find a loophole which makes you negligent and relieves them of their liability.** Always check that the details listed on a policy are correct, otherwise your policy could be void.

Rented Property: Your landlord will usually insist that you have third party liability insurance. A lease requires you to insure against 'tenant's risks', including damage you may make to the rental property and to other properties if you live in an apartment, e.g. due to flood, fire or explosion. You can choose your own insurance company and aren't required to use one recommended by your landlord.

Premiums: Premiums are usually calculated on the size of the property, either the habitable area in square metres or the number of rooms, rather than its value. The cost of household insurance in Greece is around €90 for an average home, while in Cyprus building insurance costs around CY£25 to 80 per year, depending on the value of a property, and contents insurance costs around CY£2 per CY£1,000 of the sum insured. Premiums can be much higher in high-risk areas. If you have an index-linked policy, cover is increased each year in line with inflation.

Claims: If you wish to make a claim, you must usually inform your insurance company in writing (by registered letter) within two to five days of an incident or 24 hours in the case of theft. Thefts should also be reported to the local police within 24 hours, as the police statement (of which you need a copy for your insurance company) usually constitutes irrefutable evidence of your claim. Check whether you're covered for damage or thefts that occur while you're away from a property and are therefore unable to inform your insurance company immediately.

Take care you don't under-insure your house contents and that you periodically reassess their value and adjust your insurance premium accordingly. You can arrange to have your cover automatically increased annually by a fixed percentage or amount by your insurance company. If you make a claim and the assessor discovers that you're under-insured, the amount of the claim will be reduced by the percentage you're under-insured. For example, if you're 50 per cent under-insured, your claim for €15,000 or CY£10,000 will be reduced by half to €7,500 or CY£5,000. You must usually pay an excess for each claim.

Insuring Abroad: It's possible and legal to take out building and contents insurance in another country for a property in Greece or Cyprus (some foreign insurance companies offer special policies for holiday homeowners), although you must ensure that a policy is valid under Greek or Cypriot law. The advantage is that you will have a policy you can understand and will be able to handle claims in your own language. This may seem like a good option for a holiday home in Greece or Cyprus, although it can be more expensive than insuring with a local company and can lead to conflicts when the building is insured with a local company and the contents with a foreign company, e.g. in some countries, door locks are part of the contents and in others they constitute part of the building. Most experts advise that you insure a Greek or Cypriot property (building and contents) with a local insurance company through a local agent.

Holiday & Travel Insurance

Holiday and travel insurance is recommended for all who don't wish to risk having their holiday or travel ruined by financial problems. As you're probably aware, anything can and often does go wrong with a holiday, sometimes before you even get started (particularly if you *don't* have insurance). The following information applies equally to both residents and non-residents, whether they're travelling to or from Greece or Cyprus or within either country. No-one should visit Greece or Cyprus without travel and health insurance!

Travel insurance is available from many sources, including travel agents, insurance companies and brokers, banks, automobile clubs and transport companies (airline, rail and bus). Package holiday companies and tour operators also offer insurance policies, some of which are compulsory, too expensive **and don't provide adequate cover.** You can also buy 24-hour accident and flight insurance at major airports, although it's expensive and doesn't offer the best cover. Before taking out travel insurance, carefully consider the range and level of cover you require and compare policies. Short-term holiday and travel insurance policies may include cover for holiday cancellation or interruption; missed flights; departure delay at both the start *and* end of a holiday (a common occurrence); delayed, lost or damaged baggage; personal effects and money; medical expenses and accidents (including evacuation home); flight insurance; personal liability and legal expenses and default or bankruptcy insurance, e.g. a tour operator or airline going bankrupt.

Health Cover: Medical expenses are an important aspect of travel insurance and you shouldn't rely on insurance provided by reciprocal health arrangements, charge and credit card companies, household policies or private medical insurance (unless it's an international policy), none of which may provide adequate cover (although you should take advantage of what they offer). The minimum medical insurance recommended by experts is the equivalent of around GB£250,000 for Europe and GB£1 million for North America and some other destinations. If applicable, check whether pregnancy related claims are covered and whether there are any restrictions for those over a certain age, e.g. 65 or 70 (travel insurance is becoming increasingly more expensive for those aged over 65).

Always check any exclusion clauses in contracts by obtaining a copy of the full policy document, as not all relevant information will be included in an insurance leaflet. High risk sports such as off-road trekking, para-sailing, scuba-diving, motorcycling and other 'risky' pursuits should be specifically covered and *listed* in a policy (there's usually an additional premium), as these pursuits are sometimes excluded from general cover. Special winter sports policies are available and are more expensive than normal holiday insurance.

Visitors: Travel insurance for visitors to Greece should include personal liability and repatriation expenses. If your travel insurance expires while you're visiting Greece, you can buy further insurance from a local insurance agent, although this won't include repatriation expenses. Flight and travel insurance is available from insurance desks at most airports, including travel accident, personal accident, world-wide medical expenses and in-transit baggage.

Cost: The cost of travel insurance varies considerably, depending on where you buy it, how long you intend to stay abroad and your age. Generally, the longer the period covered, the cheaper the daily cost, although the maximum period covered is usually limited, e.g. six months. With some policies a excess (deductible) must be paid for each claim. You may prefer a policy that pays a hospital directly, rather than having to pay yourself and make a claim later. If you do need to make a claim, then you must keep your medical receipts.

Note that Cyprus isn't a member of the European Union and doesn't provide reciprocal cover with EU states regarding health treatment. You should therefore have adequate cover for all risks before leaving home.

Annual Policies: For people who travel abroad frequently, whether on business or pleasure, an annual travel policy usually provides the best value, but check carefully to find out exactly what it includes. Many insurance companies, e.g. Europ Assistance, offer annual travel policies for a premium of around €180 or CY£120 for an individual (the equivalent of around three months insurance with a standard travel insurance policy), which are excellent value for frequent travellers. Some insurance companies also offer an 'emergency travel policy' for holiday homeowners who need to travel abroad at short notice to inspect a property, e.g. after a severe storm or robbery. The cost of an annual policy may depend on the area covered, e.g. Europe, world-wide (excluding North America) and world-wide (including North America), although it doesn't usually cover travel within your country of residence. There's also a limit on the number of trips a year and the duration of each trip, e.g. 90 or 120 days. An annual policy is usually a good choice for owners of a holiday home in Greece or Cyprus who travel there frequently for relatively short periods. **However, check exactly what's covered (or omitted), as an annual policy may not provide adequate cover.**

Claims: If you need to make a claim, you should provide as much documentary evidence as possible to support it. Travel insurance companies gladly take your money, but they aren't always so keen to pay claims and you may have to persevere. Always be persistent and make a claim *irrespective* of any small print, as this may be unreasonable and therefore invalid in law. Insurance companies usually require you to report a loss (or any incident for which you intend to make a claim) to the local police or carriers within 24 hours and obtain a written report. Failure to do so may mean that a claim won't be considered.

SHOPPING

Greece and Cyprus don't rate among Europe's great shopping countries, either for quality or bargains, with the exception of handmade arts and crafts, which are widely available at reasonable prices. Prices of many consumer goods such as TVs and stereo systems, computers, cameras, electrical apparatus and household appliances have fallen considerably in recent years, although they're still generally higher than in many other European countries, where there's more competition. Clothes aren't particularly good value and good quality clothing can be expensive, particularly if it's imported.

Greeks and Cypriots generally pay cash when shopping, although credit cards are widely accepted in major stores and those frequented by tourists. However, in remote areas and on some Greek islands you may find that only cash is accepted. In major cities and tourist areas you should be wary of pickpockets and bag-snatchers, particularly in markets and other crowded places. Don't tempt fate with an exposed wallet or purse or by flashing your money around.

Greece: Considering its relatively small population, Greece has a surprisingly large number of shops, practically as many as Britain, a country with four times the population. Most Greek retail enterprises are family-run and it's unusual for a large family not to own some sort of shop. Consequently, shopping is a pleasant experience and an essentially social occasion. Recent years have seen the introduction of shopping centres and hypermarkets, although these are still relatively few and far between, unlike in most other European countries where they dominate. There are several department stores in Athens, including Lambropoulos and Minion, as well as British-owned stores such as Marks & Spencer and BHS. The biggest drawback to shopping in cities and towns is parking, which can be dreadful (especially in Athens). With the exception of street markets and some souvenir shops, where haggling over the price is part of the enjoyment, retail prices are fixed.

During the hotter summer months, shops are *usually* open on Mondays, Wednesdays and Saturdays from 9am until 2.30pm, and on Tuesdays, Thursdays and Fridays from 8.30am to 2pm and from 6 to 9pm. During the cooler months, shops open around half an hour later and close an hour earlier. Opening hours are, however, somewhat erratic and also depend on national and local public holidays and individual shopkeeper's preferences, although in most tourist areas they're open all day, seven days a week during the high season. Note that butchers and delicatessens aren't allowed to sell fresh meat in the afternoon and fishmongers are only open in the mornings. It's important to shop around and compare prices in Greece, as they can vary considerably, even between shops in the same town. Note, however, that price differences often reflect different quality, so make sure that you're comparing similar products.

Among the best buys in Greece are the diverse handicrafts, including hand-woven textiles such as rugs, bags and knitwear, religious icons, ceramics, e.g. in Athens and Rhodes , leather goods (Chania on Crete has some of the best buys), Greek music and musical instruments, olive wood figures and jewellery. Gold jewellery, although of exceptional quality, is expensive and silver filigree is often cheaper and better value.

Goods made throughout Greece are available from most souvenir shops, although they're usually cheaper when purchased in the area where they're made. Local wines and olive oil are also good buys.

Cyprus: Like Greece, Cyprus isn't one of Europe's great shopping countries, although it also offers a wide choice of reasonably priced handmade arts and crafts, and clothes and shoes are also good value. As far as shopping is concerned, Cyprus is a relatively inexpensive country, although the introduction of VAT (and its recent increase to 10 per cent) on many items has helped increased the cost of living (see page 99).

Most Cypriot retail enterprises are family-run and consequently, shopping is a pleasant social experience in Cyprus, often punctuated with endless cups of Cypriot coffee. In recent years, the more traditional shopping scene has been joined by shopping centres, although these are mainly limited to Nicosia and Limassol. In these towns there are several British department stores such as Woolworths (the first department store to open on the island), Marks & Spencer and BHS. There are no large supermarkets or hypermarkets in Cyprus, although there's a profusion of small supermarkets and corner grocery shops. With the exception of street markets and some souvenir shops, where haggling over the price is part of the enjoyment, retail prices are fixed in Cyprus and prices shown include VAT.

Retail opening hours in Cyprus depend on the heat and in the hot months from May to September shops are open from 8am to 2.30pm and from 4 to 7pm. From October to April shops are open from 8am to 1pm and from 2.30 to 5.30pm. Shops are generally closed on Wednesday and Saturday afternoons and on Sundays all year round, although those in tourist areas are open on most days, including Sundays, and are usually open until later in the evening. It's important to shop around and compare prices in Cyprus, which can vary considerably, even between shops in the same town. Note, however, that price differences often reflect different quality, so ensure that you're comparing similar products.

Among the best buys in Cyprus are the diverse handicrafts that include hand-woven textiles, ceramics, leather goods, handmade lace, copper, silverware, handmade baskets, wines and spirits, and perhaps rather surprisingly, glasses. Glasses (including sunglasses) are considerably cheaper in Cyprus than in the rest of Europe and opticians offer a free eye test and can usually supply glasses to you within 24 hours. In some areas, there's even a special tourist service! Handicrafts from throughout the country are available at most souvenir shops, but are usually cheaper when purchased in the area where they're made or at the government-run 'Cyprus Handicraft Service', which has shops in major towns.

Markets

Markets are a common sight in towns and villages throughout Greece and Cyprus and are an essential part of life, largely unaffected by competition from supermarkets and hypermarkets. They're colourful, entertaining and fun, and an experience not to be missed, even if you don't plan to buy anything (you find the real country in markets). Some towns have markets on only one or two days a week, while others stage them on virtually every day of the year and many towns have permanent indoor markets selling foodstuffs. There are different kinds of markets, including indoor markets, permanent street markets and travelling street markets (*laïkí agorá*) that move from neighbourhood to neighbourhood on different days of the week or month, although they usually have a fixed day in each neighbourhood. Prices are generally lower than in shops, although much depends on your bargaining skills (haggling is expected for expensive items or when buying in bulk). There's often a large central market in cities and many towns and city neighbourhoods have indoor or covered markets. Markets usually operate from around 7am to 2pm.

A variety of goods are commonly sold in markets, including household items, dry goods (along with a vast range of herbs) and fruit and vegetables. Specialist markets in Athens and other large cities sell antiques, books, clothes, stamps, postcards, medals, coins, birds and pets. **You should be wary of bargain-priced branded goods in markets and souvenir shops, such as watches, perfume and clothes, as they're invariably fakes.**

Food markets are highly popular, despite the presence of supermarkets and hypermarkets, and there are also fish markets in coastal towns. Food is invariably beautifully presented and includes fruit and vegetables (including many exotic varieties), fish, meat, live poultry, dairy products, bread and cakes, herbs, olives and olive oil. Food is usually cheaper and fresher in markets than in supermarkets, particularly if you buy what's in season and grown locally. You should arrive early in the morning for the best choice, although bargains can often be found when stall holders are packing up for the day.

All produce is clearly marked with its price per piece or kilogramme and usually there's no haggling over the price, although near the end of the day an offer may be accepted. When shopping for food in markets, vendors may object to customers handling the fruit and vegetables, although you needn't be shy about asking to taste a piece of fruit. It's sensible to take a bag of your own when buying fruit and vegetables, as carrier bags aren't usually provided. When buying fruit and vegetables in markets, make sure that the quality of produce you're given is the same as on display, which isn't always the case. Queues at a particular stall are usually a good sign. Another good place to buy fresh fruit and vegetables is from roadside stalls set up in rural areas. Here the produce couldn't be fresher and is often grown by the seller himself.

Antique and flea markets are common throughout Greece and Cyprus. Athens in particular has several famous flea markets, including those at Monastiraki, Piraeus and Thission, which take place on Sundays from 6am to 2.30pm. The main flea and antique market in Cyprus is held in Larnaca on Sundays from 7am to 2pm. Being close to the Middle East, both countries also have several bazaars, which are well worth a visit (particularly in Athens). At antique and flea markets, you shouldn't expect to find many (or any) bargains in the major cities, where anything worth buying is snapped up by dealers, although in small towns you may find some real bargains.

You should never assume, however, that because something is sold in a market it will be a bargain, particularly when buying antiques, which aren't always authentic. **Note that in Greece it's illegal to buy, sell, possess or export antiquities that are over 100 years old and that penalties for infringement of this are second only to those imposed for drug smuggling.** In many cases the local antique shops are cheaper and in particular those selling to the local residents rather than tourists.

Always haggle over the price of expensive items. To find out where and when local markets are held, enquire at your local tourist office or town hall.

PETS

If you plan to take a pet to Greece or Cyprus, it's important to check the latest regulations. Make sure that you have the correct papers, not only for Greece or Cyprus, but for all the countries you will pass through to reach your destination. Particular consideration must be given before exporting a pet from a country with strict quarantine regulations. If you need to return, even after just a few days abroad, your pet may have to go into quarantine, which, apart from the expense, is distressing for both pets and owners. Britain has particularly strict quarantine laws, which were originally introduced to avoid importing rabies from continental Europe. However, on 28th March 2000, Britain introduced a pilot 'Pet Travel Scheme (PETS)', which replaced quarantine for qualifying cats and dogs. Under the scheme, pets must be microchipped (they have a microchip inserted in their neck), vaccinated against rabies, undergo a blood test and are issued with a 'health certificate' ('passport'). **Note, however, that the PETS certificate isn't issued until six months *after* all the above have been carried out!**

The scheme is restricted to animals imported from rabies-free countries and countries where rabies is under control – initially 22 European countries, but if successful it's expected to be extended to other countries, including North America. However, the current quarantine laws will remain in place for pets coming from Eastern Europe, Africa, Asia and South America. The new regulations cost pet owners around GB£200 (for a microchip, rabies vaccination and blood test), plus GB£60 per year for annual booster vaccinations and around GB£20 for a border check. Shop around and compare fees from a number of veterinary surgeons. To qualify, pets must travel by sea via Dover or Portsmouth, by train via the Channel Tunnel or via Heathrow airport (only certain carriers are licensed to carry animals). Additional information is available from the Department of Environment, Food and the Rural Affairs (DEFRA, formerly MAFF, ☎ UK 0845-933 5577, ✉ pets.helpline @defra.gsi.gov.uk).

If you intend to live permanently in Greece or Cyprus, most veterinary surgeons recommend that dogs and cats be vaccinated against certain diseases, and in some cases you'll need a veterinary certificate confirming that your pet has been vaccinated before it can enter the country. Note also that there are a number of diseases and dangers for pets in Greece and Cyprus that aren't found in many other European countries. You should obtain advice from a vet on arrival in Greece or Cyprus about the best way to protect your pets.

Veterinary surgeons are well trained in Greece and Cyprus, and emergency veterinary care is also provided in animal clinics, some of which provide a 24-hour emergency service. Veterinary surgeons (including many English-speaking vets), animal clinics, and kennels and catteries advertise in English-language publications in Greece and Cyprus. If you plan to leave your pet at a kennel or cattery, check whether it's a registered and bona fide establishment and book well in advance, particularly for school holiday periods. There are also foreign residents in resort areas who will look after your pets in their own homes for a reasonable fee while you're away, which many believe is preferable to leaving it at a kennel or cattery. Bear in mind that there may be discrimination against pets when renting accommodation, particularly when it's furnished (the statutes of community properties can legally prohibit pets).

Greece: You may bring a pet into Greece from another European Union country, but must present a bi-lingual export health certificate and a rabies certificate on entering the country. The export health certificate is obtainable from the Ministry of Agriculture in your home country. You complete a form that must be approved by a local veterinary inspector who will inspect your pet within 48 hours of your departure. Obtaining a rabies certificate entails a visit to a vet and paying a fee. The rabies vaccine must be administered not less than 20 days or more than 11 months before leaving your home country. On arrival in Greece you may be required to have an animal inspected by a Greek veterinary officer. Note that some Greek islands may not have a resident veterinary surgeon, meaning that if your pet requires any treatment, you could have to travel to the mainland or another island. You may also find it difficult to obtain pet supplies.

Cyprus: Cats and dogs are permitted to be brought into Cyprus provided that a licence has been obtained in advance from the Department of Veterinary Services in Nicosia and that your pet has had the appropriate vaccinations. You'll be required to produce a certificate to prove this. A period of six months' quarantine is obligatory, although a pet can be quarantined in your own home, which makes the process considerably cheaper and less traumatic.

NEWSPAPERS & MAGAZINES

Greeks are avid newspaper readers and there are some 15 daily newspapers in Greece, of which the most popular are the *Eleftheros Typos*, *Ta Nea* and *Kathimerini*, although only the latter is considered to be good quality. There are also two English-language newspapers: *Athens News*, published from Tuesdays to Saturdays and featuring world and Greek news, and the less popular *Weekly Greek News*, containing mainly Greek news. Both are widely available in Athens and the main resort areas. An English-language magazine, *Atlantis*, is published monthly and features political, travel and cultural articles. In Athens, *Scope* provides a weekly listing of entertainment in the capital and two publications from the National Tourist Information Office, *Athens Today* and *Now in Athens*, provide general information about museums, galleries and cultural performances in the city.

Many foreign newspapers and magazines are available at news kiosks in most resorts and cities, although outside the main season (May to September) they're usually available only in Athens and major resorts. Most publications arrive in Athens in the afternoon on the day of publication, although they may not be available until the next day and weekend availability varies considerably. Note that foreign publications can be quite expensive and the equivalent of around three times or more of the cover price.

Cyprus: For its size, Cyprus has an amazing number of newspapers and some 12 Greek-language newspapers are published. Freedom of the press is part of the constitution in Cyprus, although most papers are, not surprisingly, anti-Turkish. Among the English-language newspapers are the *Cyprus Mail*, published daily except Mondays, and the *Cyprus Weekly*, published on Fridays, these are the most popular.

Both include news, small ads, and TV and radio programmes. The *Cyprus Mail* also publishes a 'What's On' section on Sundays listing most events in Cyprus. *Seven Days in Cyprus* and *Nicosia this Month* are English-language magazines catering mainly for tourists and containing a calendar of events. A number of foreign-language publications are available from news kiosks, although the selection is rather limited and they can be expensive.

TELEVISION & RADIO

Greek television isn't renowned for its quality, although there's plenty of it and it's generally no worse than the fare dished up in most European countries. Satellite TV reception is generally good in Greece and is popular among the expatriate community (not that its output is much better than Greek TV). Cable TV isn't common in Greece compared with northern European countries and the USA.

There are several terrestrial TV channels as well as a number of pay-TV channels available, including two government-controlled channels, ET1 and ET2, the private Mega-Channel, New Channel, Star, Antenna and Seven-X channels. Programmes on all stations are a predictable mix of soap-operas (mainly Italian, Latin-American and Spanish), game shows, films and sports. Most British and American films and shows are broadcast in the original language with Greek subtitles, so you can enjoy re-runs of the soap operas you've come to love! All channels broadcast from early morning until late at night except for Seven-X, which starts at 7pm, and Mega-Channel which broadcasts around the clock.

The TV and radio licence in Greece payment is automatically included in your electricity bill. TV programmes are listed in Greek newspapers and TV guides. Some programmes are also listed in English-language newspapers and magazines, along with a selection of satellite TV programmes.

Cyprus: The government-controlled Cyprus Broadcasting (CyBC) has two channels: CyBC1 (daily from around 3pm to midnight) and CyBC2 (daily from 7am until 3am), which include a daily news summary in English at 9pm and bulletins from Euronews. Other channels such as ET1 and Antenna are Greek stations and there are several independent channels such as Sigma and Logos. Most channels broadcast programmes and films in English with Greek subtitles or alternatively in Greek with English subtitles. There's no TV or radio licence as such in Cyprus, although you pay around CY£7 to CyBC every two months with your electricity bill. TV programmes are listed in most Cypriot newspapers and in TV guides. Some Cypriot programmes are also listed in English-language newspapers and magazines, along with a selection of satellite TV programmes.

Standards: The standards for TV reception in Greece and Cyprus **aren't the same as in all other countries.** Local TVs and video recorders operate on the continental PAL system and TVs operating on the North American NTSC system or the British PAL system won't function in Greece. If you want a TV that will work in Greece, Cyprus and other European countries, and a VCR that will play back videos, you must buy a multi-standard TV and VCR. These are widely available and contain automatic circuitry that can switch from PAL-I (Britain), to PAL-B/G (rest of Europe) to SECAM-L (France). Some multi-standard TVs also handle the North American NTSC standard and have an NTSC-in jack plug connection allowing you to play

intermediate or advanced, and usually last from 2 to 16 weeks. Most schools offer free tests to help you find your appropriate level and a free introductory lesson.

Don't expect to become fluent in a short time unless you have a particular flair for languages or already have a good command of Greek. Unless you desperately need to learn quickly, it's best to arrange your lessons over a long period. However, don't commit yourself to a long course of study, particularly an expensive one, before ensuring that it's the right course for you. Language classes generally fall into the following categories:

Category	Hours per Week
Extensive	4–10
Intensive	15–20
Total immersion	20–40+

Some schools offer combined courses where language study is linked with optional subjects, including business Greek, Greek art and culture, reading and commentary of a daily newspaper, conversation, Greek history, and traditions and folklore. Some schools also combine language courses with a range of cultural and sports activities such as visits to monuments, tennis or water sports.

The most common language courses in Greece and Cyprus are intensive courses, providing four hours tuition a day from Mondays to Fridays (20 hours per week).

The cost of an intensive course is usually quite reasonable, e.g. a four-week intensive course costs around €180 or CY£125. The highest fees are charged in the summer months, particularly during July and August. Commercial courses are generally more intensive and expensive, e.g. around €350 or CY£250 for three weeks and a total of 60 hours tuition. Courses that include accommodation are usually good value and some schools arrange home stays with a Greek or Cypriot family (full or half board) or provide apartment or hotel accommodation. Those for whom money is no object, can take total immersion courses where study is for eight hours a day, five days a week. Whichever course you choose, you should shop around as tuition fees vary considerably. For more information contact the Greek or Cyprus national tourist office or embassy in your home country.

Private Lessons: You may prefer to have private lessons, which are a quicker, although more expensive way of learning a language. The main advantage of private lessons is that you learn at your own speed and aren't held back by slow learners or left floundering in the wake of the class genius. You can advertise for a teacher in local newspapers, on shopping centre/supermarket bulletin boards, on university notice boards, and through your or your spouse's employer. Don't forget to ask your friends, neighbours and colleagues if they can recommend a private teacher.

CRIME

Greece is one of Europe's safest countries with a low crime rate and a well-deserved reputation for honesty. If you leave some personal belongings at a bar or café, you're likely to find them in the safe-keeping of the owner awaiting your return. Greeks are generally used to leaving their possessions unattended or unlocked, although there has been an increase in theft and crimes in recent years (blamed mainly on Albanian refugees), so you should ensure that your belongings are safely locked up or supervised. The worst crime areas include Omonia in Athens, the flea markets and Athens' metro. Sexual harassment (or worse) is fairly common in Greece and women should take particular care late at night and never hitchhike alone. Some 'experts' recommend that women carry a tear gas aerosol, although they're officially illegal.

There are three types of police in Greece, including tourist police (*touristikí astinomiá*) whose job is to assist tourists (they can usually provide a wealth of local information) and carry out official inspections of hotels and restaurants. Tourist police are found in most large cities and resorts and are a division of the local police, identified by flags on their jackets indicating the languages they speak. Local police (*chorofílakes*) operate within town and city boundaries as well as in rural areas, and wear green uniforms and ride motorbikes. Athens has its own police force (*astinomiá póleon*) with dark blue uniforms and white patrol cars. All police are armed in Greece. Dial 100 in an emergency or 171 for the tourist police.

Note that the possession of illegal drugs (even small amounts) is a very serious offence in Greece, where offenders are liable to fines of up €300,000 and a prison sentence of between ten years and life!

Cyprus enjoys a remarkably low crime rate, around one-sixth of the European average and Interpol statistics reveal that in 1997 the number of serious crimes was around 600 per 100,000, far below the rate for the EU. The low incidence of crime is another reason for the country's popularity with foreign homebuyers, among whom security is a key element. Visitors are invariably surprised and reassured by this relaxed aspect of life on the island, where serious crime is virtually unheard of and theft is relatively rare. Thefts from hotels were previously also uncommon and most vehicles could be safely left unlocked, although the incidence of theft from both cars and hotels has increased markedly in recent years. Cypriot police speak English and are unarmed with the exception of those who guard airports. In an emergency you should dial 199 for the police.

PUBLIC HOLIDAYS

When a holiday falls on a Saturday or Sunday in Greece or Cyprus, another day isn't usually granted as a holiday unless the number of public holidays in a particular year falls below a minimum number. Holidays are occasionally moved to form long weekends and when a holiday falls on a Friday or Monday many businesses close for the entire holiday weekend (assuming they would normally work on a Saturday or Sunday). Note that foreign embassies and consulates in Greece and Cyprus usually observe local public holidays in addition to their own country's national holidays.

Greece: There are 11 statutory national public holidays a year plus local holidays, on which government offices, banks, post offices, most shops and restaurants, and many museums and ancient sites are closed. The following days are official national public holidays in Greece:

Date	Holiday
1st January	New Year's Day
6th January	Epiphany
Feb/March	1st Sunday in Lent
25th March	Independence Day
March/April	Good Friday
March/April	Easter Sunday
1st May	Labour Day
15th August	Feast of the Assumption
28th October	Ohi Day
25th December	Christmas Day
26th December	St Stephen's Day

In addition to national public holidays, each province or town has its own feast days, fairs and pilgrimages. Easter is the most important festival in Greece and during Easter week every town and village dedicates its energies to religious ceremonies, feasting and celebrating. The ceremonies are particularly noteworthy on the islands of Hydra, Corfu and Kios. Carnival, three weeks before Lent, is celebrated throughout Greece, with the parades and festivities in Athens and Kefallonia among the most famous and colourful. Regional holidays aren't always official public holidays, but most local businesses are closed, sometimes for a number of days. Public holidays are marked on most calendars, usually in red.

Cyprus: Cyprus has 14 statutory national public holidays per year, which are listed below:

Date	Holiday
1st January	New Year's Day
6th January	Epiphany
Feb/March	Green (Lent) Monday
25th March	Greek Independence
1st April	National Day
March/April	Good Friday
March/April	Easter Sunday
1st May	Labour Day
June	Whit Monday
15th August	Feast of the Assumption
1st October	Cyprus Independence Day
28th October	National Holiday
25th December	Christmas Day
26th December	St Stephen's Day

As in Greece, there are also local holidays and each town has its own feast days, fairs and pilgrimages, in addition to the above holidays. Easter celebrations are worth noting and go on for a week or more, mainly in coastal towns. There are huge bonfires and fireworks before the Resurrection mass as well as celebrations for the Flood Festival (*kataklismos*). Further information about holidays and festivals is contained in a *Diary of Events* published by the Cyprus Tourist Office and local tourist offices also provide a monthly update of events.

TIME DIFFERENCE

Both Greece and Cyprus are two hours ahead of Greenwich Mean Time (GMT) and three hours ahead of Britain during 'daylight-saving time', which runs from the last Sunday in March to the last Sunday in September. Time changes are announced in local newspapers and on radio and TV stations. When making international telephone calls to Greece or Cyprus, check the time difference with your home country, which is usually shown in phone books and diaries. The time difference between Greece and Cyprus at noon and some major international cities is shown below:

LONDON	CAPE TOWN	BOMBAY	TOKYO	NEW YORK
9am	11am	2.30pm	11pm	4am

3.

FINANCE

One of the most important aspects of buying a home in Greece or Cyprus and living there (even for relatively brief periods) is finance, which includes everything from transferring and changing money to mortgages and taxes. If you're planning to invest in a property or a business in Greece or Cyprus financed with imported funds, it's important to consider both the present and possible future exchange rates. On the other hand, if you live and work in Greece or Cyprus and are paid in euros or Cypriot pounds, this may affect your financial commitments abroad. **Bear in mind that if your income is received in a currency other than euros or Cypriot pounds, it can be exposed to risks beyond your control when you live abroad, particularly regarding inflation and exchange rate fluctuations.**

If you own a home in Greece or Cyprus you can employ an accountant or tax adviser to look after your financial affairs there and declare and pay your local taxes. You can also have your financial representative receive your bank statements, ensure that your bank is paying your standing orders, e.g. for utilities and property taxes, and that you have sufficient funds to pay them. If you let a home in Greece or Cyprus through a local company, the company may perform the above tasks as part of its services.

Although the Greeks and Cypriots prefer using cash to credit or charge cards, it's wise to have at least one credit card when visiting or living in Greece or Cyprus (Visa is the most widely accepted). Even if you don't like credit cards and shun any form of credit, they do have their uses, e.g. no-deposit car rentals, no pre-paying hotel bills (plus guaranteed bookings), obtaining cash 24 hours a day, simple telephone and mail-order payments, greater safety and security than cash, and above all, convenience. Note, however, that not all Greek or Cypriot businesses accept credit cards.

Wealth Warning: If you plan to live permanently in Greece or Cyprus, you must ensure that your income is (and will remain) sufficient to live on, bearing in mind devaluations (if your income isn't paid in local currency), rises in the cost of living (see page 99), and unforeseen expenses such as high medical bills or anything else that may reduce your income (such as stock market crashes and recessions). Foreigners, particularly retirees, often under-estimate the cost of living abroad and many are forced to return to their home countries after a few years.

This section includes information on importing and exporting money, banking, mortgages, taxes (property, income, capital gains, inheritance, gift and value added tax), wills and the cost of living. Unless otherwise indicated, information relates to the 2000 tax year.

GREEK & CYPRIOT CURRENCY

Greece: As you're probably aware, the Greek unit of currency was the drachma until the euro (€) took over on 1st January 2002. The Greek economy is undergoing a period of growth after many years of recession. Growth reached 3.4 per cent in 2000, when Greece qualified for the single European currency, joining 11 other EU countries (Austria, Belgium, Finland, France, Germany, Ireland, Italy, Luxembourg, the Netherlands, Portugal and Spain). The currencies of the euro zone countries were locked into a fixed exchange rate (set by the European Central Bank) against the euro and consequently against each other (there were 336.52 drachmas to one euro). Note that prices are shown only in euros in this book.

Euro notes and coins became legal tender on 1st January 2002 and for two months are to circulate alongside the drachma, which is then to be withdrawn. Greek companies and banks started to use euros for trading, accounts, statements and receipts in 2001, when shops, supermarkets and restaurants began producing receipts showing both currencies. In general, enthusiasm for the euro among the Greeks is high. (You would also be enthusiastic if you had had to put up with the drachma.)

The euro is minted in coins to the value of 1, 2, 5, 10, 20 and 50 cents (there are 100 cents to one euro) and to the value of 1 and 2 euros. Banknotes are printed in denominations of 5, 10, 20, 50, 100, 200 and 500 euros. When writing figures, a full stop (period) and not a comma is used to separate units of millions, thousands and hundreds, e.g. €2.500.000. Sums including euros and cents are normally written €0.50, etc.

Cyprus: The Cypriot currency is the Cyprus pound (CY£), which is also divided into 100 cents. Although it isn't traded internationally, it's a strong, stable currency, reflecting the stable economy on the island. Coins are minted in values of 1, 2, 5, 10, 20, and 50 cents and banknotes printed in denominations of CY£1, CY£5, CY£10 and CY£20. As with euros, sums including pounds and cents are normally written CY£0.50, etc.

It's wise to obtain some local currency banknotes and coins before arriving in the country and to familiarise yourself and your family with them. You should have some local currency in cash when you arrive, although you should avoid carrying a lot of cash. This will save you having to queue to change money on arrival at an airport (where exchange rates are usually poor).

IMPORTING & EXPORTING MONEY

Greece: Exchange controls in Greece were abolished on 1st January 1990 and there are no restrictions on the import or export of funds. A Greek resident is permitted to open a bank account in any country and to import (or export) unlimited funds in any currency. However, the importation of sums over €10,000 and the exportation of sums over €2,000 must be declared at customs. Greek residents need a certificate from the Greek tax authorities in order to export foreign currency over €10,000. If you're a Greek resident, you must also inform the Greece tax authorities in your annual tax return of any new foreign account. Sums in excess of approximately €32,700 deposited abroad, other than by regular bank transfers, must be reported to the Bank of Greece. By doing this, you make the import or export 'legal' whatever its source and you won't be investigated for fraud. Similarly, if you wish to export funds, you require written proof that the funds were obtained legally. For example, if you've sold a house, then the contract of sale (signed and stamped by either the notary or the lawyer who was present at the completion) is acceptable. A certificate from the tax authorities is also required, verifying that you don't owe any taxes to the Greek government.

Cyprus: In Cyprus, exchange distinguishes between residents and non-residents. The residence status of individuals is normally determined by reference to the place where their business is incorporated or active, and only residents are subject to exchange control restrictions on capital transfers. Individuals who aren't permanent residents of Cyprus are exempt from exchange controls, and there's no restriction on the transfer of funds abroad, which is usually handled by commercial banks in accordance with powers delegated to them by the central bank, although capital transfers must be referred to the central bank for approval. Thus non-residents owning property in Cyprus may hold and manage assets and liabilities in any foreign country, including freely convertible and transferable balances with banks on the island. A non-Cypriot resident with an external bank account can import or export foreign currency without restriction. **However, you should note that you're only permitted to import or export CY£50 in person.**

Cypriot legal entities that belong partly or wholly to non-residents carrying on business or derive income from the island are considered resident for exchange control purposes. On the other hand, Cypriot legal entities that belong wholly to non-residents carrying out business and deriving income exclusively from abroad are exempt from exchange controls.

If you sell a property in Cyprus, the entire sale proceeds cannot be remitted overseas immediately. The equivalent of the original purchase price can be remitted after a sale, but the balance, i.e. the increase in its value, less a lifetime exemption of CY£50,000 can be exported only at the rate of CY£10,000 per annum (plus any interest earned during the year), commencing the year following the sale.

International Bank Transfers

When transferring or sending money to or from Greece or Cyprus, you should be aware of the alternatives and shop around for the best deal. There are two kinds of bank-to-bank transfer, normal and SWIFT. A normal transfer is supposed to take three to seven days, but it usually takes much longer (particularly when sent by mail), whereas a SWIFT electronic transfer should be completed in as little as two hours (although it usually takes at least a day). It's usually quicker and cheaper to transfer funds between branches of the same bank or affiliated banks than between non-affiliated banks. If you intend sending a large amount of money to Greece or Cyprus or abroad for a business transaction, such as buying a property, you should ensure that you receive the commercial rate of exchange rather than the tourist rate. When you have money transferred to a bank in Greece or Cyprus, make sure that you give the name, account number, branch number and the bank code; if money is 'lost' while being transferred, it can take weeks to locate it.

Check the charges and rates in advance and agree them with your bank (you may be able to negotiate a lower charge or a better exchange rate). It's usually better to convert money to euros or Cypriot pounds before transferring it to Greece or Cyprus, in which case you shouldn't incur any charges in Greece or Cyprus, although some banks deduct commission, whatever the currency. Banks in EU countries are allowed only to to pass on to customers costs incurred by the sending bank, and the money must be deposited in a customer's account within five working days. One specialist company that claims to offer the best deal when transferring cash from Britain is Currencies Direct, 88 Kingsway, London WC2B 6AA, UK (☎ 020-7813 0332). If you routinely transfer money between currencies, you should investigate Fidelity Money Funds, which operate free of conversion charges and at wholesale rates of exchange.

Telegraphic Transfers

One of the quickest (it takes around 15 minutes) and safest methods of transferring cash is via a telegraphic transfer, e.g. Western Union, although it's also one of the most expensive, e.g. commission of 7 to 10 per cent of the amount sent! Money can be sent overseas via American Express offices by Amex card holders (using Amex's Moneygram service) to any other American Express office in just 15 minutes.

Bank Drafts & Personal Cheques

Another way to transfer money is via a bank draft , which should be sent by registered mail. However, if a bank draft is lost or stolen, it's impossible to stop payment and you must wait six months before a new draft can be issued. It's also possible to send a cheque drawn on a personal account, although it can take a long time to clear (usually several weeks) and fees are high. It's possible to pay a cheque drawn on a foreign account into a local bank account, although it can take three or four weeks to clear.

Postcheques

Giro postcheques issued by European post offices can be cashed (with a guarantee card) for up to €130 at main post offices in Greece. You can also send money to Greece via the Girobank Eurogiro system from post offices in 15 European countries (including Britain), although this service isn't available in Cyprus.

Charge, Credit & Debit Cards

An instant method of obtaining cash abroad is to use a debit, credit or charge card from an automatic teller machine (ATM). Note that you'll need a PIN number. Many foreigners living in Greece or Cyprus (particularly retirees) keep the bulk of their money in a foreign account (perhaps an offshore bank) and draw on it with a cash card locally. This is an ideal solution for holidaymakers and holiday-homeowners, although homeowners will still need a local bank account to pay their bills. Visa, Mastercard, American Express and Diners Club cards are commonly accepted in major cities and tourist areas, although in remote rural areas cash is the most common and sometimes the only form of payment acceptable.

Foreign Exchange

Most banks in major cities have foreign exchange windows and there are banks or *bureaux de change* with extended opening hours at major airports and railway stations in the main cities. Here you can buy or sell foreign currencies, buy and cash travellers' cheques, and obtain a cash advance on credit and charge cards. Note, however, that some Greek banks refuse to cash travellers' cheques. There are also automatic change machines at airports and tourist areas in major cities that accept up to 15 currencies, including US$, £sterling, marks and Swiss francs. Note, however, that airport banks and other outlets usually offer the worst exchange rates and charge the highest fees.

There are many private *bureaux de change* in Greece and Cyprus, with longer business hours than banks, particularly at weekends. Most offer competitive exchange rates and low or no commission (but always check). They're easier to deal with than banks, and if you're changing a lot of money you can also usually negotiate a better exchange rate. Never use unofficial moneychangers, who are likely to short change you or leave you with worthless foreign notes rather than euros or Cypriot pounds. The official exchange rates for most European and major international currencies are listed in banks and daily newspapers.

Travellers' Cheques

If you're visiting Greece or Cyprus, it's safer to carry travellers' cheques than cash, although they aren't as easy to redeem as in some other countries, e.g. the USA. For example, they aren't usually accepted by businesses, except some hotels, restaurants and shops, all of which usually offer a poor exchange rate. It's best to buy travellers' cheques in euros when visiting Greece and in US$ or pounds sterling for Cyprus. You can buy them from any Greek or Cypriot bank, usually for a service charge of 1 per cent. There should be no commission charge when cashing euro travellers' cheques at any bank in Greece (you must show your passport), although charges and rates vary considerably on travellers' cheques in other currencies. In Cyprus, Thomas Cook travellers' cheques can be cashed commission-free at any branch of the Bank of Cyprus. Banks usually offer a better exchange rate for travellers' cheques than for banknotes.

Always keep a separate record of cheque numbers and note where and when they were cashed. American Express provides a free, three-hour replacement service for lost or stolen travellers' cheques at all their offices world-wide, provided that you know the serial numbers of the lost cheques. Without the serial numbers, replacement can take three days or longer. Most companies provide toll-free numbers for reporting lost or stolen travellers' cheques in Greece or Cyprus.

Footnote: There isn't a lot of difference in the cost of buying Greek or Cypriot currency using cash, buying travellers' cheques or using a credit card to obtain cash from ATMs. However, many people carry only cash when visiting Greece or Cyprus, which is asking for trouble, particularly if you've no way of obtaining more cash locally, e.g. with a credit card or travellers' cheques. **One thing to bear in mind when travelling anywhere is not to rely on only one source of funds.**

BANKS

Greece: Greece generally has good banking facilities, which have improved considerably in recent years, although you may find Greek banks frustratingly slow and inefficient compared with their European counterparts. There are some 50 domestic banks operating in Greece which are divided into two groups: commercial banks and specialised credit institutions. The Bank of Greece is the central bank and monetary authority in Greece and is responsible for the supervision of credit institutions operating in the country. The main banking groups are Commercial Bank, Mortgage Bank, National Bank of Greece, Bank of Central Greece and Creta Bank, while the main specialised credit institutions are the Hellenic Bank, the National

Investment Bank, the National Mortgage Bank and the National Housing Bank. The last two dominate the housing market, although other banks also offer mortgages. Several commercial banks are currently controlled to some extent by the state, although most are in the process of being merged with other banks or privatised.

There are also around 20 foreign-owned banks represented in Greece, e.g. ANZ Grindlays Bank, Barclays Bank, Citibank, HSBC (formerly Midland Bank) and Natwest Bank, mainly in Athens (branches are rare in the provinces). Competition from foreign banks is set to increase, as EU regulations now allow any bank trading in one EU country to trade in another.

Greek banks are usually open from 8am to 2pm on Mondays to Thursdays and from 8am to 1.30pm on Fridays, although hours vary from town to town and even from branch to branch. Some branches in main cities and resorts have longer opening hours, which may include evenings and weekends. In small villages there may be a tiny bank office, open for a few hours a day or on certain days only. If you need to use teller services, you must take your passport as proof of identity and should be prepared for a *long* wait (Greek bank queues move very slowly). In many banks, transactions are performed in two parts (to keep the maximum number of people in 'employment'). A transaction involving a withdrawal must be approved or processed at one counter and then you need to queue to collect your money at the cash desk.

Cyprus: Cyprus' banking system is modelled on the British system – yet another inheritance from the country's colonial past – with banking practices, services and methods of management and control closely resembling those in Britain. Nine Cypriot commercial banks and some 30 international banking groups are represented on the island. The main domestic and foreign banks are Cyprus Popular Bank, Bank of Cyprus, Hellenic Bank, National Bank of Greece, Arab Bank, Lombard Natwest Bank and Barclays Bank. Cypriot banks are modern, efficient and equipped with the latest technology, while strong correspondent banking networks are maintained around the world by onshore and offshore banks, most of which subscribe to SWIFT, Reuters, Telerate and other services.

Banks are open from 8.15am to 12.30pm Mondays to Fridays and from 3.15pm to 4.45pm on Monday afternoons, although many branches in tourist areas offer a supplementary afternoon service on Tuesdays to Fridays from 3.30 or 4pm until 6.30pm. International banks are open from 8.30am to 5.30pm. Banking facilities are also available at the island's two international airports (Larnaca and Paphos) up to 24 hours a day.

Opening an Account

You can open a bank account in Greece or Cyprus whether you're a resident or a non-resident. It's better to open a bank account in person than by correspondence from abroad. **Before choosing a bank, you should compare the fees charged for international money transfers and other services.** Ask your friends, neighbours or colleagues for their recommendations and go along to the bank of your choice and introduce yourself. You must be over 18 years old and provide proof of identity, e.g. a passport, your local address and, in Greece, papers to show the funds you've imported and the method used. You can open a bank account before arriving in the country via an overseas branch of any Greek or Cypriot bank (or a foreign bank operating in Greece or Cyprus), but your signature must be ratified before the account can be opened. Note that various types of bank account can be opened, including current accounts, foreign currency accounts and external accounts.

It isn't wise to close your bank accounts abroad when you're living permanently in Greece or Cyprus, unless you're absolutely certain that you won't need them in future. Even when you're resident in Greece or Cyprus, it's cheaper to keep some money in an account in a country that you visit regularly than to pay commission to convert foreign currency. Many foreigners living in Greece or Cyprus maintain at least two accounts, a foreign bank account for their international transactions and a local account for day-to-day business.

Offshore Banking

If you have a sum of money to invest or wish to protect your inheritance from the tax man, it may be worthwhile looking into the accounts and services (such as pensions and trusts) provided by offshore banking centres in tax havens such as the Channel Islands (Guernsey and Jersey), Gibraltar and the Isle of Man (some 50 locations world-wide are officially classified as tax havens). The big attraction of offshore banking is that money can be deposited in a wide range of currencies, customers are usually guaranteed complete anonymity, there are no double taxation agreements, no withholding tax is payable and interest is paid tax-free. Some offshore banks also offer telephone (usually seven days a week) and Internet banking. Note that offshore banking facilities are offered by Cypriot banks, although Cyprus is officially termed a 'tax-incentive' centre rather than a tax haven. However, if you're a resident on the island, you cannot make use of its offshore banking facilities.

A large number of American, British and European banks, as well as various other international financial institutions, provide offshore banking facilities in one or more locations. Most institutions offer high-interest deposit accounts for long-term savings and investment portfolios, in which funds can be deposited in any major currency. Many people living abroad keep a local account for everyday business and maintain an offshore account for international transactions and investment purposes. However, most financial experts advise investors not to rush into the expatriate life and invest their life savings in an offshore tax haven until they know their long-term plans.

Offshore accounts have minimum deposits levels, which range from as little as GB£500 to as much as GB£100,000. In addition to large minimum balances, accounts may also have stringent terms and conditions, such as restrictions on withdrawals or high early withdrawal penalties. You can deposit funds on call (instant access) or for a fixed period, e.g. from 90 days to one year (usually for large sums). Interest is usually paid monthly or annually, with monthly interest payments slightly lower than annual payments, although monthly payments have the advantage of providing a regular income. There are usually no charges if a specified minimum balance is maintained. Many accounts offer a cash card or a credit card, e.g. Mastercard or Visa, that can be used to obtain cash via ATMs world-wide.

When selecting a financial institution and offshore banking centre, your first priority should be the safety of your money. In some offshore banking centres, bank deposits are covered by a deposit protection scheme, whereby a maximum sum is guaranteed should a financial institution go to the wall (the Isle of Man, Guernsey and

Jersey all have such schemes). Unless you're planning to bank with a major international bank (which isn't likely to fold until the day after the end of the world), you should check the credit rating of a financial institution before depositing any money, particularly if it doesn't provide deposit insurance. All banks have a credit rating (the highest is 'AAA') and a bank with a high rating will be happy to tell you (but get it in writing). You can also check the rating of an international bank or financial organisation with Moody's Investor Service. You should be wary of institutions offering higher than average interest rates; if it looks too good to be true, it probably is!

MORTGAGES

Although Greek and Cypriot banks are more keen to lend money on property than they used to be, it's difficult for a foreign non-resident to obtain a mortgage for a second home, and **in Greece non-residents (or those who don't file an annual tax declaration) aren't allowed to have a mortgage by law**. Mortgages or home loans are available from most Greek and Cypriot banks, foreign banks in Greece and Cyprus and offshore banks. Greek, Cypriot and foreign lenders have all tightened their lending criteria in the last decade owing to repayment problems experienced by many recession-hit borrowers. Note that it's unwise to over-stretch your finances when taking out a mortgage, as there will inevitably be added costs that you haven't bargained for. Some foreign lenders apply stricter rules than Greek and Cypriot lenders regarding income, employment and the type of property on which they will lend, although some are willing to lend more. Some lenders, e.g. offshore lenders, don't permit long-term or regular letting, and some banks demand a guarantee from a third party. If you raise a mortgage outside Greece or Cyprus for a property in either country, you should be aware of any impact this may have on your foreign or your Greek or Cypriot tax liabilities. Most financial experts advise clients to obtain a mortgage from a large reputable bank, rather than a small one.

Most banks are willing to finance the construction of a house, although you will usually need to pay for the land out of your own resources. A bank usually advances the mortgage to the builder or developer in stages in line with the agreed stage payments. Lenders usually require a life policy and building insurance for a property's full value. It's customary for a property in Greece or Cyprus to be held as security for a home loan, i.e. the lender takes a first charge on the property, which is recorded at the property registry. If a loan is obtained using a property as security, additional fees and registration costs are payable to the notary for registering the charge against the property.

To obtain a mortgage from a local bank, you must usually provide proof of your monthly income and outgoings such as existing mortgage payments, rent and other loans or commitments (although some lenders offer 'non-status' loans at higher interest rates). Mortgage arrangements in Cyprus are usually made by the solicitor in charge of the conveyancing and completion of a sale. If you want a Greek or Cypriot mortgage to buy a property for commercial purposes, you must provide a detailed business plan in Greek. Note that a mortgage can usually be taken over by a new owner when a property is sold.

Greece: In Greece, all private commercial banks provide retail mortgages, but the mortgage market is dominated by two state controlled banks: the National Mortgage Bank of Greece and the National Housing Bank. Some mortgage facilities are subsidised by the state and other organisations. You can usually borrow up to 70 per cent of a property's value over a term of five to 15 years, although longer terms, e.g. 20 or 25 years, are available. Traditionally, mortgages have been very expensive in Greece compared with other western European countries, although rates have come into line with other euro zone countries from 2001. You should carefully check all commissions and fees before signing.

Bear in mind that you must add expenses and fees totalling around 15 per cent of the purchase price of a property. For example, if you're buying a property for €75,000 and obtain a 70 per cent mortgage, you must make a 30 per cent deposit (€25,000) plus around 15 per cent fees (€11,250), making a total of around €36,250. There are various fees associated with mortgages, e.g. all lenders levy an 'arrangement' fee, and banks also insist on a valuation survey (see page 145) before they grant a loan.

Cyprus: In Cyprus all private banks offer retail mortgages, but bank loans (mortgages or otherwise) are rarely granted to non-resident, foreign property buyers, who may need to borrow from foreign or offshore banks. Some brokers offer mortgages on Cypriot properties from UK banks, for example. The minimum sum for a mortgage loan is CY£35,000 and you can borrow up to around 75 per cent of a property's value, with interest rates around 2.5 per cent above the basic rate. You're required to pay a commitment fee of at least 1 per cent of the loan. Terms are usually five or ten years; longer terms are difficult to obtain. There are various fees associated with mortgages, although these are usually included in the solicitor's fees, as it's common practice for the solicitor handling a sale to arrange the mortgage. A solicitor's fees (including mortgage arrangement, general contract work and stamp duty) are typically around CY£750. **Note also that many developers offer schemes whereby you can pay for a home over three to five years.**

Buying through an Offshore Company

Properties in both Greece and Cyprus can be purchased in the name of an offshore company. If a property in Cyprus is purchased via an offshore company, exchange controls don't affect the sale of a property and full repatriation of funds is possible. In addition, no land registry fees are payable, which can represent a large saving. The shares of an offshore company can be used to secure a loan for the purchase of the property, the shares being charged to the bank in return for a loan equal to a percentage of the value of the property. Buying through an offshore company is also useful to avoid inheritance tax. Before buying a property through a offshore company, it's essential to obtain expert legal advice and weigh up the long-term advantages and disadvantages.

Mortgages for Second Homes

If you have spare equity in an existing property in your home country, it may be more cost effective to re-mortgage (or take out a second loan) on that property than to take out a new mortgage for a second home. It involves less paperwork and therefore lower legal fees, and a plan can be tailored to your requirements. Depending on the equity in your home and the cost of the property abroad, this may also enable you to pay cash for a second home. Note, however, that when a mortgage is taken out on a Greek or Cypriot property, it's based on that property and not the individual, which could be important if you get into repayment difficulties. If you let a second home, you may be able to offset the interest (pro rata) on your mortgage against letting income and reduce your taxes.

Foreign Currency Loans

It's possible to obtain a foreign currency mortgage, i.e. other than in euros or Cypriot pounds. In previous years, high Greek interest rates meant that a foreign currency mortgage was a good option for many foreigners. However, you should be wary about taking out a foreign currency mortgage, as interest rate gains can be wiped out overnight by currency swings and devaluations. It's generally recognised that you should take out a mortgage in the currency in which you're paid if not in the currency of the country where your property is situated. Note that the Cypriot pound is generally a stable currency which isn't traded internationally and consequently isn't prone to currency fluctuations. A CY£ loan may therefore be more secure than one in a foreign currency.

When choosing between a euro or Cypriot pound loan and a loan in another currency, ensure that you take into account all costs, fees, interest rates and possible currency fluctuations. Irrespective of how you finance the purchase of a second home in Greece or Cyprus, you should obtain professional advice. Note that if you have a mortgage in a currency other than that in which you're paid, you must usually pay commission charges each time you transfer money into euros or Cypriot pounds and remit money abroad.

VALUE ADDED TAX

Greece: Value added tax (*foros prostithemenis axias*), was introduced in Greece on 1st January 1986, when the country joined the European Union. Most prices in stores are quoted inclusive of value added tax (VAT), although sometimes exclusive prices are quoted, e.g. for commercial goods. Certain goods and services are exempt from VAT, including medical services, legal and notarial services, post office services, building leases, agriculture and imports from other EU states. Exports are also exempt from VAT. On all other goods Greece levies three rates of VAT, as follows:

Rate	Applicability
4% (low)	Books and other printed materials; theatre tickets.
8% (reduced)	Food products; pharmaceutical products; medical equipment and ancillary goods; public transport; homes; food and drink in coffee shops, cafeterias and restaurants; products and services relating to agricultural production.
18% (standard)	All other goods and services.

On some of the Greek island groups such the Dodecanese, north-eastern Aegean and the Sporades, the 18 and 8 per cent rates are reduced by 30 per cent (to 12.6 per cent and 5.6 per cent respectively) on all goods with the exception of tobacco products and vehicles.

All businesses in Greece must register for VAT and returns are normally filed monthly and due within two months of the end of the month to which they relate. Smaller enterprises with annual sales below a certain amount are permitted to file quarterly returns. Any tax due must be paid when the return is filed. VAT fraud is rife in Greece and payments are often paid in cash to avoid VAT. Note that it's necessary to have legitimate bills showing registered names and VAT numbers in order to reclaim VAT. Furnished property lettings are exempt from VAT, although you may need to charge clients VAT if you provide certain services.

VAT is payable on goods imported from outside the EU, but not on goods purchased from another EU country where VAT has already been paid, although you may be asked to produce a VAT receipt. Enterprises located in other EU countries may obtain a refund of VAT paid on goods and services purchased in Greece, and VAT may also be refunded to enterprises in a non-EU country when Greece has a reciprocity agreement with that country.

Cyprus: VAT was introduced in Cyprus on 1st July 1992. In 2000, several changes were made to rates, the most significant of which was an increase in the standard rate from 8 to 10 per cent, and the introduction of a 5 per cent rate on hotel and restaurant bills and alcoholic drinks. As in Greece, most prices in shops are quoted inclusive of VAT, although sometimes exclusive prices are quoted, e.g. on commercial goods. Many products and services, including agricultural machinery and products, bank transactions, books, bus fares, children's clothing, exports, financial services, medicines, and most food items are exempt from VAT. On other goods and services Cyprus levies two rates of VAT, as follows:

Rate	Applicability
5% (reduced)	Hotel and restaurant bills; alcoholic drinks.
10% (standard)	All other goods and services.

SOCIAL SECURITY TAXES

The social security systems in Greece and Cyprus are administered by the state and, in principle, apply to all individuals working in either country, whether employed or self-employed. They provide benefits for health care (see page 45), sickness, retirement, disability, death and old age, maternity, paternity and adoption. Note, however, that benefits are reduced considerably when you're self-employed. Both employers and employees must register and make social security contributions. Voluntary registration can also be made by those who aren't required to register. An employer must notify the authorities when a new employee starts work and deduct contributions from his gross salary and, in Greece, make payments to the authorities at the end of each month. All compulsory social security contributions are tax deductible (in Greece and Cyprus).

Social security contributions are payable on the following:

- all remuneration, including payments in kind, e.g. accommodation or food;
- regular bonus payments, commission and prizes;
- overtime payments;
- Christmas and holiday bonuses (Greece only);
- unsociable hours payments, e.g. shift work;
- remuneration resulting from suspension due to disciplinary action;
- compensation for unfair dismissal or termination of a contract;
- early retirement premiums;
- danger money. (It's especially important to declare this for social security purposes!)

The following income is exempt from social security contributions:

- travel expenses;
- subsistence allowances;
- payments in lieu of holidays;
- sick pay and pensions;
- payments made during military service;
- payments made towards the education of children (including university education);
- payments made towards medical bills;
- redundancy payments when made to all employees;
- profit-related pay.

Greece: Social security contributions are regarded as a form of tax in Greece, where the system governing social security payments is complicated and several groups of employees have their own funds (other than the state IKA fund) for main and auxiliary insurance. Employees' contributions are normally based on their gross monthly income up to a maximum salary of €1,747.30, although this ceiling doesn't apply to employees insured after 1st January 1993 and those in certain occupations pay a fixed sum. The percentage payable varies with the region where you're employed, the number of 'occupational hazards' and working conditions, but in all cases is extremely high. In occupations that aren't classified as dangerous, employees pay 15.9 per cent and employers 27.26 per cent. Employees of international organisations and diplomatic missions are exempt from paying social security contributions in Greece.

Note that because Greek employers pay 14 'monthly' salaries, the extra payments being made at Easter (half a month's salary), summer (half a month's salary) and Christmas (one month's salary), 14 social security contributions are made per year.

Self-employed individuals in Greece must also pay social security contributions, although benefits are limited. For example, the self-employed aren't entitled to unemployment or accident benefits. As with salaried employees, the amount paid depends on your profession, although it's usually between €178 and 208 monthly.

Greece has reciprocal social security agreements with Argentina, Austria, Belgium, Brazil, Canada, Cyprus, the Czech Republic, Denmark, Egypt, Finland, France, Germany, Hungary, Iceland, Ireland, Italy, Libya, Liechtenstein, Luxembourg, the Netherlands, New Zealand, Norway, Poland, Portugal, Slovakia, Spain, Sweden, Switzerland, the United Kingdom, the United States, Uruguay and Venezuela. These agreements allow for social security contributions paid in one country to be taken into account under the social security schemes of another country. Employees from the above countries who are transferred to Greece for a limited period and who continue to contribute to their home country's social security scheme are exempt from paying contributions in Greece for a year. This exemption may be extended for a further year or, in certain circumstances, five years. However, once the exemption period has elapsed, employees must pay social security contributions in Greece.

Cyprus: Employees' contributions are based on their gross monthly income up to a maximum salary of CY£1,647. Both employees and employers pay 6.3 per cent, plus a 2 per cent contribution to the national defence fund. The self-employed contribute 11.6 per cent of their gross monthly income plus 3 per cent towards the national defence fund. Minimum and maximum monthly incomes for the self-employed are classified depending on the type of business, profession or vocation. As in Greece, employees of international organisations and diplomatic missions are exempt from paying social security contributions in Cyprus.

Cyprus has social security agreements only with Greece and the United Kingdom, under which overseas cover is usually permitted for one to three years. During this time, employees who are transferred to Cyprus for a limited period and who continue to contribute in Greece or the UK are exempt from paying contributions in Cyprus. Once the exemption period has elapsed, employees must pay social security contributions in Cyprus.

INCOME TAX

Greece: Greek income tax (*foros issodimatos*) is near the EU average, particularly for large families. However, when income tax is added to the high social security contributions (see above) and other indirect taxes, Greek taxes are among the highest in Europe. Employees' income tax is deducted at source (i.e. pay-as-you-earn) by employers in Greece and employees aren't responsible for paying their own income tax, although most must still file a tax return. Non-residents who receive income from a Greek source must also file a return with the main tax office in Athens, which deals with Greeks and non-Greeks residing abroad with assets in Greece. All individuals or companies acquiring property in Greece or receiving income from property need to obtain a Greek tax registration number and must file an income tax return annually. The tax registration number, necessary not only for tax purposes but also for transactions such as registering for electricity and water bills and obtaining a telephone line, is available from local tax offices.

Like most people, the Greeks hate paying taxes and tax evasion is a national sport. Most Greeks don't consider cheating the tax man a crime, and it's estimated that many non-salaried people don't declare a substantial part of their income. However, if your tax affairs are investigated and you're found to have made a false declaration, even as a result of an 'innocent' mistake, the authorities often take a hard line. The tax authorities maintain computer records of tax declarations, employers and bank accounts to help them expose fraud, and if your perceived standard of living is higher than would be expected on your declared income, you may be suspected of fraud – which is why many Greeks contrive to appear poor.

Interest paid on deposit accounts in euros is subject to 15 per cent tax, whereas deposit accounts held by non-residents in foreign currencies aren't subject to tax.

Cyprus: As in Greece, salaried employees have their income tax deducted at source on a pay-as-you-earn (PAYE) basis. Uniquely, Cyprus taxes the assets of expatriates only on a remittance basis, meaning that many expatriates can keep assets free of tax in an offshore bank, investments or trust, and simply transfer to Cyprus what they need for their day-to-day expenses. Foreign residents are taxed at a basic flat rate of 5 per cent on pension and investment income brought into Cyprus above CY£4,000 per person or CY£8,000 for a couple. This is obviously a big attraction compared with many other countries, where property owners are subject to tax rates of up to 60 per cent. However, residents in Cyprus usually need to show a minimum income of CY£7,000 (CY£10,000 for a married couple). Double taxation agreements (see page 88) enable foreigners to receive both state and private pensions free of tax.

There are many other tax advantages for expatriates in Cyprus. For example, expatriate employees of offshore entities are taxed only on income earned in Cyprus. Those living and working in Cyprus are taxed at half the standard rate, i.e. from 0 to 20 per cent rather than 0 to 40 per cent. The foreign employees of offshore companies working abroad, but receiving their salary via Cyprus pay just 10 per cent of the standard rate and those who don't receive their salary in Cyprus pay no Cypriot tax at all. There are further tax incentives for the Larnaca tax-free zone. Offshore companies themselves also benefit from a business tax rate of just 6 per cent per year. Insurance pensions can be paid to retirees in Cyprus on a similar tax-free basis and are index-linked under reciprocal agreements, compared with their 'frozen' status in other countries.

Dividends and interest paid on non-resident deposit accounts are subject to 20 per cent tax, although this is increased to 25 per cent on interest paid to non-residents in excess of CY£40,000 annually. Interest accrued on foreign currency deposited in a Cyprus bank is tax free.

Liability

Greece: Your liability for Greek income tax (and certain other taxes) depends on where you're domiciled. Your domicile is normally the country you regard as your permanent home and where you live most of the year. For example, a foreigner working in Greece for a Greek company who has taken up residence in Greece and has no income tax liability abroad is considered to have his tax domicile in Greece. A person can be resident in more than one country at any given time, but can be domiciled only in one country. The domicile of a married woman isn't necessarily the same as her husband's, but is determined using the same criteria as an independent person. Your country of domicile is particularly important when it comes to inheritance tax (see page 97). You're considered to be a Greek resident and liable to Greek tax if *any* of the following apply:

- Your permanent home, i.e. family or principal residence, is in Greece.
- You spend over 183 days in Greece during any calendar year.
- You're employed or carry out paid professional activities in Greece, except when secondary to business activities conducted in another country.
- Your centre of vital economic interest, e.g. investments or business, is in Greece.

If you intend being self-employed in Greece, depending on the type of business or occupation, you may be required to register with the Chamber of Trade and Commerce and the Artisans and Tradesmen's Insurance scheme (TEVE) or the alternative Merchants' Insurance Fund (TAE).

You must complete an income tax return in Greece if your annual income is over €1,188.63 (€2,377.26 if you're a salaried employee). Even if you have no taxable income at all, you must file a tax return if you happen to meet *any* of the following conditions:

- You own a private car, a motorcycle with an engine capacity of more than 500cc, a pleasure boat or an aircraft.
- You have a domestic servant.
- You're a partner in a Greek partnership, limited liability company or joint venture.
- You have income of more than €148.60 from the letting of property or land.
- You're purchasing or constructing a building.
- You own a house with more than 150m² of floor space or a second house.

Married couples file joint returns, although tax is calculated separately on the income of each spouse, and a net loss of one spouse may not be offset against the income of the other. The husband is responsible for filing the return of a married couple and declaring his wife's income.

Cyprus: Your liability for taxes in Cyprus depends on where you're domiciled, which is usually the country you regard as your permanent home and where you live most of the year. Cypriot law doesn't specifically define residence, although any person who spends over 183 days in any calendar year in Cyprus or who has a place of abode there is usually considered resident. However, if your income doesn't exceed CY£5,000 per annum, you aren't required to file a tax return. Married couples resident in Cyprus are taxed separately on all income.

Double Taxation

Greek and Cypriot residents are taxed on their world-wide income, subject to certain treaty exceptions, although citizens of most countries (the USA is a rare exception) are exempt from paying taxes in their home country when they spend a minimum period abroad, e.g. one year. The Greek and Cypriot governments have double taxation treaties with many countries, which are designed to ensure that income that has already been taxed in one treaty country isn't taxed again in another.

Treaties establish a tax credit or exemption on certain kinds of income, either in the country of residence or the country where the income is earned, and where applicable a double taxation treaty prevails over domestic law. Many people living abroad switch their investments to offshore holdings to circumvent often complicated double taxation agreements. If you're in doubt about your tax liability in your home country or another country where you have assets or from where you receive income, contact the tax authorities there for a ruling. Note that if you aren't living in Greece or Cyprus but have assets there, you're usually obliged by law to file a tax return listing your assets and any income you receive from them.

If you plan to live permanently in Greece or Cyprus, you should notify the tax authorities in your present country (you will be asked to complete a form, e.g. a P85 in Britain). You may be entitled to a tax refund if you depart during the tax year, which necessitates the completion of a tax return. The authorities may require evidence that you're leaving the country, e.g. evidence of a job abroad or of having purchased or rented a property there. If you move to Greece or Cyprus to take up a job or start a business, you must register with the local tax authorities soon after your arrival.

Note that moving to Greece or Cyprus may offer opportunities for 'favourable tax planning', i.e. tax avoidance, rather than tax evasion. To take the maximum advantage of your situation, you should obtain professional advice from a tax adviser who's familiar with both the Greek or Cypriot tax system and that of your present country of residence.

Greece: Greece has double taxation treaties with many countries, including Argentina, Austria, Belgium, Canada, Cyprus, the Czech Republic, Denmark, Egypt, Finland, France, Germany, Hungary, Iceland, Ireland, Italy, the Republic of Korea, Luxembourg, the Netherlands, Norway, Poland, Romania, the Slovak Republic, Sweden, Switzerland, the United Kingdom and the USA.

Cyprus: Cyprus has double taxation treaties with Austria, Bulgaria, Canada, China, the Czech Republic, Denmark, Egypt, France, Germany, Greece, Hungary, India, Italy, Kuwait, Malta, Norway, Poland, Romania, Russia, South Africa, Sweden, Syria, the UK, the USA and Yugoslavia.

Deductions & Allowances

Before you're liable for income tax, you can subtract certain deductions and allowances from your gross income. Income tax is calculated upon both earned and unearned income, and your gross income includes earnings from employment as well as business profits, rental income, capital gains, overseas and cost of living allowances, bonuses (annual, performance, profit share, etc.), relocation allowances, payments in kind (such as free accommodation or meals, language lessons provided for a spouse, personal company car, and children's education), stock options, home leave or holidays paid by your employer, and property and investment income (dividends and interest).

Deductions are amounts that are subtracted from your gross income to arrive at your net income. A number of allowances are then deductible from this figure to give your taxable income. In order to claim allowances relating to personal expenditure or family circumstances, it's usually necessary to produce receipts.

Greece: The following items are deductible from your gross income:

- social security contributions;
- medical expenses for you and dependent family members – 100 per cent up to €29,716 and 50 per cent between €29,716 and 44,574;
- 100 per cent of interest on loans taken out to buy your primary residence;
- rent payments up to €742.90;
- life and accident insurance premiums for you and your dependants up to €742.90;
- tuition fees for you or your dependent children up to €742.90 per person;
- donations to the Greek state under certain conditions and up to a certain amount;
- 30 per cent of family expenditure for purchases of certain goods or services up to €891.50.

The following family allowances can be claimed:

- €89.15 for a family with one child;
- €104 per child for a family with two children;
- €148.58 per child for a family with three children;
- €178.30 per child for a family with four children;
- an additional €29.72 per child for a family with more than four children.

Note that non-residents who earn income from Greek sources aren't entitled to any of the above deductions, unless they're EU citizens who earn at least 90 per cent of their total income in Greece.

Cyprus: The following items are deductible from your gross income:

- social security contributions;
- interest up to CY£500 on housing loans;
- rent relief up to CY£300;
- life assurance premiums;
- professional tax paid to municipalities;
- membership fees for trade and professional organisations, if membership is mandatory;
- 100 per cent of documented charitable donations up to CY£20,000 and 50 per cent above CY£20,000.

Taxpayers aged over 65 also receive an allowance of CY£1,500.

In addition to the above deductions and allowances, the following types of income are tax-free for foreign residents in Cyprus:

- up to CY£2,000 of foreign investment income (including dividends, interest, royalties and rental income) remitted to Cyprus;
- interest on foreign funds deposited with any bank in Cyprus;
- up to CY£5,000 of pension payments (from employment outside Cyprus) remitted to Cyprus. For amounts exceeding CY£5,000, there's a flat tax rate of 5 per cent.

Married couples and families also receive the following tax credits:

- CY£500 for a husband or wife (apportioned when both have taxable income);
- CY£500 for each child under 16 who isn't receiving secondary education;
- CY£500 for each child receiving secondary education;
- CY£1,500 for each child receiving higher education in Cyprus.

Rates

Greece: Families are taxed as a single entity in Greece, and a husband's return normally includes his wife and children's income, although he can elect for a dependent child's income to be taxed separately if this is advantageous. A wife may be taxed separately only if she's separated from her husband. Net income is subject to the rates of tax shown in the table below (for income earned in 2001). The second column shows the tax rate payable on the income band shown in the first column. For example, if your taxable income is €15,000, you pay no tax on the first €5,843, 5 per cent tax on the next €2,209 (= €110.45), 15 per cent on the next €4,828 (= €724.20) and 30 per cent on the remaining €2,118 (= €635.40), making a total tax bill of €1,470.05.

Taxable Income (€)	Tax Rate (%)
up to 5,843	0*
5,843–8,053	5
8,054–12,882	15
12,883–22,525	30
22,526–48,244	40
over 48,244	45

* Individuals domiciled abroad are taxed at 5 per cent on income up to €5,843 unless they're EU residents who earn at least 90 per cent of their total income in Greece.

Cyprus: Net income after deduction of allowable expenses is subject to income tax at the rates shown in the table below (for an explanation, see **Greece** above):

Taxable Income (CY£)	Tax Rate (%)
up to 5,000	0
5,001–8,000	20
8,001–11,000	30
over 11,000	40

Note that imported foreign pension and investment income above CY£4,000 (CY£8,000 for a couple) is taxed at 5 per cent.

Calculation

The following examples of tax calculations are for the tax year 2000.

Greece: The following calculation is for a married employee with two children, employment income only (based on 14 payments of €3,000), with a non-working spouse, social security paid in Greece and no expenses.

Item	Sum (€)
Gross Annual Income	42,000.00
Deductions:	
Social security (14 x €1,747.30 x 15.9%)	(3,889.50)
Net Income	38,110.50
Tax (see table above)	9,957.20
Tax Credits:	
Children (2)	(280.00)
Total Tax Payable	9,677.20

Cyprus: The following tax calculation is for a married employee with two children with employment income only (based on 12 payments of CY£1,666), a non-working spouse, social security paid in Cyprus and no expenses.

Item	Sum (CY£)
Gross Annual Income	20,000.00
Deductions:	
Social security (6.3%)	(1,260.00)
Net Income	18,740.00
Tax (see table above)	4,596.00
Tax Credits:	
Children (2)	(1,000.00)
Total Tax Payable	3,596.00

Property Income

Greece: Income tax is payable in Greece on rental income from a property, even if you live abroad and the money is paid there. If you receive income from property in Greece you must have a tax registration number (see page 86). All rental income must be declared to the Greek tax authorities, whether you let a property for a few weeks to a friend or 52 weeks a year on a commercial basis. You're eligible for deductions such as repairs and maintenance, security, cleaning costs, mortgage interest, management and letting expenses (e.g. advertising), local taxes, and an allowance to cover depreciation and insurance. You should seek professional advice to ensure that you're claiming everything to which you're entitled. Many people find that there's little or no tax to pay after deducting their expenses.

Non-resident property owners who receive an income from a Greek property (or any Greek source) must file a tax return, available from local tax offices in Greece or Greece consulates abroad. Completed forms must be sent to the tax office by 15th March each year. You should keep a copy of your return and send it by registered letter, so that there's no dispute over whether it was received. Some months after filing you will receive a tax assessment detailing the tax due. Failure to file a tax return carries a minimum penalty of €60. The tax authorities have many ways of detecting people letting homes and not paying tax and have been clamping down on tax evaders in recent years.

Non-residents must also declare any income received in Greece on their tax return in their country of residence, although tax on Greek letting income is usually paid only in Greece. However, if you pay less tax in Greece than you would have paid in your home country, you must usually pay the difference. On the other hand, if you pay more tax in Greece than you would have paid on the income in your home country, you aren't entitled to a refund!

Cyprus: Property letting isn't generally permitted by non-resident foreigners in Cyprus.

Returns & Bills

Greece: The tax year in Greece is the same as the calendar year, i.e. 1st January to 31st December, and residents are sent an annual tax return by the tax authorities at the beginning of each year. If you aren't sent a form you can obtain one from your local tax office. An income tax return must be submitted if the your taxable income exceeds €1,188.64 or €2,377.27 for salaried employees. Married couples file joint returns, although tax is calculated separately on the income of each spouse and a net loss by one spouse cannot be offset against the income of the other. The husband is responsible for filing a family's return and declaring his wife's income. Foreigners planning to leave Greece (and Greeks going abroad for more than a year) must file a tax return and pay any tax due from the beginning of the current tax year up to the date of their departure.

Tax returns must be filed by 1st March for the previous tax year, e.g. the return filed in March 2001 is for the year 2000. The deadline is extended to 16th April if your declared income includes income from individual commercial enterprises and to 2nd May for income including employment or pensions and foreign income. Non-residents also have until 2nd May to file a return. No extensions are usually permitted and late filing attracts a penalty. The fine for failing to file a tax return is equal to 3.5 per cent (5 per cent for withholding taxes and VAT) of the tax due per month of delay up to a maximum of 300 per cent. There's a fine of 1.5 per cent (2.5 per cent for withholding taxes and VAT) of the tax due per month of delay up to a maximum of 200 per cent. The penalty for filing an incorrect return is a fine of 3 per cent (4.5 per cent for withholding taxes and VAT) of the tax due per month of delay up to a maximum of 300 per cent. For gross violations, offenders may be liable for criminal penalties, including imprisonment.

Employers must withhold income tax from salaries, wages and other forms of remuneration paid to employees. Any difference between the amount of tax paid and the amount that should have been paid according to the tax laws is billed (or refunded) by the tax authorities. The tax liability of individuals who aren't salaried employees is calculated by deducting from the tax due any advance payments, taxes withheld at source and any creditable amounts of foreign taxes paid. An advance payment of 55 per cent of the current year's tax liability must be paid, based on the previous year's income tax, less any tax withheld at source during the year. The total amount due, including the advance payments of the current year's tax, is payable in three equal bimonthly instalments. However, the tax can be paid in a lump sum, in which case a 2.5 per cent discount is granted.

Greek tax returns are complicated, despite attempts to simplify them in recent years. The language used is particularly difficult for foreigners (and many Greeks) to understand. However, local tax offices will usually help you to complete your tax return. You can make an appointment for a free consultation with your local tax inspector at your town hall. (Unless your Greek is fluent, you should take a translator with you). Alternatively, you can employ a tax accountant to complete your return.

If a you believe that your tax assessment is incorrect, you can try to come to an agreement with the tax authorities through an administrative appeals procedure or, failing that, appeal to a tax court. All tax returns are subject to audits by the tax authorities. Note that the statute of limitations for income tax verification is 11 years after the end of the accounting year.

Cyprus: The income tax year in Cyprus is the calendar year, i.e. 1st January to 31st December. Income tax returns need only be submitted if your taxable income exceeds CY£5,000. If you earn more than this amount, you must give notice to the Commissioner of Income Tax no later than 30th April of the year following the income year and taxes are payable by 1st August, e.g. taxes for the year 2000 must be paid by 1st August 2001. Businesses must make an estimate of tax due by 1st August of the current tax year and pay provisional tax in three instalments on 1st August, 30th September and 31st December.

Income tax returns are available in English and contain instructions regarding their completion on the reverse. However, unless you're 100 per cent sure how to complete the form, you should seek professional help. Free assistance is available from the income tax district offices in Larnaca, Limassol, Nicosia and Paphos, either by telephone or in person (you must make an appointment with a tax inspector). Alternatively, you can employ an accountant or tax expert to complete your tax return for you.

PROPERTY TAXES

Greece: All Greek property owners are liable for property taxes with the exception of Greek citizens and foreign residents buying their first home in Greece, who are exempt for a period. Otherwise, tax is levied at a rate of between 0.25 and 0.35 per cent on a property's market value by local municipalities, who also charge other fees and taxes to pay for local services, either directly or indirectly.

A kind of wealth tax on property was re-introduced in Greece in 1997 (it had been formerly been abolished in 1993) and applies to all individuals and legal entities owning property there valued at over €205,000, although there are allowances for families and those with children. Allowances are €410,000 for a couple and €52,000 for each child. After the deduction of allowances, tax is payable on a progressive scale ranging from 0.3 per cent to 0.8 per cent, as shown in the table below:

Taxable Amount (€)	Tax Rate (%)
up to 148,580	0.3
148,581–297,160	0.4
297,161–445,740	0.5
445,741–742,900	0.6
742,901–1,040,060	0.7
over 1,040,060	0.8

This means that a couple with two children (with a total allowance of €514,000) owning a house worth €750,000 would pay tax only on €236,000 – the first €148,580 at 0.3 per cent (= €445.74) and the remaining €87,420 at 0.4 per cent (= €349.68), making a total tax bill of €795.42.

For companies and other legal entities there's a flat rate tax of 0.7 per cent on the value of property in excess of €51,625. In this case there are no allowances, although there are certain exemptions. e.g. when a company uses a property for production or commercial activities. Hotels are taxed at 50 per cent of their value.

Cyprus: Property owners in Cyprus are liable for local authority taxes (rates) and an immovable property tax, irrespective of their residence status. Local authority taxes are levied for rubbish collection, street lighting, road maintenance and other services. The total tax bill for an average property is usually between CY£30 and 100 per year, depending on its location and size. Taxes are generally higher in towns than in villages and rural areas. Properties valued at over CY£35,000 are subject to an additional charge of between CY£1.50 and 3.50 per CY£1,000 value.

The government imposes an annual immovable property tax on the registered owners of property in Cyprus. The amount payable is from 2 to 3.5 per cent of a property's official value, as shown in the table below:

Value of Property (CY£)	Tax Rate (%)
up to 100,000	0
100,001–250,000	2
250,001–500,000	3
over 500,000	3.5

CAPITAL GAINS TAX

Greece: Profits made by individuals in Greece on the sale of assets and property aren't generally subject to capital gains tax (CGT). Companies are, however, liable for CGT at the rate of 30 per cent on gains from the transfer of any right connected with the company, e.g. a sublease, and at 20 per cent on gains from the transfer of the entire company or the transfer of shares.

Cyprus: Capital gains tax at a rate of 20 per cent is levied on profits from the sale of property in Cyprus or from the disposal of shares in companies whose assets include property. Profits are adjusted for inflation to arrive at the taxable gain. There are lifetime (i.e. once only) exemptions from profit made on the sale of a property, as shown in the table below:

Type of Property	Amount of Exemption (CY£)
Private residence	50,000
Agricultural land	15,000
Other property	10,000

Note, however, that when you sell a property in Cyprus you're allowed to export the original cost plus CY£50,000 profit, but any balance can be exported only at the rate of CY£50,000 per year (plus interest), commencing the year following the sale. Note also that profits from the sale of property acquired with imported foreign currency in the period 1st August 1980 to 13th July 1990 is exempt from CGT.

INHERITANCE & GIFT TAX

As in most countries, dying doesn't free you (or more correctly, your beneficiaries) from the clutches of the tax man. Both Greece and Cyprus impose inheritance and gift taxes, called estate tax or death duty in some countries. **It's important for both residents and non-residents with property in Greece or Cyprus to decide in advance how they wish to dispose of their property, which if possible should be decided before buying a property.** Inheritance laws are complicated and professional advice should be sought from an experienced lawyer who understands both Greek or Cypriot inheritance law and the law of any other countries involved. Your will (see below) is also a vital component in reducing Greek or Cypriot inheritance and gift taxes to the minimum or delaying their payment.

Greece: Greece imposes inheritance tax on the world-wide assets of a deceased person who was domiciled in Greece. Similarly, property located in Greece and movable property situated abroad given by a Greek national or by a foreigner to a person domiciled in Greece is subject to gift tax. The tax rates for inheritance and gift tax are the same, although the amount of tax payable varies with the relationship of the beneficiary to the deceased or donor. Relationships are categorised into four groups: spouse, children and parents (category A); other descendants and ascendants, brothers and sisters and other relatives of the third degree, i.e. nephews/nieces and uncles/aunts (category B); foster parents, children from previous marriages of the spouse, and sons or daughters-in-law (category C); distant relatives and non-relatives (category D). Each category is taxed according to a different scale of rates, the highest rate in each case applying to property valued at over €178,295, and each category is entitled to a different allowance, as shown in the table below. The fourth column shows the amount of tax payable on the first €178,295 of a property's value, taking into account the relevant allowance and scale of tax rates; the fifth column indicates the total tax payable on a property valued at €250,000, by way of an example:

Category	Scale of Tax Rates (%)	Allowance (€)	Tax on first €178,295 (€)	Tax on €250,000 Property (€)
A	5–25	153,780	21,518	39,444
B	10–35	112,772	30,074	55,171
C	20–50	51,260	54,692	90,544
D	35–60	30,760	81,385	124,408

The tax on gifts of up to €59,432 made by parents to their children is reduced to 50 per cent of the tax applicable to gifts in category A. The €59,432 limit applies to each child and to cumulative gifts made by parents to the same child.

The recipient of an inheritance or donation must file a tax return within six months of the date of death or receipt of a gift. Greece has inheritance tax treaties with Germany, Italy, Spain and the USA to prevent double taxation of inheritances. Inheritance tax on property can be avoided by buying a home through an offshore company (see page 82).

Cyprus: Cyprus imposes inheritance tax on the world-wide assets of a deceased person who was domiciled in Cyprus. However, property acquired after January 1976 that was purchased with foreign funds is exempt, provided that the deceased had been resident outside Cyprus at some time. For non-residents, inheritance tax applies only to property situated in Cyprus, including movable and immovable property, money, investments and other assets, as well as gifts made within three years of death. Before an estate is subject to inheritance tax, the following allowances apply:

Relationship to the Deceased	Allowance (CY£)
Surviving spouse	75,000
Each child under 21	150,000
Each child over 21	75,000
Each disabled child over 21	150,000
Each predeceased child with own children	50,000
Donations to charitable institutions	Up to 50,000
Donations to the Cyprus government or any local authority for public purposes	Total Donation

After deduction of allowances, inheritance tax is applied at the rates shown in the table below:

Value of Estate (CY£)	Tax Rate (%)
up to 20,000	0
20,001–25,000	10
25,001–35,000	13
35,001–55,000	15
55,001–80,000	17
80,001–105,000	20
105,001–150,000	23
over 150,000	30

For example, an estate worth CY£425,000 inherited from a person with a surviving spouse and two children under 21 would be subject to tax on CY£50,000 – the first CY£20,000 at 0 per cent, the next CY£5,000 at 10 per cent (= CY£500), the next CY£10,000 at 13 per cent (= CY£1,300) and the remaining CY£15,000 at 15 per cent (= CY£2,250), making total inheritance tax of CY£4,050.

There's no gift tax in Cyprus.

WILLS

It's an unfortunate fact of life that you're unable to take your hard-earned assets with you when you take your final bow. All adults should make a will, irrespective of how large or small their assets, and each spouse should make a separate will. If a foreigner dies intestate in Greece or Cyprus, i.e. without a will, his estate may be automatically disposed of under local law. The disposal of your estate depends on your country of domicile (see **Liability** on page 87). As a general rule, Greek and Cypriot law permits a foreigner who isn't domiciled there to make a will in any language and under the law of any country, provided that it's valid under the law of that country. However, a foreigner resident in Greece or Cyprus is usually permitted to dispose of his assets there according to the law of his home country, provided that his will is valid under the law of that country. If you've lived abroad for a long time, it may be necessary for you to create a legal domicile in your home country for the purpose of making a will.

Although it isn't necessary to have a Greek or Cypriot will for a home and other assets in these countries, it's wise to have a separate will for every country in which you own property. If a person has a local will, his assets can be dealt with immediately under local law without having to wait for the granting of probate in another country. (The administration of the estate is also cheaper.) Having a local will for your assets speeds up the will's execution and saves the long and complicated process of having a foreign will executed abroad. Note that if you have two or more wills, you *must* ensure that they don't contradict or invalidate one another, and you should also periodically review your will to ensure that it reflects your current financial and personal circumstances. All previous wills can be revoked by writing a new one, indicating that a past will has been cancelled.

Note that Greek law applies forced heirship, whereby the closest relatives (which include the surviving spouse, children and parents) of a deceased person are entitled to half of the estate and cannot be disinherited. If there are surviving children, the deceased's parents are excluded and the surviving spouse's share of the estate is reduced from a half to as little as an eighth, depending on the number of children.

Wills can be drawn up by qualified lawyers and notaries in your home country, but it's cheaper to do it in Greece or Cyprus. Note that a will in Cyprus must be signed in the presence of a lawyer or notary and, where applicable, the rules relating to witnesses are strict; if they aren't followed precisely a will can be rendered null and void. You'll also need someone to act as the executor (or personal representative) of your estate, which can be particularly costly for modest estates. Your bank, lawyer (the least expensive, but far from cheap) or other professional will usually act as executor, although this should be avoided if possible, as the fees can be astronomical. **It's best to appoint your beneficiaries, who can then instruct a lawyer after your death if they need legal assistance.** Keep a copy of your will(s) in a safe place and another copy with your lawyer or the executor of your estate. Don't leave them in a bank safe deposit box, which in the event of your death is usually sealed for a period. You should keep information regarding bank accounts and insurance policies with your will(s), but don't forget to tell someone where they are!

Note that inheritance law is a complicated subject and it's important to obtain professional legal advice when writing or altering your will(s).

COST OF LIVING

It's virtually impossible to calculate an average cost of living in Greece or Cyprus, as it depends on each individual's circumstances and lifestyle. For example, the difference in your food bill will depend on what you eat and where you lived before arriving in Greece. Nevertheless, the following information gives an indication of how far your euros or Cypriot pounds will stretch and how much (if any) you will have left after paying your bills.

Greece: Greece has enjoyed a stable and strong economy in recent years, reflected in the strong drachma and the entry of the country into the single European currency, the euro. Salaries are generally high and Greeks enjoy a high standard of living, although social security costs are very high, particularly for the self-employed, and the combined burden of social security, income tax and indirect taxes make Greek taxes among the highest in Europe. Anyone planning to live in Greece, particularly retirees, should also take care not to underestimate the cost of living, which has increased considerably in the last decade. However, Greece is still a relatively inexpensive country by American and northern European standards, particularly if your income is earned in a strong currency that has appreciated against the drachma in recent years. Nevertheless, you should be wary of published cost of living comparisons with other countries, which are often wildly inaccurate (and usually include non-essential items which distort the results).

With the exception of Athens, other major cities and some islands such as Hydra and Mykonos, the cost of living in Greece is around 30 per cent below the average of other northern European countries. Food costs less than in many other European countries and around the same as in the USA, although you may have to modify your diet. In fact, it's possible to live very frugally in Greece if you're willing to forego luxuries and live largely 'off the land'. Shopping for 'luxury' items such as cars, stereo equipment, household apparatus, electrical and electronic goods, computers and photographic equipment abroad, e.g. via the Internet can also result in significant savings, as well as offering a wider choice.

Cyprus: Recent statistics showed Cyprus to be one of the least expensive countries in Europe, with prices around 25 to 50 per cent lower than most northern European countries. The island has a solid economy and one of the highest GNPs in the Mediterranean (around US$15,000 in 1999), yet the cost of living on the island is relatively low. According to the UBS Switzerland world-wide survey carried out in 2000, Nicosia has the lowest cost of living of any capital city in western Europe and one of the lowest of any in the world. However, the cost of living is rising and British expatriates find that many goods cost the same in CY£ as they do in pounds sterling at home, which means they're in fact some 15 per cent more expensive. On the other hand, there are many tax incentives available to expatriates in Cyprus, which allow you to invest your money in the most advantageous way, e.g. offshore, yet pay relatively little in taxes.

4.

FINDING YOUR DREAM HOME

Having decided to buy a home in Greece or Cyprus, your first tasks will be to choose the region and what sort of home to buy. **If you're unsure where and what to buy, the best decision is usually to rent for a period.** The secret of successfully buying a home abroad (or anywhere else for that matter) is research, research and more research, preferably before you even set foot there. You may be fortunate and buy the first property you see without doing any homework and live happily ever after. However, a successful purchase is much more likely if you thoroughly investigate the towns and communities in your chosen area, compare the range and prices of properties and their relative values, and study the procedure for buying property. It's a wise or lucky person who gets his choice absolutely right first time.

Greece has a fairly lively property market, although until the last decade or so it attracted few foreign buyers, mainly because of restrictions on foreign ownership. Until around 1990 there were few estate agents offering services to prospective foreign buyers, although more have appeared as Greece has become more popular. Greece is largely undeveloped with most areas as unspoilt as Portugal and Spain were 20 or 30 years ago. It has a largely untapped holiday-home market and many areas have good investment potential. There are strict controls over development and renovation to ensure that the local character is maintained, particularly in coastal and country areas. Old village houses are reasonably priced and in plentiful supply in most areas, although they usually require extensive modernisation and renovation and are seldom a good investment. Many foreign buyers buy a plot of land and build a new house. Note that you can expect to pay a premium for a coastal or island property.

Prices are stable in most areas and largely unaffected by world recessions. The main foreign buyers are the British, Germans and Scandinavians, who have been joined by Russian and other Eastern European buyers in recent years. The British tend to prefer the islands and the Germans the mainland.

Cyprus has a flourishing property market and is a popular location for both holiday and retirement homes, particularly among the British. Most property for sale is in the Greek part of the island, although the Turkish Cypriots have been trying to attract buyers in recent years. A wide range of properties are available, both new and old, including restored and unrestored old village houses. There are many new developments, although they're often uninspiring and few have swimming pools or sports facilities such as tennis courts. Over-development and mass-market tourism has ruined many coastal areas, although most inland villages are unspoilt and full of character. The Cyprus property market is disproportionately large considering the size of the country's economy, and property development is its largest sector.

Restrictions: There are a few restrictions on foreign property ownership in Greece for security reasons, e.g. in all border areas and islands close to Turkey (such as the Dodecanese Islands). Generally non-EU citizens aren't allowed to purchase property in the restricted areas or even engage in long-term rental contracts. Waivers can be obtained but the process is long and very expensive. European Union citizens have the same rights as Greeks in most of Greece. In Cyprus, foreigners are permitted to own one building plot or property only, usually up to two donums, i.e. 2,675m^2 /28,800ft^2 or approximately two-fifths of a hectare (two-thirds of an acre). In certain cases foreigners can own up to three donums (0.4ha/1 acre) but only if the building occupies more than two donums or the land is for professional or commercial use. Permission to buy more than two donums must be sought from the Council of Ministers. Note that applications for more than one residence in Cyprus are rarely approved.

One of the things that attracts many buyers to Greece and Cyprus is the relatively low cost of property compared to many other European countries. Home ownership is high compared with many other countries, although the locals don't generally buy property as an investment, and you shouldn't expect to make a quick profit when buying property in Greece or Cyprus. Property values generally increase at an average of around 5 per cent a year or in line with inflation, meaning that you must own a house for around two years simply to recover the fees associated with buying. Property prices rise faster than average in some fashionable areas, although this is generally reflected in higher purchase prices. The stable property market acts as a discouragement to speculators wishing to make a quick profit.

In Greece, most foreigners live in and around Athens, the Peloponnese, and the islands, particularly Crete, the Cyclades, the Dodecanese and the Ionian Islands. In Cyprus, most foreigners live around the major coastal cities of Larnaca, Limassol and Paphos. A slice of the good life needn't cost the earth, with 'old' village homes requiring renovation available from as little as €15,000 to 30,000/CY£10,000 to 20,000, modern apartments from around €60,000/CY£40,000 and detached villas from €90,000/CY£60,000. However, if you're seeking a substantial home with a large plot of land and a swimming pool, you will usually need to spend over €120,000/CY£80,000 (depending on the area). For those with the financial resources the sky's the limit, with luxury apartments and villas costing well over €150,000/CY£100,000. In recent years prices have risen sharply throughout Greece and Cyprus – both in resort areas and the major cities.

This chapter is designed to help you decide what sort of home to buy and, most importantly, where to buy. It will also help you avoid problems and contains information about regions, research, location, renting, the cost, fees, buying new and resale, community properties, timesharing (and other part-ownership schemes), estate agents, inspections and surveys, conveyancing, purchase contracts, completion, renovation and restoration, moving house, security, utilities, heating and air-conditioning, property income and selling a home.

REGIONS

Greece

For the purpose of this book, Greece has been divided into the following 12 regions: Attica, central Greece, Crete, the Cyclades Islands, the Dodecanese Islands, Epirus and the west, Evia and the Sporades, the Ionian Islands, the north-eastern Aegean Islands, northern Greece, Peloponnese and the Saronic Gulf Islands, all of which are shown on the maps on page 6 and in **Appendix D**.

Attica

The region of Attica lies at the south-eastern end of mainland Greece and includes the capital city of Athens. The Apollo coast is home to a number of crowded and overdeveloped resorts such as Glyfádha and Vouliagméni, which are popular with both visitors and Athenians at weekends, and home to a sizeable expatriate population. The famous historical sites of the Temple of Poseidon and Marathon are situated in Attica, while Mount Párnitha in the north has spectacular forests and rock scenery. The region is also noted for its extensive olive and grape production. The climate in Attica is temperate with hot summers, mild winters and low rainfall, although it can snow in Athens.

Athens (pop. 4.5m) is the oldest city in Europe and the birthplace of western civilisation and democracy, with a history dating back some 7,000 years. Many cultures have passed through Athens (named after the Greek goddess Athena), which in 1834 (soon after the end of Ottoman rule) was declared the capital of Greece. It remained a relatively small city until 1923, when a huge influx of refugees from Turkey forced a rapid expansion of the city, which now covers some 450km² (174mi²). In the intervening years Athens has grown from a population of less than 500,000 to over 4 million, which has created considerable urban and environmental problems. The city is largely a vast sprawl of virtually identical six-storey, cement apartment blocks known as 'multiple dwellings', hurriedly constructed to house the influx of immigrants, and is home to over two-thirds of the country's cars which create endless traffic jams. Their fumes and the oppressive heat combine to envelop Athens in a thick, acrid smog (called *néfos*) for days at a time during summer, added to which is the congestion wrought by some 4 million tourists who visit the cradle of Greek civilisation annually.

However, despite the smog, congestion and endless traffic noise, Athens has the best medical and education facilities in the country. The standard of living is also higher than in the rest of Greece and job opportunities are plentiful, as over half of the country's industry is concentrated around the capital, which is the political, commercial and cultural centre of Greece. Athens is an interesting amalgamation of cultures where east meets west in a vibrant, exciting ambience, with traditional coffee-houses and donkey carts vying for space with modern office blocks, deluxe hotels and the ubiquitous motor vehicles. Despite its rapid expansion, Athens is really a string of small villages, its people are friendly and gregarious, and many suburbs are relatively calm and peaceful with beautiful restored 19th century mansions. When the hustle and bustle becomes too much, an escape to the tranquillity of the surrounding mountains and countryside is never far away, and, as a small compensation, you can marvel at the Acropolis, which dominates the skyline from practically every street corner.

Communications are good in Athens and the city has comprehensive bus and metro services, the latter undergoing a huge expansion programme, and a new and modern international airport opened at Spata in 2001. There are ambitious plans to transform Athens into a 'new' city in time for the 2004 Olympic Games with an improved road and public transportation system, more areas of greenery and a cleaner environment. Trains and buses leave the capital at regular intervals for the rest of the country and at Piraeus, Athens' port and one of the Mediterranean's busiest, ferries and hydrofoils service most of the islands. Athens is connected by road to western and northern Greece by the E75 motorway. In keeping with the high standard of living, house prices in Athens and the surrounding beach resorts are the highest in the country and are spiralling even higher in anticipation of the 2004 Olympic Games.

Central Greece

The land of the mythical centaur, central Greece is home to flourishing fruit orchards and dense oak and beech forests. The region is dotted with some of the prettiest villages in Greece, including Makrinítsa with its outstanding churches and monasteries. Local architecture is a unique blend of whitewashed, half-timbered houses, which are often decorated with intricate frescoes. The Aegean-facing east coast has some excellent beaches and popular resorts such as Platanías and Áfissos. The area is much cooler in summer than the rest of mainland Greece, which, when added to its natural charm, makes it extremely popular in summer and more expensive than many other areas.

Communications are quite good between the main towns, most of which are served by trains and buses and have reasonable roads. Outside the main areas, however, there are narrow mountain roads and infrequent bus services, particularly outside the summer season, when private transport is a must. Larissa has a domestic airport serving a limited number of routes.

Central Greece comprises two large regions: Stereá Ellhada and Thessaly, which offer some of the country's most varied scenery.

Stereá Ellhada, situated north-west of Athens, was the only independent Greek territory during the 19th century and encompasses a vast expanse of wild, mountainous countryside punctuated by small towns (the region was largely depopulated in the 20th century). Its most famous sights are at Delphi, Greece's most ancient oracle with its unique amphitheatre and Temple of Apollo, and Mount Parnassós, site of two ski resorts.

Thessaly lies to the north of Stereá Ellhada and consists of a vast, rich agricultural plain surrounded on three sides by mountain ranges, including Mount Olympus to the north. The region's main towns include Larissa, a busy market centre, Vólos, a rapidly expanding industrial area and busy port, and Kalambáka, a modern town and the base for visitors to the nearby spectacular Metéora rock monasteries. The earliest Orthodox religious communities made their homes on the black pinnacles of the naturally sculptured rock, which is one of the great sights on the Greek mainland. Vólos has excellent hydrofoil and ferry communications from the nearby Sporades and lies just west of the popular Mount Pílion peninsula.

In the north of Thessaly, near Larissa, is the Vale of Témbi, one of the country's most famous and popular beauty spots, which meanders 10km (6mi) through a spectacular mountain gorge carved by the River Pinio. The coastline beyond Témbi has been heavily developed and is popular with Greek tourists. North of Larissa is Mount Olympus National Park containing the country's highest peak, Mount Olympus (2,972m/9,751ft), legendary home of the gods. It's snow-capped for much of the year and offers spectacular hiking in a unique terrain carpeted with wild flowers.

Crete

Crete (pop. 500,000) is the largest Greek island (almost a country on its own) and the fifth-largest in the Mediterranean, and for many is the quintessential Greek island. It's noted for its mild winter climate, beautiful beaches, hospitable people, and as a botanical and ornithological paradise (it's a great place for walkers). These attractions have made Crete the destination of a quarter of all tourists visiting Greece and the most popular region for holiday homes, and consequently it has a large number of resident expatriates. It was home to Europe's first civilisation, the Minoans, and their ancient sites are scattered throughout the island. Crete has a flourishing agricultural economy and is one of the few places in Greece that could survive without the tourist trade, although much of the coast has been developed as resort areas.

Communications in the north of the island are excellent, with international airports at Heráklion and Chania (Haniá), and a small domestic airport at Sitia There are six ferry ports with frequent, fast services in summer and a reduced service during the winter months. A dual carriageway runs along the north coast linking the main cities and resorts and there's a good bus service, in contrast with the south, where there are few roads and infrequent buses (private transport is usually a must here).

Crete's climate is mild in winter with almost guaranteed sunshine, although there's often snow on the highest peaks. Summers are hot, with the highest temperatures in Greece (which is very hot!). In general, the island is more expensive than other parts of Greece and a two-bedroom apartment on the north coast costs around €90,000, although there's an abundance of cheaper, secluded rural properties on offer, many requiring complete restoration. The island is divided into four administrative prefectures: Chania, Heráklion, Lassithi and Rethimnon.

Heráklion, the capital, lies on the north coast of the island and is the fifth-largest city in Greece and home to nearly half of the island's population. It has the highest per capita income in the country, although its wealth isn't reflected in the infrastructure. The city has a glorious past, particularly during the Middle Ages, a splendour that's reflected in its Venetian architecture and city walls. Heráklion is a busy city with a vibrant night-life. Knossos, the main Minoan site and largest palace is situated close to the city.

To the east of the capital is the area known as the 'Cretan Riviera', packed with popular resorts such as Hersonissos, Malia and Stalidha, and bustling beaches. Aghios Nikolaos (known as 'Ag Nik') was once the 'St Tropez of Crete' and has the best and most expensive hotels on the island. Inland is the rich agricultural plain of Lasithi, famous for its windmills that are used for irrigation. On the east coast, Sitia has a busy port and is the site of a number of new residential developments, although this part of the island is relatively unspoilt. Europe's only palm tree forest is at Vái on the east coast. In the south, the numerous gorges and cliffs mean there are few towns, although Mátala has a well-known beach and Arvi's microclimate permits the cultivation of bananas and pineapples. Samariá Gorge in the White Mountains (Lefka Ori) is the longest ravine in Europe and one of Greece's most visited natural spots.

The west of the island is the least inhabited and although there are a number of resorts, they're less developed than those in the east. Rethimnon, a town of many contrasts, is the smallest of Crete's four major towns and the least visited. It has an attractive Venetian harbour surrounded by fish restaurants and a handsome old town with a wealth of Venetian buildings from the 13th to 17th centuries. Crete's second-largest city Chania, like Rethimnon a former Venetian town, was the island's capital until 1971. The old city around the Venetian harbour has retained its unique charm and is home to many expatriates.

The Cyclades Islands

The Cyclades (pop. 95,000), a group of 56 islands (of which 24 are inhabited), is one of the most popular locations for holiday homes in Greece. Their name derives from the circle they form around the island of Delos, the birthplace of Apollo and once the centre of religion and commerce in the central Mediterranean. The islands form a disparate group and are mostly different in character, yet small and close enough to allow easy 'island hopping'. They all share the characteristic Greek, whitewashed architecture, blue domed churches and the warm hospitality of the inhabitants.

The Cyclades enjoy mild winters, although they experience strong winds virtually all year round. The summer *meltémi* can sometimes disrupt ferry schedules, although it reduces the heat, and in winter strong north winds often make ferry travel impossible. Rainfall can be scarce and water shortages are commonplace.

Communications with mainland Greece and between the islands is mainly by ferry, where Paros is the main port of call for most inter-island services. During the summer there are frequent ferry services linking the islands, although services are severely curtailed in winter and can be suspended altogether when the weather is bad. Six of the islands have airports, although only two, Mykonos and Paros, cater for international flights. Bus services are provided on most islands, although the quality of buses and frequency of services varies greatly, and the inaccessibility of some areas means private transport is often essential.

The most visited islands are the following:

Ios (pop. 2,000) is especially popular with the younger generation.

Mykonos (pop. 6,000) receives around a million visitors a year, who come to enjoy a hedonistic lifestyle, and is the most expensive of all the Greek islands.

Naxos (pop. 15,000) is the largest and most fertile of the Cyclades and is largely self-sufficient. It's also the most scenic of the islands and has their highest mountain, Mount Zas.

Paros (pop. 9,500) is the third-largest of the Clyclades group with excellent beaches and a hectic nightlife. It's the hub of the ferry services linking the Cyclades and attracts thousands of foreign homebuyers, particularly the British.

Santorini (pop. 9,500), the most spectacular of all Greek islands, is a partly submerged volcanic crater thought to be the legendary city of Atlantis. It's an important port of call for cruise ships and is famous for its black-sand beaches.

Tinos (pop. 8,000), with its charming traditional villages and famous 'lacework' dovecotes, is the Greek Lourdes with its church of Panayia Evangelistria and miraculous icon attracting thousands of Greek Orthodox pilgrims each year.

Syros (pop. 20,000), the most populated of the Cyclades Islands, also contains its administrative centre, the attractive town of Ermoúpolis. Syros, **Andros**, **Kéa** and **Kythnos** are popular with Athenians for weekend breaks and summer holidays.

The islands of **Anafi**, **Folégandros**, **Milos** and **Sikinos** are barely populated and practically untouched by tourism (and thus are good places to experience the 'real' Greece).

The Dodecanese Islands

The Dodecanese (pop. 170,000) form an archipelago of 12 islands off the west coast of Turkey and are Greece's southernmost and most recent territorial acquisition. The islands' history and architecture reflect their previous occupants, although each island has a distinctive landscape. Many are popular with tourists, particularly Rhodes and Kos, while others are barely touched by modern life and many of the local women still wear traditional dress. The islands are a paradise for water-sport lovers and divers, although scuba diving is strictly controlled in some areas.

As with all Greek islands, communication is mainly by boat, and services are frequent in summer but few and far between in winter or cancelled altogether when the weather is bad. Rhodes is the hub of the inter-island ferries, which also serve the mainland. The islands have three international airports, on Rhodes, Karpathos and Kos, which also have domestic connections. The larger islands have good bus services, although these are limited on the smaller islands. Private transport can be useful, although some of the islands have poor to non-existent roads.

Rhodes (pop. 100,000) is an alluring mixture of sun, sea and beautiful landscapes and is the best known of the islands and the most popular with tourists and holiday homebuyers. It enjoys a unique climate with over 300 days of sunshine annually (it's the sunniest spot in Greece) and excellent beaches on the east coast. Most of the island has been heavily developed for the flourishing tourist trade, although Rhodes Town remains one of the architectural treasures of the Mediterranean with its medieval walls and monuments. (It also has an exciting nightlife.) The city of Lindos (with its stunning Acropolis) in the south-east is an attractive car-free resort.

Kos (pop. 26,500), birthplace of Hippocrates, the father of medicine, has the second-largest population of the group. It's one of Greece's most beautiful islands, essentially flat and fertile with some of the country's best beaches. It's popular with tourists and has many resorts, although it isn't as heavily developed as Rhodes. Property prices on Kos are higher than on the other Dodecanese islands.

Other islands of note in the group include **Karpathos** with its excellent beaches, **Kálymnos** (reached by boat from Kos), a centre of sponge fishing with its attractive port of Póthia, **Symi**, known as the 'jewel of the Dodecanese' on account of its well-preserved 19th century neo-classical architecture, **Tílos** with fine beaches and excellent hiking, and **Níssyros**, one of the most fertile islands thanks to its dormant volcano.

Epirus & The West

The regions of Epirus and Western Macedonia share their borders with Albania and the former Yugoslav Republic of Macedonia, and their scenery provides a stark contrast to 'tourist' Greece. This is a land of rocky peaks, deep river gorges (including Vikos Gorge, the world's deepest), lakes and forests, where poor communications mean that much of the area is barely inhabited. However, extensive government investment in recent years has improved communications and many villages and towns have been restored and offer quality tourism for hikers and nature lovers. There are several national parks in the area which have unique wildlife, including bears, wolves and lynx, and offer excellent hiking. Communications away from the coast remain limited and private transport is essential. The west is the rainiest region of the country and its winters are cold with heavy snowfalls. The coastal area in the north-west around Parga is heavily developed with many hotels and several villages are popular tourist and hiking centres. However, the region isn't popular with holiday homebuyers and unless you're looking for a remote rural dwelling to restore, it's of little interest.

Evia and The Sporades

The island of **Evia** (pop. 66,000), the second-largest in Greece after Crete, lies just off the coast of mainland Greece (to which it's joined by a suspension bridge), north of Athens. The main town, Halkída is a big industrial centre and port, and is of little interest to visitors. There are some beautiful villages in the centre and north of the island, including Stení, the starting point for the climb to the top of Mount Dirfys (1,743m/5,718ft), Evia's highest mountain. The southern part of the island has a number of resorts, although they're generally more popular with Greeks than foreigners. There are some good beaches to the north and east.

The **Sporades** (pop.15,000) lie to the north and east of Evia and are a collection of 11 islands, of which only four are inhabited: Alonnisos, Skiathos, Skopelos and Skyros. **Alonnisos** is a green island and the least developed of the four, with many natural harbours (no mooring fees). Its surrounding waters are a 'marine conservation park' and a paradise for divers. **Skiathos** is one of Greece's most attractive islands with an abundance of dense woods, rugged mountains, golden-sand beaches, azure seas and enchanting villages – many believe it's the most beautiful island in the Aegean. It's a popular tourist destination and home to a relatively large expatriate population, although it's also one of Greece's most expensive islands. **Skopelos** is extensively cultivated and less developed due to its pebbly beaches, although is popular with hikers. The capital, Skopelos town, is one of the prettiest towns in the Aegian and the island is more of a retreat than a resort. **Skyros** is different from the other Sporades and is more reminiscent of the Cyclades in its architecture, although it's just as developed.

Communications in the region vary considerably, although as would be expected, Evia is well served with connections to the mainland by road and train. Bus and ferry services are also good on the island. Skiathos and Skyros both have international airports, although flights are infrequent outside the summer tourist season. There's a regular ferry service between the islands and the mainland in summer, but this is much reduced in winter. Although there are bus services on the islands, private transport is often essential.

The property market on the Sporades varies considerably from island to island, and some, such as Skiathos, have few homes and little land for sale and prices are consequently relatively high. However, on Alonissos, for example, there's plenty of property for sale, with prices for plots starting at around €20,000 and two-bedroom properties from around €75,000.

The Ionian Islands

The Ionian Islands (pop. 200,000) consist of seven main islands (Corfu, Ithaki, Kefallonia, Kythira, Lefkas, Paxos, Zakynthos) off the west coast of mainland Greece, which, thanks to abundant rainfall, are the greenest and most verdant of all the Greek islands. The Ionian Islands are all beautiful and most have superb beaches. Their culture and cuisine are quite different from other parts of Greece and they've a distinct Venetian character.

The Ionian climate is the wettest in Greece, particularly Corfu, and outside the summer season the weather is often unsettled with heavy rains. The summers can be extremely hot, as unlike many other islands they don't benefit from cooling winds. However, in late spring and early autumn the weather is usually perfect.

Communications are generally excellent and Corfu, Kefallonia and Zakynthos all have international airports and good connections with Athens. In the summer there are frequent ferry services between the islands and the mainland, which although severely curtailed during winter, remain reasonable. Bus services on Corfu and Zakynthos are good, but poor on Kefallonia (although improving) and private transport is useful on all the islands.

Corfu (pop. 110,000) is the most popular of all the Greek islands and synonymous with package holidays; it's over-developed in parts, although due to its size it's easy to escape the tourist resorts. It's the greenest of the Greek islands (dubbed the 'emerald isle') thanks to its abundance of ancient olive groves and fir trees, with tiny fishing villages in sheltered coves on the east coast and sandy beaches on the west. The capital, Corfu Town, is one of the country's most charming and sophisticated island capitals, with an elegant blend of Venetian, French and Greek architecture. Paleokastrítsa on the west coast is a picturesque, unspoilt resort, while the main family resorts tend to be on the north side. Further to the east between Kassiopi and Barbati (the gem is San Stefano) are some favourite hideaways of the expatriate population, mainly British, where there's an abundance of villas. There are beautiful sandy beaches on the west coast and the Korísson Lagoon in the south is a large nature reserve and a paradise for ornithologists. Corfu also has several attractive satellite islands. It has been called 'the bridge connecting Greece with the rest of Europe' and is served by both international and domestic flights, plus ferries from Brindisi and Ancona (Italy), and Patra and Igoumenitsa on the mainland.

Ithaki (pop. 3,100) off the north-east of Kefallonia, was Odysseus' long lost home (ancient Ithaca) and is one of the least spoilt islands in Greece. Most boats dock at the main town of Vath″, situated at the end of a deeply set bay, which was badly damaged in a earthquake in 1953, but has since been rebuilt in the old style.

Kefallonia (pop. 32,500) is gradually developing as a tourist destination and is the largest and most mountainous of the group, where Mount Enos is the highest peak on the islands. Its capital, Argostóli, is a large thriving town and Sami is its main port. The north and west coasts have excellent sandy beaches and there are several expatriate developments, particularly around Argostóli.

Kythira (pop. 3,000), around 30km (19mi) long and 18km (11mi) wide, is an island of some 600 churches. It's essentially a bleak plateau crossed by well-watered ravines and forms part of a sunken land bridge between the Peloponnese and Crete. Geographically it's an extension of the Peloponnese, but historically it's part of the

Ionian archipelago. Kythira town is one of the best preserved capital towns of the Aegean, with fine medieval mansions and Venetian fortifications. Until recently Kythira was little visited by tourists and is consequently unspoiled, although it's becoming more popular.

Lefkas (pop. 21,000) is connected to the mainland by a long causeway through lagoons and hardly feels like an island at all. It's reached from mainland Greece via a floating drawbridge over a canal that was dug by the Corinthians in the seventh century (historically it has always been an important strategic site). It's a fertile island and the main industry is agriculture rather than tourism, although the resort of Vassilikí in the south is reputedly Europe's largest windsurfing centre and Nidrhí in the east has good beaches.

Paxos (pop. 2,000) is the smallest of the main Ionian islands and the least developed. It has no sandy beaches or historical sites, few hotels and a serious water shortage, despite which it's extremely popular in summer. Paxos is also a favourite stopping-off point for visiting yachts, which has helped make it one of the most expensive islands in the group.

Zakynthos (pop. 32,500), also called Zante, like Corfu, features heavily on the package tour circuit, although the island is less developed. It's exceptionally beautiful – the Venetians called it 'the flower of the East' – with some of the best beaches in Greece.

The North-eastern Aegean Islands

The north-eastern Aegean islands (pop. 175,000) are a collection of seven major islands that are grouped together for convenience rather than any administrative or historical reason. Nearly all the islands are closer to Turkey than Greece and are less visited than the Cyclades and Dodecanese islands. The scenery on the islands is mountainous and forested, and hiking is a popular pastime.

All the north-eastern Aegean islands except Samothraki have airports, with good domestic and international connections, although the latter are infrequent in winter. Samos is the ferry hub of the north-eastern Aegean, with good services during the summer. There are also boats to mainland Greece, and several islands have (relatively expensive) services with Turkey. Road transport varies considerably on the islands, and public transport is limited in the more remote parts.

Chios (pop. 30,000) is a relatively large island (reputedly the birthplace of Homer and Christopher Columbus) that has traditionally been the home of Greek ship-owners, and therefore less dependent on tourism. In the south is the Mastihohoria area, noted for its mastic gum production and characteristic architecture of white lime and black sand decoration, which is particularly vibrant at Pyrgi, one of the most extraordinary villages in Greece. Off the north-east coast lie nine tiny islets, the Inousses, home to many wealthy ship-owners who have built luxury villas there. Chios is more expensive than other islands in the group.

Ikaria (pop. 9,000) is a fertile, mainly agricultural island, famous for its spa resort, Therma, with its therapeutic radioactive springs. The island is little developed and has a low-key tourist industry.

Lesbos (pop. 90,000) is largely influenced by its proximity to Turkey and is known as the 'Garden of the Aegean' thanks to its fertile soil that produces the best olive oil in Greece (it also claims to make the finest *ouzo*). Trekking and bird-watching are popular activities on the island, which has one of only two fossilised forests in the world (on the west side). Lesbos is popular with Greek holidaymakers, particularly Molivos, a beautiful resort in the north of the island.

Limnos (pop. 10,000) is one of the Aegean's best kept secrets and is largely unspoilt with many fine beaches, despite having a large military air base. (Limnos is close to Turkey.) The capital, Myrina, is the main port, with an impressive Byzantine fortress.

Samos (pop. 32,000) is situated just 3km from the Turkish mainland and is the closest of all Greek islands to Turkey. It's the most visited island in the group and the east coast is particularly developed with many resorts. Its verdant landscape is famous for its vines and orchids, which give it an exotic flavour, and makes the island a popular destination for ramblers and hikers. Samos was devastated by a forest fire in July 2000, which destroyed a vast area of woodland.

Samothraki (pop. 3,000) is a small island but scenically one of the most dramatic, with dense forests dominated by Mount Fengari, the highest peak in the Aegean. The island is mainly agricultural and one of the most ecologically conscious in Greece.

Thassos (pop. 13,000), 175km (110mi) from Thessalonika, is a relatively unknown island outside Greece, although it has plenty to offer in terms of wild, wooded countryside and fine beaches. There are strict building regulations on the island and new properties must conform to traditional styles and proportions. A wide range of new and old property is available on the island and prices are generally low, e.g. from €90,000 for a new villa on a small plot.

Northern Greece

Northern Greece comprises two regions, Macedonia and Thrace, and is the least visited part of the country. The region's climate is quite different from the rest of Greece: the short summers are hot and humid, the winters very cold, and there's less rainfall than in most other areas. Communications between Macedonia and the rest of mainland Greece are excellent, with well maintained, fast roads and frequent bus and coach services linking the major towns. Thessalonika has an international airport and there are smaller airports at Kavala and Alexandroupolis with limited international services. There's also a regular train service between most towns, although journeys are slower than by bus. In the more remote areas, private transport is essential.

Macedonia is the largest prefecture in Greece and its capital is Thessalonika (pop. 750,000), a lively, sophisticated Byzantine city set on the edge of the Thermaic Gulf, whose port is the natural gateway to the Balkans. The area's three highlights are Pella, the birthplace of Alexander the Great, Vergina, site of the royal tombs of several Macedonian monarchs, and Dion, Macedonia's sacred city. In the north-west are the attractive Prespa lakes and in the south, Mount Olympus (see **Thessaly** above), surrounded by a large national park with excellent hiking.

To the south of Thessalonika and separated by two large lakes lies the region of Halkidiki, whose south coast consists of three peninsulas: Cassandra, Sithonia and Athos. The peninsulas have a coastline of over 500km (312mi) and superb sandy beaches, making them a popular resort area. Cassandra is the favourite among package tourists and includes Greece's largest resort, Sani Beach. Sithonia is greener and less developed, although it has an abundance of villas and its resorts of Neos Marmatas and Porto Karrás are two of Greece's largest holiday complexes. The third peninsula, Athos, is where the Virgin Mary is said to have landed and declared it her garden, and Mount Athos is the holiest of places for the Orthodox religion. Nowadays it's a semi-autonomous, 'theocratic republic' run by Orthodox monks, who live in some 20 monasteries with access strictly controlled and restricted to men.

Thrace is Greece's most recent acquisition (1923) and is something of a backwater, being tucked away in the north-east corner of the country. The architecture and culture of the region are largely Turkish. The area's main towns are Kavala, the principal port for northern Greece and one of the most attractive Greek cities, Komotini, where the population is half Greek and half Turkish, and Alexandroupolis, an important military garrison. The country's vast tobacco industry is centred in Thrace, where sunflower oil and cotton are also produced. Close to the border with Turkey, the Evros delta is one of Europe's most important wetlands, and Dhadhiá Forest is an important nature reserve.

The Peloponnese

The Peloponnese (pop. 375,000) peninsula is the southernmost part of the Greek mainland, lying south-east of Athens. The Peloponnese is practically an island, joined to the Greek mainland by the man-made Corinth canal crossing the narrow isthmus in the north-west. The peninsula takes its name from the legendary Greek hero, Pelops, and is reputed to have the best of everything Greek. It's an area of outstanding natural beauty with high, snow-covered mountains and some of the most famous archaeological sites in Greece, notably the ancient citadel of Mycenae, the sanctuary of Zeus at Olympia (where the first recorded games were held in 776BC), and the theatre at Epidaurus. Parts of the east and north coasts are fast developing into resort areas, although the peninsula as a whole remains more popular with Greeks than with foreigners. The beaches on the relatively undeveloped west coast are among the best in the country.

The climate in the Peloponnese varies considerably. The west has hot and dry summers, but rainfall is among the highest in the country and its winters are less severe than other parts of mainland Greece. The mountains in the central Peloponnese are snow-covered for much of the winter, and the nights can be cold even in summer. The east experiences very hot summers and is influenced by the strong north wind, the *meltemi.*

Communications in the northern Peloponnese are among the best in Greece, although there's no airport in the area. The north and west coasts as far as Olympia and south to the city of Tripoli (soon to be extended to Kalamata) are served by motorways and there are frequent bus and train services to most destinations in the north of the peninsula and to the rest of the mainland. Getting around in the southern part of the Peloponnese is more difficult, and private transport is essential if you wish to travel at a reasonable speed. Kalamata in the south-west has an international airport with limited connections.

There's plenty of property for sale in the Peloponnese and you can choose between rural dwellings requiring total restoration from around €30,000, modern apartments from around €100,000 and villas in resort areas starting from around €150,000.

The Peloponnese is divided into seven prefectures and there are several important cities in the region. **Corinth**, at the canal entrance to the Peloponnese, is a busy city famous world-wide for its currants. South of Corinth is the vast plain of **Argos**, where much of the Peloponnese's agricultural production of citrus, grapes and olives is concentrated. On the Argos coast are some of the most popular resorts on the peninsula, including **Killini** and **Porto Heli**, which have some of the most expensive property in Greece. Nearby are **Náfplio**, one of the most beautiful towns in the Peloponnese, **Epidauros** with its spectacular Greek theatre, and the ancient town of **Mycenae**. Further south is the prefecture of **Lakonia** with its dramatic, harsh landscape. The famous town of **Sparta** is also located here as well as the remote region of **Maní**, noted for its fierce opposition to both foreign and home rule. Off the southern tip of Lakonia is the island of **Kythira**, a relatively expensive island with excellent beaches and developing resorts.

In the south-west is **Messinia**, one of the least-known and least developed regions of Greece. Kalamata, the capital town of Messinia, is essentially a military town and has the Peloponnese's main airport. On the west coast are some of the best beaches in Greece, although their remoteness and the general lack of development in the area make them rather inaccessible. Inland at **Arcadia**, as the name suggests, is the best agricultural land in Greece, surrounded by mountains and medieval villages. In the north-west lies the city of **Patra** (pop. 150,000), Greece's third-largest city and a major port serving the western Mediterranean, particularly Italy.

The Saronic Gulf Islands

The Saronic Gulf Islands (pop. 45,000) form a rocky, volcanic chain, known as the 'Athenian Riviera', running south of the mainland and east of the Peloponnese peninsula. They're the closest islands to the capital and popular with wealthy Greeks, particularly Athenians, many of whom own second homes there. The Saronic Gulf Islands have good communications with the mainland and with each other through frequent ferry and hydrofoil services. The climate is temperate with hot summers and mild winters. There are five main islands in the group:

Salamis (pop. 23,000), birthplace of one of the great Greek playwrights, Euripedes, is barely 1km from Piraeus and consequently is almost an extension of Athens. As a result the island is heavily developed and industrialised.

Aegina (pop. 11,000) is the largest island in the Saronic Gulf group and lies close enough to the mainland to be a popular commuter base and to be packed with Athenians at weekends. Due to its ideal strategic position, the island has a glorious past and was briefly the capital of Greece – Aegina is the site of the Temple of Aphaia, one of the most complete ancient buildings in Greece. It's a verdant and beautiful island blessed with magnificent mountain scenery and many secluded rocky coves.

Hydra (pop. 3,000), a popular venue with artists and writers during the '60s, is a national monument and one of the most popular and expensive resorts in Greece. Hydra Town has an attractive waterfront and gracious stone mansions, a legacy of its wealthy shipbuilding past, and has a sizeable expatriate population. Motorised vehicles are banned on the island, where the only means of transport is the donkey.

Poros (pop. 4,000) is a forested island close to the Peloponnese peninsula, separated from the mainland at Galatas by a narrow channel of water. Most inhabitants live in Poros Town, the only settlement apart from the many tourist hotels around the island. It's a popular holiday destination, particularly with the British.

Spétses (pop. 3,750) is a pine covered island with small coves and the best beaches in the islands, and is popular with foreign holidaymakers and Athenians. It's less spoilt than its neighbours and only certain vehicles are allowed on the island, so there's little traffic. Spétses is one of the most expensive islands in Greece, with prices starting at around €150,000 for a three-bedroom property or around double those in Hydra.

Cyprus

Cyprus (pop. 750,000) is the most easterly of the Mediterranean islands and the third-largest after Sicily and Sardinia. It covers 9,251km² (3,572mi²) and stretching 240km (150mi) from west to east and 96km (60mi) from north to south. Cyprus has been home to Assyrians, Egyptians, Persians, Alexander the Great, Romans, Byzantines, Crusaders, Lusignans, Venetians and the British – it has been termed the meeting point of the continents of Europe, Asia and Africa – and has developed a unique character and traditions. It's also an island of great beauty with a wide variety of contrasting landscapes ranging from sandy beaches to unspoilt villages nestling in vine-clad foothills, from citrus and olive groves to pine and cedar forests. Its wealth of fascinating remains include Roman temples, Byzantine churches and medieval castles, which co-exist with cosmopolitan hotels, bustling shopping centres and modern housing developments. Water-sports, particularly snorkelling, are popular on the coast, while the central area is the island's market garden.

Communications in the Republic of Cyprus are generally good and there are two international airports at Larnaca and Paphos with frequent international connections. The roads connecting the main cities are good dual carriageways, although off the main routes 'roads' can be mere tracks and rather dangerous. There's a good bus service between the main cities and taxis are relatively cheap, although if you plan to buy a home inland or in the mountains, private transport is essential. The climate is mild, although the summers are very hot except in the Troodos Mountains, where temperatures are much lower than on the coast. The island has little rainfall, most of which is in the winter months. Paphos has the best climate on the island with short, mild winters and some 340 days of sunshine per year. House prices in the Republic vary from around CY£20,000 to 25,000 for an average-size inland plot; one-bedroom apartments start at around CY£40,000 and villas at around CY£100,000.

Since 1974 the island has been divided into two parts: the pariah 'state' of the Turkish Republic of Northern Cyprus (covering 37 per cent of the island), occupied and recognised only by Turkey, and the Republic of Cyprus in the south. This book deals exclusively with the Republic of Cyprus, which for convenience has been divided into five regions: Larnaca, Limassol, Paphos and the west, south Nicosia and its environs, and the Troodos Mountains, which are shown on the map in **Appendix D**.

Larnaca: Larnaca (pop. 65,000) is situated in the south-east of the island and is one of the oldest cities in the world, with numerous monuments that bear witness to its colourful history, including several Byzantine churches. Larnaca is also a modern tourist centre with good shopping and is a popular holiday destination, particularly during the summer. It's one of two major ports in the south of the island and also has a large yacht marina. Nearby is the Hala Sultan Tekke Mosque, a site of Muslim pilgrimage, and the Larnaca Salt Lake, an important migration spot for many birds, including flamingos. To the east of Larnaca is the resort of Agia Napa, a once quiet fishing village that's now a busy, sophisticated tourist centre, with many luxury hotels and an exciting nightlife. The beaches in this area are generally good, particularly Nissi Beach, which is reminiscent of the Caribbean and rated among the best in Cyprus. Nearby is the resort of Protaras, a relatively new and popular development.

Limassol: Cyprus' second-largest city (pop. 150,000), Limassol is and the main passenger ferry port on the island. Its ten miles of coastline are extensively developed and the area is popular with tourists year round, making it the busiest winter resort in Cyprus. There are extensive fruit (mainly citrus) plantations in the countryside around Limassol, which is also the centre of a thriving wine industry. The city has a large marina, and there are a number of golf courses nearby. To the west of Limassol on the Akrotiri peninsula is the Akrotiri Salt Lake, home to migrating colonies of flamingos in winter, and the impressive cliff-top ruins of Kourion, capital of the ancient Hellenic kingdom. To the west towards Paphos lies the popular resort of Pissouri, boasting excellent beaches. The main British military bases, known as Sovereign Base Areas (SBAs), are situated in this area and much of the land west of Limassol lies within their boundaries.

Paphos and the West: The south-west of Cyprus, the birthplace of Aphrodite, has always been the remotest and least developed part of the island. However, the expanding tourist industry has made its mark here in recent decades, particularly around Paphos, and it's now the most popular spot for foreign homebuyers, although it remains largely unspoilt and traditionally Cypriot. The town of Paphos (pop. 30,000) is the tourist capital of Cyprus. In fact it comprises two separate towns: Ktima, the old town on the hill; and Kato Paphos where the harbour, luxury hotels and nightlife are situated. The area around Paphos contains some of Cyprus' finest archaeological treasures, such as the Temple of Aphrodite and the Tomb of the Kings. The Paphos countryside is hilly, its river valleys dotted with small villages that are popular with holiday homebuyers.

To the north of the area are the villages of Kamares and Coral Bay, two popular new developments consisting mainly of apartments and villas, while the resort of Polis is cheaper than Paphos and has some good beaches. Paphos has the most expensive property in Cyprus but is one of the most unspoilt locations, as it was among the last to be developed and has strict planning regulations. The Akamas Peninsula is home to the recently established Akamas National Park, noted for its magnificent jagged coastline, pine forests and a host of unique flora and fauna. The beaches here are among the best on the island.

South Nicosia and its Environs: Nicosia (pop. 200,000) is the capital and largest city in the Republic of Cyprus. It's divided in half by two walls: the 16th century Venetian walls separating the new city from the old, and the 'green line' that divides Northern Cyprus from the south after the Turkish invasion of 1974. The city has a strong business tradition and remains the commercial heart of the island, its narrow, pedestrianised streets lined with craftsmen. Although the city receives many day-trippers, it isn't a popular tourist destination and outside the summer season facilities are limited.

The Troodos Mountains: Mount Olympus (1,951m/6,400ft), the highest mountain in Cyprus and not to be confused with the mountain of the same name in Greece, is part of the Troodos range, which stretches almost the length of southern Cyprus. Some of the most spectacular scenery in Cyprus is to be found here, with carefully preserved pine forests and a wealth of Byzantine monasteries and churches in the villages. Platres on the southern slopes is the most popular of the hill resorts and has many hotels, although outside the summer season it's relatively quiet. Fikardhou and Lazania are officially 'preserved' villages containing houses from the Ottoman period. Around Platres there are many forest hiking trails and there's a winter ski resort at Mount Olympus.

RESEARCH

As when buying property anywhere, it isn't wise to be in too much of a hurry when looking for a home in Greece or Cyprus. It's a wise or lucky person who gets his choice absolutely right first time, which is why most experts recommend that you rent before buying unless you're absolutely sure of what you want, how much you wish to pay and where you want to live. Have a good look around in your chosen region(s) and obtain an accurate picture of the types of property available, their relative prices and what you can expect to get for your money.

However, before doing this, you should make a comprehensive list of what you want and don't want from a home, so that you can narrow the field and save time on wild goose chases. In most areas, properties for sale include derelict, unmodernised and modernised farmhouses and village homes, modern townhouses and apartments with all mod cons, and a wide choice of detached villas. You can also buy a plot of land and have an individual, architect-designed house built to your own specifications.

To reduce the chances of making an expensive error when buying in an unfamiliar region, it's often prudent to rent a house for a period (see **Renting** on page 127), taking in the worst part of the year (weather-wise). This allows you to become familiar with the region and the climate, and gives you plenty of time to look around for a home at your leisure. There's no shortage of properties for sale in Greece or Cyprus (indeed, in many areas there's a glut) and whatever kind of property you're looking for, you'll have an abundance from which to choose. Wait until you find something you fall head over heels in love with and then think about it for another week or two before rushing headlong to the altar! One of the advantages of buying property in Greece or Cyprus is that there's often another 'dream' home around the next corner – and the second or third dream home is often even better than the first. **However, don't delay too much, as good properties at the right price don't remain on the market for long.**

If you're looking for a holiday home, you may wish to investigate mobile homes or a scheme that restricts your occupancy of a property to a number of weeks each year. These include shared ownership, leaseback, time-sharing and a holiday property bond (see page 143). Don't rush into any of these schemes without fully researching the market and before you're absolutely clear about what you want and what you can realistically expect to get for your money. The more research you do before buying a property abroad the better, which should (if possible) include advice from those who already own a home there, from whom you can usually obtain invaluable information (often based on their own mistakes). Many people set themselves impossible deadlines in which to buy a property or business, e.g. a few days or a week, and often end up bitterly regretting their rash decision. Although mixing a holiday with a property purchase is common practice, it isn't advisable as most people are inclined to make poor decisions when their mind is fixed on play, rather than business.

Publications & Exhibitions: Outbound Publishing (1 Commercial Road, Eastbourne, East Sussex BN21 3XQ, UK, ☎ 01323-726040, ✉ outbounduk@aol. com) publish *World of Property*, a quarterly magazine containing many properties for sale in Greece and Cyprus (and other countries) and organise property exhibitions in the south and north of England. Other international property exhibitions that include homes in Greece and Cyprus are organised by Homebuyer Events, Mantle House, Broomhill Road, London SW18 4JQ, UK (☎ 020-8877 3636, 🖥 www.homebuyer. co.uk) and Homes Overseas Magazine, Blendon Communications, 46 Oxford Street, London W1N 9FJ, UK (☎ 020-7636 6050, 🖥 www.homes overseas.co.uk). Property is also advertised for sale in many English-language newspapers and magazines in Greece, Cyprus and abroad (see **Appendix A**) and on the Internet.

AVOIDING PROBLEMS

The problems associated with buying property abroad have been accentuated in the last decade or so, during which the property market in many countries has gone from boom to bust and back again. From a legal viewpoint, both Greece and Cyprus are relatively safe places in which to buy a home, with buyers having a high degree of protection under local law. However, the pitfalls must never be ignored! The possible dangers haven't been highlighted in order to discourage you, but simply to ensure that you go into a purchase with your eyes open and to help you avoid problems (forewarned is forearmed!).

Legal Advice: It cannot be emphasised too strongly that anyone planning to buy property abroad *must* take expert, independent legal advice. *Never* sign anything, or pay any money, until you've sought legal advice in a language in which you're fluent, from a lawyer who's experienced in local property law. If you aren't prepared to do this, you shouldn't even think about buying property abroad! It has been estimated that most property buyers abroad don't take independent legal advice and most people who experience problems take no precautions whatsoever. Of those who take legal advice, many do so only after having already paid a deposit and signed a contract or when they hit problems. (It's said that there are two types of property buyers: those with a lawyer and those who wish they had one!) You will find that the relatively small price – in comparison with the cost of a home – of obtaining legal advice to be excellent value for money, if only for the peace of mind it affords. Trying to cut corners to save on legal costs is foolhardy in the extreme when tens of millions of drachmas or tens of thousands of Cyprus pounds are at stake. **However, be careful whom you engage, as some lawyers are sometimes part of the problem rather than the solution!** Don't pick a lawyer at random, but hire one who has been highly recommended by someone you can trust.

Employing Professionals: There are professionals speaking English and other languages in some areas of Greece and throughout Cyprus, and expatriate estate agents, architects, builders and surveyors also practise in these countries. However, don't assume that because you're dealing with a fellow countryman that he'll offer you a better deal or do a better job than a local person, as the opposite may be the case. It's wise to check the credentials of professionals you employ, whatever their nationality. Note that it's *never* advisable to rely solely on advice proffered by those with a financial interest in selling you a property, such as a builder, developer or estate agent, although their advice may be excellent and totally unbiased. **You should also avoid 'cowboy' agents and anyone who does property deals on the side (such as someone you meet in a bar), as dealing with them often leads to heartache.**

Problems: Among the possible problems associated with buying property abroad are: properties bought without a legal title; properties built illegally without planning permission; properties sold that are subject to embargoes; properties sold with forged deeds; properties with missing infrastructure; builders or developers going bust; developer's loans being undischarged after completion and undischarged mortgages from the previous owner; intermediaries disappearing with the seller's proceeds; overcharging by vendors (particularly when selling to foreigners); property being difficult to sell in some areas, particularly if there are problems with a development; properties sold to more than one buyer; and even properties sold that don't exist!

Note that old properties often have a number of owners, all of whom must agree to sell, and that trees, e.g. carob, citrus and olive, can be owned by a number of people who don't own the land! Properties my not have been legally inherited by the heirs and there have been cases where the buyers have had to pay the inheritance taxes. Title deeds have been a big problem in the past, although this is rarer nowadays. Buyers must also accept their share of the blame. It's a common adage that many buyers 'leave their brains behind at the airport' when buying property abroad and it's certainly true that some people do incredibly irresponsible things, such as (on occasion) literally handing over bags full of cash to agents or owners without any security. **It's hardly surprising that people are occasionally defrauded!**

Mistakes: Common mistakes made by buyers in Greece and Cyprus include: not using the services of a good lawyer; buying in the wrong area (**rent first!**); buying a home that's unsaleable; buying a property for renovation and grossly underestimating the restoration costs; not having a survey done on an old property; not taking legal advice; not including the necessary conditional clauses in the contract; buying a property for business, e.g. to convert to self-catering accommodation, and being too optimistic about the income; and taking on too large a mortgage. It's normal practice abroad to declare a lower price in the title deed than actually paid, although you must take care that you don't declare too low a price. Checks must be carried out both before signing a contract *and* before signing the deed of sale. Note that if you get into a dispute over a property deal it can take years to get it resolved in the courts, and even then there's no guarantee that you will receive a satisfactory outcome.

Buying Off Plan: Many problems can arise when buying off plan, i.e. unbuilt properties, or a property on an unfinished development. Because of the problems associated with buying off plan, such as the difficulty in ensuring that you actually get what's stated in the contract and that the developer doesn't go bust, some experts have even advised buyers against buying an unfinished property. However, this isn't practical, because in a seller's market it's essential to buy off plan if you wish to buy a home in a popular development. A 'finished' property is a property where the building is complete in every detail (as confirmed by your own lawyer or architect), communal services have been completed, and *all* the infrastructure is in place such as roads, parking areas, external lighting, landscaping, water, sewerage, electricity and telephone services. A builder or developer is supposed to provide buyers who purchase off-plan through stage payments with an insurance policy that protects them against the builder going bust before construction is completed.

Take Your Time: Many people have had their fingers burnt by rushing into property deals without proper care and consideration. It's all too easy to fall in love with the attractions of a home in the sun and to sign a contract without giving it sufficient thought. If you aren't absolutely certain, don't allow yourself to be rushed into making a hasty decision, e.g. by fears of an imminent price rise or of losing the property to another buyer who has 'made an offer'. Although many people dream of buying a holiday or retirement home in Greece or Cyprus, it's vital to do your homework thoroughly and avoid the 'dream sellers' (often fellow countrymen), who will happily prey on your ignorance and tell you anything in order to sell you a home.

CHOOSING THE LOCATION

The most important consideration when buying a home in Greece or Cyprus is usually its location – or, as the old adage goes, the *three* most important points are location, location and location! A property in a reasonable condition in a popular area is likely to be a better investment than an exceptional property in a less attractive location. There's usually no point in buying a dream property in a terrible location. Greece and Cyprus offer a wide choice of homes to suit practically everybody, but you must choose the right property in the right spot *to suit you*. **The wrong decision regarding location is one of the main causes of disenchantment among foreigners who have purchased property abroad.**

Where you buy a property in Greece or Cyprus will depend on a range of factors, including your personal preferences, your financial resources and, not least, whether you plan to work or not. If you've got a job abroad, the location of your home will probably be determined by the proximity to your place of employment. However, if you intend to look for employment or start a business, you must live in an area that allows you the maximum scope. Unless you've good reason to believe otherwise, it would be foolish to rely on finding employment in a particular area. If, on the other hand, you're looking for a holiday or retirement home, the whole of Greece or Cyprus is your oyster.

A large number of regions and islands attract foreign property buyers in Greece. The most popular islands include Crete, the Cyclades, e.g. Ios, Mykonos, Naxos, Paros, the Dodecanese, e.g. Rhodes, Kos, Kalymnos, the Ionian Islands, e.g. Corfu, Paxos, Zakynthos, the Sporades, e.g. Skiathos, Skopelos, Alonissos and Skyros, and the Saronic Gulf Islands. Crete is the most favourable location if you're seeking winter sunshine, while the most popular mainland area among foreigners is the Peloponnese. The most popular areas for foreign buyers in Cyprus are in and around the coastal towns of Ayia Napa, Limassol, Larnaca and Paphos, while the Troodos mountains are also popular. When seeking a permanent home, don't be too influenced by where you've spent an enjoyable holiday or two. A town or area that was adequate for a few weeks' holiday may be totally unsuitable for a permanent home, particularly regarding the proximity to shops, medical services, and sports and leisure facilities.

If you've little idea about where you wish to live, read as much as you can about the different regions (see **Regions** on page 105) and spend some time looking around your areas of interest. Note that the climate, lifestyle and cost of living can vary considerably from region to region (and even within a particular region). Before looking at properties, it's important to have a good idea of the type of property you want and the price you wish to pay, and to draw up a shortlist of the areas and towns of interest. Most importantly make a list of what you want and don't want in a property – if you don't do this you're likely to be overwhelmed by the number of properties to be viewed.

The 'best' area in which to live depends on a range of considerations, including proximity to your place of work, schools, coast or town, shops, public transport, entertainment and sports facilities, swimming pool, restaurants, bars, etc. There are beautiful areas to choose from throughout Greece and Cyprus, most within easy travelling distance of a town or city. Don't, however, accept at face value the travelling times and distances stated in adverts and quoted by estate agents. According to many developers and agents, everywhere in the Greek islands is close to an international airport (this is generally true in Cyprus due to the relatively small size of the island). When looking for a home, bear in mind travelling times and costs to your place of work, shops and schools (and the local bar/restaurant). If you buy a remote country property, the distance to local amenities and services could become a problem, particularly if you plan to retire abroad. If you live in a remote rural area you will need to be much more self-sufficient than if you live in a town and you will also need to use the car for everything, which will increase your cost of living.

If possible, you should visit an area a number of times over a period of a few weeks, both on weekdays and at weekends, in order to get a feel for the neighbourhood (it's better to walk rather than drive around). A property seen on a balmy summer's day after a delicious lunch and a few glasses of wine may not be nearly so attractive on a subsequent visit without sunshine and the warm inner glow. If possible, you should also visit an area at different times of the year, e.g. in both summer and winter, as somewhere that's wonderful in summer can be forbidding and inhospitable in winter (or vice versa if you don't like extreme heat). In any case, you should view a property a number of times before deciding to buy it. If you're unfamiliar with an area, most experts recommend that you rent for a period before deciding to buy (see **Renting** on page 127). This is particularly important if you're planning to buy a permanent or retirement home in an unfamiliar area. Many people change their minds after a period and it isn't unusual for buyers to move once or twice before settling down permanently.

If you will be working abroad, obtain a map of the area where you will be based and decide the maximum distance that you'll consider travelling to work, e.g. by drawing a circle with your work place in the middle. Obtain a large-scale map of the area and mark the places that you've seen, at the same time making a list of the plus and minus points of each property. If you use an estate agent, he will usually drive you around and you can then return later to the properties that you like best at your leisure – provided that you've marked them on your map! (The best maps of Greece are produced by Road Editions.) Note, however, that agents may be reluctant to give you the keys to visit a property on your own.

There are many points to consider regarding the location of a home, which can roughly be divided into the local vicinity, i.e. the immediate surroundings and neighbourhood, and the general area or region. Take into account the present and future needs of all members of your family, including the following:

Climate: Do you want or need winter *and* summer sunshine? If you want a relatively warm winter climate, then the best choice is Crete or Cyprus. Note, however, that although the days are mild and pleasant in winter with daytime maximum temperatures in the southernmost Greek islands and Cyprus around 15 to 20°C (60 to 68°F), this will seem quite cool if you're accustomed to the blazing heat of high summer (when air-conditioning is a blessed relief). In winter, it's too cold for sea bathing anywhere in Greece or Cyprus. Bear in mind both the winter and summer climate, position of the sun, average daily sunshine, plus the rainfall and wind conditions (see **Climate** on page 42). The orientation or aspect of a building is vital and if you want morning or afternoon sun (or both) you must ensure that balconies, terraces and gardens are facing the right direction (some people take a compass when house hunting).

Natural Disasters: Check whether an area is liable to natural disasters such as earthquakes, floods, forest fires or severe storms. If a property is located near a waterway, it may be expensive to insure against floods (or flash floods) which are a threat in some areas. Note that in areas with little rainfall there may be frequent droughts, severe water restrictions and high water bills.

Noise: Noise can be a problem in some areas, particularly in summer. Although you cannot choose your neighbours, you can at least ensure that a property isn't located next to a busy road, industrial plant, commercial area, building site, discotheque, night club, bar or restaurant (where revelries may continue into the early hours). Look out for objectionable neighbouring properties that may be too close to the one you're considering and check whether nearby vacant land has been zoned for commercial activities. In community developments, e.g. apartment blocks, many properties are second homes and are let short-term, which means you may have to tolerate boisterous holiday-makers as neighbours throughout the year (or at least during the summer months). In towns, traffic noise, particularly from motorcycles, can continue all night! **Outside the summer season, Greek islands are blissfully quiet and a haven of tranquillity.**

Tourists: Bear in mind that if you live in a popular tourist area, i.e. almost anywhere on the coast or the islands, you will be inundated with tourists in the summer. They won't only jam the roads and pack the beaches and shops, but will also occupy your favourite table at your local bar or restaurant (heaven forbid!). Bear in mind that while a 'front-line' property on a beach sounds attractive and may be ideal for short holidays, it isn't always the best solution for permanent residents. Many beaches are hopelessly crowded in the peak season, streets may be smelly from restaurants and fast food joints, parking may be impossible, services stretched to breaking point and the incessant noise may drive you crazy. You may also have to tolerate water shortages, power cuts and sewage problems. Some people prefer to move inland or to higher ground, where it's less humid, you're isolated from the noise and can also enjoy excellent views. Note, however, that getting to and from hillside properties is often precarious and the often poorly-maintained roads (usually narrow and unguarded) are for sober, confident drivers only.

Community: Do you wish to live in an area with many other expatriates from your home country or as far away from them as possible? If you wish to integrate with the local community you should avoid the foreign 'ghettos' and choose a village, area or development with mainly local inhabitants. However, unless you speak good Greek or intend to learn it, you should think twice before buying a property in a Greek village, although residents in rural areas who take the time and trouble to integrate into the local community are invariably warmly welcomed. Most Greek Cypriots speak English, as do many Greeks in resort areas.

Neighbours: If you're buying a permanent home, it's important to check your prospective neighbours, particularly when buying an apartment. For example, are they noisy, sociable or absent for long periods? Do you think you will get on with them? **Good neighbours are invaluable, particularly when buying a second home in a village.**

On the other hand, if you wish to mix only with your compatriots and don't plan to learn Greek, then living in a predominantly foreign community may be ideal. Note that some developments and areas are inhabited largely by second homeowners and are like ghost towns for much of the year. In these areas many facilities, businesses and shops are closed outside the main tourist season, when even local services such as public transport may be severely curtailed.

Environment: Do you wish to be in a town or do you prefer the country? Inland or by the sea? How about living on an island? Live on a Greek island is more restricted and remote, e.g. you cannot jump into your car and drive to Athens or another large town or 'pop' over the border into a neighbouring country. You should also bear in mind that many Greek islands have only a restricted ferry service in winter and are often cut off for days at a time due to rough seas. If you buy a property in the country you will have to tolerate poor public transport, long travelling distances to a town of any size, solitude and remoteness, and the high cost and amount of work involved in the upkeep of a country house and garden. You won't be able to nip to the local shop for fresh bread, drop into the local taverna for a glass of your favourite tipple with the locals, or have a choice of restaurants on your doorstep. In a town or large village, the weekly market will be just around the corner, the doctor and pharmacy close at hand, and if you need help or run into any problems, your neighbours will be near by.

On the other hand, in the country you will be closer to nature, will have more freedom, e.g. to make as much noise as you wish, and possibly complete privacy, e.g. to sunbathe or swim *au naturel*. Living in a remote area in the country will suit those looking for peace and quiet who don't want to involve themselves in the 'hustle and bustle' of town life (not that there's a lot of this in Greek or Cypriot rural towns). If you're after peace and quiet, make sure that there isn't a busy road or railway line nearby or a local church within 'donging' distance. Note, however, that many people who buy a remote country home find that the peace of the countryside palls after a time and they yearn for the more exciting city or coastal night-life. If you've never lived in the country, it's advisable to rent before buying. Note also that while it's cheaper to buy in a remote or unpopular location, it's usually much more difficult to find a buyer when you want to sell.

Garden: If you're planning to buy a country property with a large garden or plot of land, bear in mind the high cost and amount of work involved in its upkeep. If it's to be a second home, who will look after the house and garden when you're away? Do you want to spend your holidays gardening and cutting back the undergrowth? Do you want a home with a lot of outbuildings? What are you going to do with them? Can you afford to convert them into extra rooms or guest accommodation?

Employment: How secure is your job or business and are you likely to move to another area in the near future? Can you find other work in the same area, if necessary? If there's a possibility that you may need to move in a few years' time, you should rent or at least buy a property that will be relatively easy to sell and recoup the cost. Consider also your partner's job and children's job prospects.

Schools: What about your children's present and future schooling? What is the quality of local schools? Note that even if your family has no need or plans to use local schools, the value of a home may be influenced by the quality and location of schools.

Health Services: What local health and social services are provided? How far is the nearest hospital with an emergency department? Are there English-speaking doctors and dentists, and private clinics or hospitals in the area?

Shopping: What shopping facilities are provided in the neighbourhood? How far is it to the nearest sizeable town with good shopping facilities, e.g. a supermarket or hypermarket? How would you get there if your car was out of order? Note that many rural villages are dying and have few shops or facilities, so they aren't usually a good choice for a retirement home.

Sport & Entertainment: What is the range and quality of local leisure, sports, community and cultural facilities? What is the proximity to sports facilities such as beaches, golf courses, ski resorts or waterways? Bear in mind that properties in or close to coastal resorts are generally more expensive, although they also have the best letting potential.

Public Transport: Is the proximity to public transport, e.g. an international airport, port or railway station, or access to a motorway important? Don't believe all you're told about the distance or travelling times to the nearest airport, port, railway station, motorway junction, beach or town, but check for yourself.

Parking: If you're planning to buy in a town or city, is there adequate private or free on-street parking for your family and visitors? Is it safe to park in the street? Note that in cities it's important to have secure off-street parking if you value your car. Parking is a problem in cities and most large towns, where private garages or parking spaces are unobtainable or expensive. Traffic congestion is also a problem in many towns and tourist resorts, particularly during the high season. Bear in mind that an apartment or townhouse in a town or community development may be some distance from the nearest road or car park. How do you feel about carrying heavy shopping hundreds of metres to your home and possibly up several flights of stairs? If you're planning to buy an apartment above the ground floor, you may wish to ensure that the building has a lift.

Crime: What is the local crime rate? In many resort areas the incidence of housebreaking and burglary is high, which also results in more expensive home insurance. Check the crime rate in the local area, e.g. burglaries, housebreaking, stolen cars and crimes of violence. Is crime increasing or decreasing? Note that crooks love isolated houses, particularly those full of expensive furniture and other belongings that they can strip bare at their leisure. You're much less likely to be the victim of thieves if you live in a village, where crime is virtually unknown – strangers stand out like sore thumbs in villages, where their every move is monitored by the local populace.

Municipality: Is the local council well run? What are the views of other residents? If the municipality is efficiently run you can usually rely on good local services and amenities.

RENTING

If you're uncertain about exactly what sort of home you want and where you wish to live, you should rent for a period in order to reduce the chances of making a costly error. **Renting long-term before buying is particularly prudent for anyone planning to live abroad permanently!** If possible, you should rent a similar property to that which you're planning to buy, during the time of year when you plan to occupy it. Renting allows you to become familiar with the weather, the amenities and the local people; to meet other foreigners who have made their homes abroad and share their experiences; and, not least, to discover the cost of living at first hand. Provided that you still find Greece or Cyprus alluring, renting 'buys' you time to find your dream home at your leisure. You may even wish to consider renting a home long term (or even 'permanently') as an alternative to buying, as it saves tying up your capital and can be surprisingly inexpensive in many regions. Some people let their family home and rent one abroad – and often make a substantial profit!

If you're looking for a rental property for a few months, e.g. three to six months, it's best not to rent unseen, but to rent a holiday apartment for a week or two to allow yourself time to look around for a longer-term rental. Properties for rent are advertised in local newspapers and magazines, particularly expatriate publications, and can also be found through property publications in many countries (see **Appendix A** for a list). Many estate agents offer both short and long-term rentals and developers may also rent properties to potential buyers. Holiday companies also rent properties, although only short-term. A rental contract is necessary when renting property abroad, whether long or short-term.

Long-term Rentals: Greece and Cyprus don't have flourishing long-term (i.e. one year or longer) rental markets in resort areas, where it's more common for people to buy, and it can be difficult to find good long-term rentals for a reasonable rent. Most rental properties in resort areas, whether long or short-term, are let furnished and long-term unfurnished properties are difficult to find. However, in major cities the opposite is the case, with long-term rental properties usually let unfurnished and furnished properties in short supply. Rental costs vary considerably depending on the size (number of bedrooms) and quality of a property, its age and the facilities provided. However, the most significant factor affecting rents is the region, the town and the particular neighbourhood. A small, one or two-bedroom, unfurnished apartment, e.g. 50 to 75m^2, which rents for between €450 to 750 per month in an average Athens suburb or CY£300 to 500 in Nicosia, costs around 50 per cent less in most rural and resort areas outside the main tourist season. You should be able to strike a good bargain when renting out of the main season, when there's a glut of properties for rent.

Short-term Rentals: Short-term rentals are always furnished and are usually for holiday lets or periods of up to a year. A short-term or temporary contract is necessary, which provides tenants with fewer rights than a long-term contract. There's an abundance of self-catering properties for rent in Greece and Cyprus, including apartments, cottages, farmhouses, townhouses and villas. Rents for short-term rentals are usually higher than for long lets, particularly in popular holiday areas, where many properties are let as self-catering holiday accommodation. However, many agents let self-catering properties in resort areas at a considerable reduction during the 'low season', e.g. October to March. The rent for an average one or two-bedroom furnished apartment or townhouse during the low season is usually between €300 to 600 per month or CY£200 to 400 in Cyprus, for a minimum one or two-month let. Rent is usually paid one month in advance with one month's rent as a deposit. In Cyprus if you rent by the month you will be billed separately for electricity. Lets of less than a month are more expensive, e.g. €300 or CY£200 per week for a two-bedroom apartment in the low season, which is some 50 per cent (or less) of the rental charged in the high season. Many hotels and hostels also offer special low rates for long stays during the low season (see below). Note, however, that when the rental period includes the peak letting months of July and August, the rent can be prohibitively high.

Standards vary considerably, from dilapidated, ill-equipped apartments to luxury villas with every modern convenience. Always check whether a property is fully equipped (which should mean whatever you want it to mean) and whether it has central heating if you're planning to rent in winter. Rentals can be found by contacting owners advertising in the publications listed in **Appendix A** and through estate agents in most areas, many of whom also handle rentals. The Cyprus Tourist Office publishes an accommodation handbook with short-term rental listings.

Hotels & Motels: Hotel rates in Greece and Cyprus vary depending on the time of year, the exact location and the individual establishment, although you may be able to haggle over rates outside the high season and for long stays, for which many hotels offer special rates. Hotels located in large towns, cities and coastal resorts are the most expensive, and rates in cities such as Athens and Nicosia (while lower than in other European capitals) can be very high. However, inexpensive hotels can be found in most towns, where a single room can usually be found for €15 to 30 or CY£10 to 20 and a double for €20 to 35 or CY£15 to 30, although usually without a private bath or shower.

Minimum and maximum rates are set according to the facilities and the season, although there's no season in the major cities. Rates are considerably higher in tourist areas during the high season of July and August, when rooms at any price are hard to find. On the other hand, outside the main season, particularly in winter, many hotels offer low half or full board rates (even better rates are offered for stays of a week or longer). Hotels aren't a cost-effective, long-term solution for home hunters, although there's usually little choice if you need accommodation for a short period only. Bed and breakfast accommodation is also available in Greece and Cyprus, although it isn't usually budget accommodation, in which case you need to choose a hostel.

Home Exchange: An alternative to renting is to exchange your home abroad with one in Greece or Cyprus for a period. This way you can experience home living abroad for a relatively small cost and may save yourself the expense of a long-term rental (if you decide you don't want to buy a home there). Although there's an element of risk involved in exchanging your home with another family – depending on whether your swap is made in heaven or hell! – most agencies thoroughly vet clients and have a track record of successful swaps. There are home exchange agencies in most countries, many of which are members of the International Home Exchange Association (IHEA).

The best place to find or contact home exchange organisations is via the Internet. The following is a selection of sites you may find useful:

- ▣ www.digsville.com (American-oriented with a retro-hippy feel);
- ▣ www.echangedemaison.com (mostly French properties);
- ▣ www.gti-home-exchange.com (Green Theme International – mostly European);
- ▣ www.homebase-hols.com;
- ▣ www.homexchange.com (boasts 250,000 requests per month from over 70 countries, although most properties are in North America);
- ▣ www.homelink.org.uk (over 12,000 members – one of the largest and best known companies);
- ▣ www.home-swap.com (many Australian properties);
- ▣ www.intervac.com (long-established, large membership);
- ▣ www.landfair.com (offers a custom matching service for US$250);
- ▣ www.webhomeexchange.com (American oriented);
- ▣ www.worldxchange.net (a free service).

There are also many specialist agencies for particular groups such as teachers (▣ www.teacherstravelweb.com), Christians (▣ www.christianhomeexchange. com) and gays (▣ www.well.com/user/homeswap).

COST

Property prices in Greece and Cyprus have risen considerably in the last decade, although not by as much as in some other countries. Property in Cyprus is around a third cheaper than in other popular Mediterranean countries such as Greece, Portugal and Spain. The biggest rises have been seen on some popular Greek islands, where prices have risen at a much faster rate since the country joined the European Union and restrictions on foreign ownership was largely abolished for EU citizens. Note that there's sometimes a tendency to over-charge foreigners in some areas of Greece, therefore it's important to compare local prices (i.e. what the locals are paying!) or find a good agent. In contrast to the wild fluctuations seen in some countries, property prices generally rise slowly and steadily in Greece and Cyprus, and are usually fairly stable, particularly in rural areas where there's little local demand and few non-resident owners.

Apart from obvious factors such as size, quality and land area, the most important consideration influencing the price of a house is its location. Property is cheapest in rural areas (on the mainland in Greece), where a farmhouse or village house may cost the same as a studio apartment on a popular island or in a fashionable resort. The quality of properties varies considerably in respect to materials, fixtures and fittings, and workmanship. Value for money also varies enormously and you should compare at least five to ten properties to get a good idea of their relative values. Most property is sold freehold.

When property is advertised, the total living area in square metres (written as m^2) and the number of bedrooms are usually stated. When comparing prices, compare the cost per square metre of the habitable or built area, excluding patios, terraces and balconies, which should be compared separately. If you're in any doubt about the size of rooms you should measure them yourself, rather than rely on the measurements provided by the vendor or agent. Note that a garage is rarely provided with apartments or townhouses, although there may be a private parking space or a communal off-road parking area. Some apartment blocks have underground garages, and lock-up garages may be sold separately for apartments and townhouses. Villas usually have their own car port or garage. Note that without a garage, parking can be a nightmare, particularly in cities or busy resort towns and developments in summer.

Greece: Costs vary considerably depending on the location and whether you buy a new or an old property. Athens is expensive – not that many foreigners would choose to live here unless they work in the capital. New apartments on the islands cost from around €60,000 for one bedroom, €80,000 for two bedrooms and €105,000 for three bedrooms, although they can be much higher in a fashionable resort or on a popular island. A new two-bedroom townhouse or villa costs from around €105,000, although prices rise to €150,000 or more in a good location on a small island. A three-bedroom, two-bathroom villa costs from around €150,000 (around €20,000 for a pool) and a four-bedroom villa on a large plot at least €200,000. Inland properties are much cheaper than coastal properties. Old stone houses are common in many areas (particularly Crete) and can be purchased from as little as €15,000. However, renovation costs are likely to be at least three times the purchase price, depending on how much of the original structure you can retain. Note that most old village houses tend to be small, e.g. 50 to 75m^2 , with only a few rooms.

Cyprus: A wide choice of properties is available, including apartments, townhouses and villas. Prices vary considerably depending on location, size and quality. One-bedroom apartments cost from around CY£25,000, two-bedroom apartments from CY£35,000, two-bedroom townhouses from CY£45,000, and two-bedroom detached bungalows and villas from around CY£60,000. The cost of a modern three-bedroom villa with swimming pool is usually well over CY£100,000. Front-line beach properties attract a premium of around 20 per cent. Resale properties are often sold furnished. The cost of building land varies with the area, from around CY£400 to 1,000 per m^2 . Renovated village houses are cheaper, costing from around CY£50,000 for two bedrooms and from around CY£65,000 for three bedrooms. Note that Cypriot developers often offer a form of hire purchase, whereby you pay for a property over a period, usually three to five years (in effect you receive a short-term mortgage from the developer).

Athina Tsakirakis
Advocate

ATS

Law Firm

ATS – multilingual lawyers situated in Athens, Greece

Areas of expertise: Property law for the purchase, sale or lease of private and commercial property (including flats, houses, hotels and building plots) throughout Greece.

Services: We perform the necessary searches and draw up the appropriate contract for the transaction. We also prepare power of attorney, tax documents and advise on Greek property taxes. ATS also specialise in the following:

- Construction law
- General commercial, corporate and business law and investments
- Offshore company formation
- Family law
- Inheritance law and wills

Our competitive advantages: We provide detailed invoices including all costs, fees and services provided; oral and written communications in English throughout our business transactions; accurate, honest and prompt service regardless of the complexity of the case; and give personal attention to each and every case.

35 Megalou Alexandrou Street • 171 21 Nea Smirni • Athens Greece • Tel. +301 93 19 411 • Mobile +309 44 544 297 Fax +301 93 28 468 • E-mail: atslaw@internet.gr Internet: www.internet.gr/ats

FEES

When you buy a property in Greece or Cyprus, you must pay a variety of fees, which are higher than in many other countries in the case of Greece and lower in Cyprus.

Greece: The fees associated with buying a home in Greece are high and usually total around 15 per cent (excluding agents' fees – see below). The main fee is purchase tax, which is based on the declared price. Note that, as in many other countries, there are usually two prices for property in Greece: the declared price or objective government price (OGP) and the actual buying price (ABP). In cities, the OGP is based on official valuation rates (which are published), calculated according to location, quality, size, construction and amenities. For rural properties the OGP is assessed by the local tax office, based on tables issued by the Ministry of Finance. The OGP usually amounts to around two-thirds of the ABP. Purchase tax is payable by the buyer at a flat rate of 10 per cent, which is increased by 2 per cent if the property is in an area served by a public fire protection service. In certain parts of Greece a further tax of 3 per cent may be levied, depending on certain conditions and the location. The intricacies of purchase tax make it particularly recommended to take legal advice before proceeding with a property purchase.

Other property fees include: lawyer's fees (usually 1 to 2 per cent); notary fees (1 to 2 per cent of a property's OGP); and land registry fees (0.3 per cent of the OGP plus a small sum for stamp duties and certificates). A community tax at 3 per cent of the property transfer tax is paid to the local municipality for general public services such as road maintenance. Note that this tax is paid at the same time as the purchase tax to the central tax office. There may also be additional costs such as certificates proving the property has been built to legal standards and that it has not been affected by an earthquake. Estate agent's fees are usually paid by the vendor, although an allowance is usually made when setting the sale price, so in effect the buyer pays.

Cyprus: The fees payable when buying a property in Cyprus total around 6 per cent of the purchase price and are among the lowest in western Europe. A lawyer's fees are between CY£200 and CY£500 or 1 per cent of the purchase price up to CY£75,000. Stamp duty is CY£1.50 per CY£1,000 of a property's value up to CY£100,000 and CY£2 per CY£1,000 of its value above CY£100,000, e.g. CY£75 for a CY£50,000 property and CY£350 for a CY£250,000 property. Stamp duty is payable within 30 days of signing a contract. The application to the Council of Ministers costs around CY£200, although this is due to be abolished for EU nationals. Land registry fees (transfer tax) are levied at between 3 and 8 per cent, depending on the value of the property. The tax is payable once the title deeds for the property have been issued by the relevant government authority and are as shown in the table below:

Value (CY£)	Transfer Tax (%)
up to 50,000	3
50,001–100,000	5
over 100,000	8

For example, on a property costing CY£100,000 the buyer pays CY£1,500 on the first CY£50,000 and CY£2,500 on the next CY£50,000, making a total of CY£4,000.

However, when a couple are buying a property together and are registered as co-owners, they can split the transfer tax between them. Therefore in the above example each would pay CY£1,500, making a saving of CY£1,000.

Note that the fees and rules associated with buying property in Cyprus have been changing rapidly in recent years, so you should check exactly what they are before signing a contract.

Running Costs: In addition to the fees associated with buying a property, you should also take into account running costs. These include local property taxes or rates (see page 94); community fees for a community property (see page 138) garden and pool maintenance (for a private villa); household, i.e. building and contents, insurance (see page 51 standing charges for utilities, e.g. electricity, gas, telephone and water; and a caretaker's or management fees if you leave a home empty or let it. Annual running costs usually average around 2 to 4 per cent of the cost of a property.

BUYING A NEW HOME

New properties are widely available in both Greece and Cyprus, and include coastal and city apartments and townhouses, golf and marina developments, and a wide range of individually designed villas. Many new properties, particularly in Cyprus, are part of purpose-built developments, which are planned as holiday homes and may not be attractive as permanent homes. If you're buying an apartment or house that's part of a community development, check whether your neighbours will be mainly locals or foreigners. Some people don't wish to live in a community consisting mainly of their fellow countrymen (or other foreigners) and this may also deter buyers when you wish to sell. On the other hand, some foreigners don't want to live in a Greek or Cypriot community, particularly if they don't speak the language.

Prices of new properties vary considerably according to their location, size and quality (see **Cost** on page 129). Most new homes have a steel (earthquake resistant) frame with a reinforced concrete slab and hollow clay bricks, although you can also have a new stone house built, which is environmentally friendly and benefits from modern building methods, materials and amenities. Building plots in Greece cost from around €18,500 and building costs are usually between €1,000 and 1,500 per m^2, while a typical 2,000m^2 plot in Cyprus costs from around CY£20,000. Planning permission in Greece costs from €3,000 to 9,000. Most apartments are relatively small, e.g. 75m^2, while villas are usually between 100 and 150m^2. When sales are slow, some developers offer inducements to buyers, which may include 'free' inspection flights and accommodation. Bear in mind, however, that the cost of these 'gifts' is included in the price and you may be able to get an equivalent (or even larger) cash reduction by haggling.

It's often cheaper to buy a new home than an old property requiring modernisation or renovation, as the price is fixed, unlike the cost of renovation which can soar way beyond original estimates (as many people have discovered to their cost). If required (and permitted), a new property can usually be let immediately and modern homes have good resale potential and are considered a good investment by local buyers. New properties are also covered by a warranty against structural defects. On the other hand, new homes may be smaller than older properties, have smaller gardens and rarely come with a large plot of land.

Most new properties are sold directly by property developers or builders, although they may also be marketed by estate agents. New developments may also have a sales office and/or a show house or apartment on site. When a building is purchased off plan, payment is made in stages as building work progresses. Homes can often be built in less than six months, although building work may not take place during the summer. **Note that it's important to ensure that each stage is completed satisfactorily before making payments.** If you're unable to do this yourself, you must engage an independent representative, e.g. an architect, to do it on your behalf. It isn't uncommon to have problems when buying a property off plan. According to investigations in various countries, many new properties have construction defects or deficiencies and in many cases the contract conditions aren't adhered to, particularly regarding the completion date (properties are rarely completed on schedule) and the quality of materials used.

When buying a property off plan, you can usually choose the colour of your bathroom suites, wall and floor tiles, carpets, internal walls, external wall plaster, shutters, doors and timber finish. You may also be able to alter the interior room layout, although this may increase the price. Note that you should make any changes or additions to a property during the design stage, such as including a more luxurious kitchen, a chimney or an additional shower room, which will cost much more to install later.

The quality of new property in Greece and Cyprus is extremely variable and may be poorer than in northern European countries and North America, although the quality of construction is generally high. More expensive properties use a high proportion of imported fixtures and fittings, and many building materials may also be imported. The quality of a building and the materials used will be reflected in the price, so when comparing prices ensure that you're comparing similar quality. Cheaper properties aren't usually the best built, although there are exceptions. If you want a permanent rather than a holiday home, you're better off opting for high quality construction and materials.

New homes usually contain a high level of 'luxury' features, which may include: a full-size, fully-fitted kitchen (possibly with a microwave, hob/oven with extractor hood, dishwasher, fridge/freezer and washing machine); a utility room; large bathrooms (possibly en suite to all bedrooms); a separate shower room and guest toilet; fitted carpets in bedrooms; double-glazing and shutters on all windows; stone wood-burning fireplace; stone, ceramic or marble floors in kitchens and bathrooms, and terracotta-tiled floors in other rooms; tiled verandas, terraces and patios; oak wood doors; fitted wardrobes; communal satellite TV and telephone outlets. Options may include a Jacuzzi, barbecue, swimming pool, sauna/steam bath, wooden/parquet floors, pergolas, walkways/paved surfaces, landscaping, garage or car port, central heating and air-conditioning. Larger homes may have maid's quarters or a separate guest apartment and a study.

Luxury properties that are part of a large development (see **Community Properties** on page 138) also have a wide range of communal facilities such as a swimming pool (or a number), tennis courts and landscaped gardens. If you wish to furnish a property for letting, many developers can do this for you and they may offer furniture packages which are generally good value.

Resale 'New' Homes: There are many advantages to buying a modern resale home rather than a brand new one in which you're the first occupant. These may include: a range of local services and facilities within an established development; the absence of 'teething troubles'; furniture and other extras included in the price; a mature garden and trees; and a larger plot of land. With a resale property, you can see exactly what you're getting for your money and the previous owners may have made improvements or added extras such as a swimming pool, which may not be fully reflected in the asking price. See also **Buying a Resale Home** on page 137.

BUILDING A HOME

If you want to be far from the madding crowd, you can buy a plot of land and have an individual architect-designed house built to your own design and specifications or to a standard design provided by a builder. Note, however, that building a home abroad isn't recommended for the timid. Red tape and local business practices can make building your own home a nightmare, and it's fraught with problems. Nevertheless, there are many excellent builders in Greece and Cyprus, and building your own home allows you not only to design your home, but to ensure that the quality of materials and workmanship are first class. Note, however, that properties must be built in the architectural styles of the region.

The Cost: Land is expensive in Greece and Cyprus and there are minimum plot sizes for each size of building. Land area is expressed in *stremmattas* (units of 1,000m^2 or around a quarter of an acre). In Greece, outside towns and villages a building plot must usually be over 4,000m^2, although special permission can sometimes be obtained for smaller plots. Inside town limits, a plot must be at least 250m^2 to be developed. Building permits, which can be obtained through registered architects and engineers, are also costly. Fees are regulated by the government and are around €35 to 45 per m^2, i.e. €7,000 to 9,000 for a 200m^2 house. Half the permit fee is paid before work starts and the remainder later on. In Greece, the average cost of a 2,000m^2 plot in a rural area is around €30,000, although building plots vary considerably in price and a small, e.g. a 250m^2 plot near the coast can cost as little as €18,500. A typical 2,000m^2 plot in Cyprus costs from around CY£20,000. Note also that providing services to a property in a remote rural area may be prohibitively expensive.

Buying a Building Plot: You must take the same care when buying land as you would when buying a home. The most important point is to ensure that it has been approved for building and that the plot is large enough and suitable for the house you plan to build. Minimum plot sizes vary and depend on whether the site is in a community, e.g. a village, or in the country. For smaller plots, the permitted floor area is usually a maximum of 60 to 70 per cent of the plot size. It may be possible to build on agricultural land, but there are strict limits on plot and building sizes. If the plot is part of a development, the contract must state that the plan has been approved and give the date and authority. You should consult an architect before deciding to buy a plot, as it may be unsuitable for building, e.g. too steep or requiring prohibitively expensive foundations. Also check that there aren't any restrictions such as high-tension electricity lines, water pipes or rights of way that may prohibit or limit building plans. You should also check that the boundaries are correct, as title deeds can be vague regarding measurements.

Always get confirmation in writing from the local town council that land can be built on and has been approved for road access (without which building isn't possible), whether building is restricted, and if so, in what way, whether the road is subject to a widening scheme, and whether electricity and water services can be provided and at what cost. Before buying land for building, ensure that the purchase contract is dependent on obtaining the necessary planning permission. Obtain a receipt showing that the plot is correctly presented in the local property register and check for yourself that the correct planning permission has been obtained (don't simply leave it to the builder). If planning permission is flawed, you may need to pay extra to improve the local infrastructure or the property may even have to be demolished! Note that it can take a long time to obtain planning permission.

Most builders and developers offer package deals that include the land and the cost of building a home. However, it isn't always wise to buy the plot from the builder who's going to build your home and you should shop around and compare separate land and building costs. **If you decide to buy a package deal from a builder, you *must* insist on separate contracts for the land and the building and obtain the title deed for the land before signing a building contract.**

Finding an Architect & Builder: When looking for an architect and builder, you should obtain recommendations from local people you can trust, e.g. neighbours and friends. Note that estate agents and other professionals aren't always the best people to ask, as they may receive commissions. You can also obtain valuable information from expatriates in local bars and from owners of properties in an area that you particularly like. Many Greek and all Cypriot architects speak English, and there are also architects from other EU countries working in Greece. Note that architects' fees are usually fixed and calculated as a percentage of the total cost of the work. For example, in Cyprus fees are set by the Institute of Architects and Civil Engineers and are 4 per cent of the construction cost for design services and 3 per cent of the construction cost for supervisory services.

An architect should be able to recommend a number of reliable builders, but you should also do your own research, as the most important consideration when building a new home is the reputation (and financial standing) of the builder. You should also be wary of an architect with his 'own' builder (or a builder with his own architect), as it's the architect's job to ensure that the builder does his work according to the plans and specifications – so you don't want their relationship to be too cosy. Inspect other homes a builder has built and check with the owners as to what problems they've had and whether they're satisfied. If you want a house built exactly to your specifications, you will need to supervise it every step of the way or employ an architect to do so for you. Without close supervision it's highly likely that your instructions *won't* be followed.

Contracts: You should obtain written quotations from a number of builders before signing a contract. Note that one of the most important features of a home must be good insulation (against both heat and cold) and protection against humidity. The contract must include: a detailed building description and a list of the materials to be used (with references to the architect's plans); the exact location of the building on the plot; the building and payment schedule, which must be made in stages according to building progress; a penalty clause for late completion; the retention of a percentage, e.g. 2 to 5 per cent, of the building costs as a 'guarantee' against defects; and how disputes will be settled. It may be difficult or impossible to get the builder to accept a penalty clause for late completion, as buildings are rarely completed on time. It should also be spelt out in the contract *exactly* what 'complete' means, as it's is open to local interpretation.

Ensure that the contract includes: all costs, including the architect's fees (unless contracted separately); landscaping (if applicable); *all* permits and licences; and the connection of utilities (water, electricity, gas, etc.) to the house, not just to the building site. The only extra is usually the cost of electricity and water meters. Before accepting a quotation, you should have it checked by a building consultant to confirm that it's a fair deal. You should check whether the quotation (which must include taxes) is an estimate or a fixed price, as sometimes the cost can escalate wildly due to contract clauses and changes made during building work. **It's vital to have a contract checked by a lawyer, as building contracts are often heavily biased in the builder's favour and give clients very few rights.**

Warranties: Greek and Cypriot law requires a builder to guarantee his work against structural defects. An architect is also responsible for defects due to poor supervision, incorrect instructions given to the builder, or problems caused by poor foundations, e.g. subsidence. Note that it isn't uncommon to have problems during construction, particularly regarding material defects. If you experience problems, you must usually be extremely patient and persistent in order to obtain satisfaction. You should have a completed building checked by a structural surveyor and a report drawn up; if there are any defects, he should determine who was responsible for them.

BUYING A RESALE HOME

Resale properties often represent good value, particularly in resort areas, where many apartments and townhouses are sold fully furnished, although the quality of furnishings varies considerably and may not be to your taste. (Luxury properties and villas, e.g. costing upwards of around €150,000/CY£100,000, are rarely sold furnished.) Another advantage of buying a resale property is that you can see exactly what you will get for your money and will save the cost of installing water and electricity meters and telephone lines, or the cost of extending these services to a property. When buying a resale property in a development, you should ask the neighbours about any problems, community fees, planned developments and anything else that may affect your enjoyment of the property. Most residents are usually happy to tell you, unless of course they're trying to sell you their own property!

If you want a property with abundant charm and character, a building for renovation or conversion, outbuildings, or a large plot of land, you'll probably have to choose an old property. Although you can buy a new stone home, they invariably have less character than old renovated properties. Note, however, that many old homes are small, although they generally offer better value per m$^{\approx}$ than the same size new home. Traditional stone-built houses are common throughout Greece, particularly in Crete, although the prices for 'ruins' are often farcical and have been driven up by demand in recent years. Old village houses are also popular in the interior of Cyprus. Note that you can buy a ruin from as little as €18,000/CY£10,000, but you will need to carry out major renovation and modernisation which will greatly increase the price. A structurally sound property may cost as much as €50,000/CY£30,000.

Many old homes lack basic services such as electricity, a reliable water supply and sanitation. Note that in Greece in order to obtain an electricity supply for older properties you may have to provide legal documentation showing the property's age. Because the purchase price is usually low, many foreign buyers believe they're getting a wonderful bargain, without fully investigating the renovation costs. If you aren't into do-it-yourself in a big way, you may be better off buying a new or recently built property, as the cost of restoring an old property can be prohibitive. If you're planning to buy a property that needs restoration or renovation and you won't be doing the work yourself, obtain an *accurate* estimate of the costs *before* signing a contract. You should also consider having a survey carried out (see page 145) on a resale property, particularly a detached house, as major problems can even be found in properties less than five or ten years old. Be wary of buying a property designed for tourist accommodation, as these were often built with inferior materials and workmanship – cavity walls and good insulation are essential if a property is to be used as a permanent home.

Bear in mind that, if you buy and restore a property with the intention of selling it for a profit, you must take into account not only the initial price and the restoration costs, but also the fees and taxes included in the purchase and possibly capital gains tax. It's often difficult to sell an old renovated property at a higher than average market price, irrespective of its added value. The locals have little interest in old restored properties, which is an important point if you need to sell an old home quickly in an area that isn't popular with foreign buyers. **If you're buying for investment, you're usually better off buying a new home.**

Owners often advertise properties in the local and expatriate press (see **Appendix A**) or by simply putting a 'for sale' sign in a window. Note that, although you can save money by buying direct from an owner, particularly when he is forced to sell, you should *always* employ a lawyer to carry out the necessary checks (see **Conveyancing** on page 147). If you're unsure of the value of a property, you should obtain a professional valuation.

COMMUNITY PROPERTIES

Community properties are those with elements (whether a building, amenities or land) shared with other properties. They include apartments, townhouses, and single-family (detached) homes on a private estate with communal areas and facilities. In fact, the only properties that don't belong to a community are detached houses built on individual plots in public streets or on rural land. Community properties are owned through a system of co-ownership (similar to that of a condominium in the USA) whereby each property owner also owns a share of the common elements of the building or development, including foyers, hallways, passages, lifts, patios, gardens, roads, and leisure and sports facilities (such as swimming pools and tennis courts). When you buy a community property, you automatically become a member of the community of owners.

Many community properties are located in or near coastal resorts and offer a range of communal facilities, which may include a golf course, swimming pools, tennis courts, a gymnasium or fitness club, and a bar and restaurant. Most developments have landscaped gardens and some also offer high security and a full-time caretaker. At the other extreme, cheaper, older developments may consist of tiny cramped studio apartments with few, if any, amenities. Note that some community properties are planned as holiday homes and aren't attractive as permanent homes.

Advantages: The advantages of owning a community property include: increased security; lower property taxes than detached homes; a range of communal sports and leisure facilities; community living with lots of social contacts and the companionship of close neighbours; adequate off-road parking; no garden, lawn or pool maintenance; fewer of the responsibilities of home ownership; ease of maintenance; and the opportunity to live in an area where owning a single-family home would be prohibitively expensive, e.g. a beach front or town centre.

Disadvantages: The disadvantages of community properties may include: excessively high community fees (owners may have no control over increases); restrictive rules and regulations; a confining living and social environment and possible lack of privacy; noisy neighbours (particularly if neighbouring properties are let to holidaymakers); limited living and storage space; expensive covered or secure parking (or insufficient off-road parking); and acrimonious owners' meetings where management and factions may try to push through unpopular proposals (sometimes using proxy votes).

Research: Before buying a community property, you should ask current owners about the community. For example; do they like living there, what are the fees and restrictions, how noisy are other residents, are the recreational facilities easy to access, would they buy there again (why or why not), and, most importantly, is the community well managed? You may also wish to check on your prospective neighbours and if you're planning to buy an apartment above the ground floor you may want to ensure that the building has a lift. Note that upper floor apartments are both cooler in winter and hotter in summer, and you may incur extra charges for the use of lifts (they do, however, offer more security than ground floor apartments). An apartment that has other apartments above and below it will generally be more noisy than a ground or top floor apartment.

Cost: Community properties vary enormously in price and quality, e.g. from around €30,000/CY£20,000 for a studio or one-bedroom apartment in an average location to €150,000/CY£100,000 or more for a luxury apartment, townhouse or villa in a prime location. Garages and parking spaces must usually be purchased separately, and a lock-up garage or a space in an underground car park can cost €7,500 to 18,500/CY£5,000 to 10,000. If you're buying a resale property, check the price paid for similar properties in the same area or development in recent months, but bear in mind that the price you pay may have more to do with the seller's circumstances than the price fetched by other properties. Find out how many properties are for sale in a particular development; if there are many on offer you should investigate why, as there could be management or structural problems. If you're still keen to buy, you can use any negative points to drive a hard bargain.

Community Fees: Owners of community properties must pay fees for the upkeep of communal areas and for communal services. Charges are calculated according to each owner's share of a development or apartment building, and *not* whether they're temporary or permanent residents. Shares are usually calculated according to the relative size of properties, e.g. the owners of ten properties of equal size usually each pay 10 per cent of community fees. The percentage to be paid is detailed in the property deed. Shares not only determine the share of fees to be paid, but also voting rights at general meetings.

Fees go towards: road cleaning; green zone maintenance (including communal and possibly private gardens); cleaning, decoration and maintenance of buildings; caretaker or concierge; communal lighting in buildings and grounds; water supply, e.g. swimming pools and gardens; insurance; administration fees; community rates; maintenance of radio and TV aerials; and satellite TV charges. Always check the level of general and any special charges before buying a community property. Fees are usually billed at fixed periods during the year and are adjusted at the end of the year when the actual expenditure is known and the annual accounts have been approved by the committee. If you're buying an apartment from a previous owner, ask to see a copy of the service charges for previous years and the minutes of the last annual general meeting, as owners may be 'economical with the truth' when stating service charges, particularly if they're high.

Community fees vary considerably according to the location and the communal facilities provided. Fees for a typical two-bedroom apartment costing around €75,000/CY£50,000 are generally in the region of €225 to 450/CY£150 to 300 per year, although they can be much (much) higher for a luxury penthouse in a prestigious development. Note that high fees aren't necessarily a negative point (assuming you can afford them), provided that you receive value for money and the community is well managed and maintained. The value of a community property depends to a large extent on how well the development is maintained and managed. Note that if you own a holiday home, it's important to ensure that bills are paid in your absence.

Maintenance & Repairs: Owners can be required to pay an additional amount to make up any shortfall of funds for maintenance or repairs. You should check the condition of the common areas (including all amenities) in an old development and whether any major maintenance or capital expense is planned for which you could be liable. Old run-down apartment blocks can have their community fees increased substantially to pay for new installations and repairs (such as a new water supply or sewage installation). Always enquire about any planned work and obtain a copy of the minutes of the last annual meeting, where important matters are sure to have been raised. Owners' meetings can become rather heated when finances are discussed, particularly when assessments are being made to finance capital expenditure.

Restrictions: Community rules allow owners to run a community in accordance with the wishes of the majority, while safeguarding the rights of the minority. Rules usually include: noise levels; the keeping of pets (usually permitted, although some communities prohibit all pets); renting; exterior decoration and plants, e.g. the positioning of shrubs; rubbish disposal; the use of swimming pools and other recreational facilities; exterior decoration and adornments (such as sun blinds); the activities of children, e.g. no ball games or cycling on community grounds; parking; business or professional use; the installation and positioning of satellite dishes; use of a communal laundry room; and the hanging of laundry. Check the rules and discuss any restrictions with residents.

Holiday Homes: If you're buying a holiday home that will be vacant for long periods (particularly in winter), don't buy in an apartment block where heating and/or hot water charges are shared, or you will be paying towards your co-owners' bills. You should also check whether there are any rules regarding short or long-term rentals or leaving a property unoccupied for long periods. Note that when buying in a large development, communal facilities may be crowded during peak periods, e.g. a large swimming pool won't look so big when 100 people are using it, and getting a game of tennis can be difficult.

TIMESHARE & PART-OWNERSHIP SCHEMES

If you're looking for a holiday home abroad, you may wish to investigate a scheme that provides sole occupancy of a property for a number of weeks each year. These include co-ownership, leaseback, timeshare and a holiday property bond. **Don't rush into any of these schemes without fully researching the market and before you're absolutely clear what you want and what you can realistically expect to get for your money.**

Co-ownership: Co-ownership includes schemes such as a group of people buying shares in a property-owning company and co-ownership between family, friends or even strangers. Co-ownership allows you to recoup your investment in savings on holiday costs while retaining equity in a property. A common deal is a four-owner scheme (which many consider to be the optimum number of co-owners), where you buy a quarter of a property and can occupy it for up to three months a year. However, there's no reason why there cannot be as many as 12 co-owners, with a month's occupancy each per year (usually divided between high, medium and low seasons).

Co-ownership offers access to a size and quality of property that would otherwise be unimaginable, and it's even possible to have a share in a substantial mansion, where a number of families could live together simultaneously and hardly ever see each other if they didn't want to. Co-ownership can be a good choice for a family seeking a holiday home for a few weeks or months a year and has the added advantage that (because of the lower cost) a mortgage may be unnecessary. Note that it's cheaper to buy a property privately with friends than to buy from an agent or developer who offers this sort of scheme, in which case you may pay well above the market value for a share of a property (check the market value of a property to establish whether it's good value). **Co-ownership is much better value than a timeshare and needn't cost much more.** Note, however, that a water-tight contract must be drawn up by an experienced lawyer to protect the co-owners' interests.

One of the best ways to get into co-ownership, if you can afford it, is to buy a property yourself and offer shares to others. This overcomes the problem of getting together a consortium of would-be owners and trying to agree on a purchase in advance, which is difficult unless it's just a few friends or family members. Many people form a local company to buy and manage a property, which can in turn be owned by a company in the co-owners' home country, thus allowing any disputes to be dealt with under local law. Each co-owner receives a number of shares according to how much he has paid, entitling him to so many weeks' occupancy a year. Owners don't need to have equal shares and can all be made direct title holders. If a co-owner wishes to sell his shares, he must usually give first refusal to the other co-owners, although if they don't wish to buy them and a new co-owner cannot be found, the property will need to be sold.

Sale & Leaseback: Leaseback or sale and leaseback schemes are designed for those seeking a holiday home for a limited number of weeks each year. Properties sold under a leaseback scheme are located in popular resort areas, e.g. golf, ski or coastal resorts, where self-catering accommodation is in high demand. Buying a property through a leaseback scheme allows a purchaser to buy a new property at less than its true cost, e.g. 30 per cent less than the list price. In return for the discount the property must be leased back to the developer, usually for around ten years, so that he can let it as self-catering holiday accommodation. The buyer owns the freehold of the property and the full price is shown in the title deed.

The purchaser is also given the right to occupy the property for a period each year, usually six or eight weeks, spread over high, medium and low seasons. These weeks can usually be let to provide income or possibly be exchanged with accommodation in another resort (as with a timeshare scheme). The developer furnishes and manages the property, and pays for maintenance and utilities, etc. during the term of the lease, even when the owner occupies the property. Note that it's important to have a contract checked by a legal expert to ensure that you receive vacant possession at the end of the leaseback period, *without* having to pay an indemnity charge, otherwise you could end up paying more than a property is worth. In some cases you can buy out of a sale and leaseback scheme after a period, e.g. two years.

Timeshare: Also known as holiday ownership, vacation ownership, co-ownership or holidays for life, timeshare is a popular form of part-ownership, although there are few timeshare resorts in Greece and Cyprus compared with, for example, Spain. The best timeshare developments are on a par with luxury hotels and offer a wide range of facilities, including bars, restaurants, entertainment, shops, swimming pools, tennis courts, health clubs, and other leisure and sports facilities. If you don't wish to holiday in the same place each year, you should choose a timeshare development that's a member of an international organisation such as Resort Condominium International (RCI) or Interval International (II), which allow you (usually for an additional fee) to exchange your timeshare with one in another area or country.

Timeshare has earned a poor reputation in some countries, although things have improved in recent years since the introduction of new EU regulations to protect buyers, including a requirement that buyers have secure occupancy rights and that their money is properly protected prior to the completion of a new property. Timeshare companies are required to disclose information about the vendor and the property and to allow prospective buyers a ten-day 'cooling off period', during which they may cancel a sales agreement they've signed without penalty. Timeshare purchases can now be registered with a notary and inscribed in the registry at the buyer's request (it isn't mandatory). A guarantee must be provided by the timeshare company that a property is as advertised and, where applicable, the contract must be in the language of the EU country where the buyer is resident or the language of the buyer's choice (you cannot sign away any of your rights irrespective of what's written in the contract). If a new contract isn't in accordance with the new law, it's null and void.

The best timeshares cost around €12,000/CY£8,000 or more for one week in a one or two-bedroom apartment in a top-rated resort, to which must be added annual management fees of €225 to 300/CY£150 to 200 or more for each week and other miscellaneous fees. Most experts believe that there's little or no advantage in a timeshare over a normal holiday rental and that it's simply an expensive way to pay for your holidays in advance. It doesn't make sense to tie up your money for what amounts to a long-term reservation on an annual holiday (usually you don't actually 'own' anything). Most financial advisers believe that you're better off putting your money into a long-term investment, where you keep your capital and may even earn sufficient interest to pay for a few weeks' holiday each year. For example, €12,000/CY£8,000 invested at just 5 per cent yields €600/CY£400 a year, which when added to the saving on management fees makes a total of around €900 or CY£600 – sufficient to pay for a week's holiday in a self-catering apartment outside the 'high season' almost anywhere.

Often timeshares are difficult or impossible to sell at any price. **Note that there's no real resale market for timeshares, and if you need to sell you're highly unlikely to get your money back.** If you want to buy a timeshare, it's best to buy a resale privately from an existing owner or a timeshare resale broker, when they sell for a fraction of their original cost. When buying privately, you can usually drive a hard bargain and may even get a timeshare 'free' simply by assuming the current owner's maintenance contract. Further information about timesharing can be obtained from the Timeshare Council (☎ UK 020-7821 8845) and the Timeshare Helpline (☎ UK 020-8296 0900) in Britain. The Timeshare Consumers Association (Hodsock, Worksop, Notts, S81 0TF, UK, ☎ 01909-591100, ✉ tca@netcomuk.co.uk) publishes a useful booklet entitled *Timeshare: Guide to Buying, Owning and Selling*.

Holiday Property Bond: A holiday property bond is a good alternative to timesharing for those with a minimum of around GB£2,000 to invest. Holiday Property Bond (operated by the Villa Owners Club Ltd., HPB House, Newmarket, Suffolk CB8 8EH, UK, ☎ 01638-660066) owns over 600 properties in many countries, including Greece and Cyprus. Each GB£1 invested is equal to one point and each week's stay in a property is assigned a points rating depending on its size, location and the time of year. There are no extra fees apart from a small 'user' charge when occupying a property to cover cleaning and utility costs. Furthermore, there's a buy-back guarantee after two years, when an investment can be sold at its current market value.

ESTATE & PROPERTY AGENTS

The vast majority of property sales in Greece and Cyprus are handled by estate agents or developers' agents, particularly those involving overseas foreign buyers. It's common for foreigners in many countries, particularly Britain, to use an agent in their own country who works in co-operation with a foreign agent or developer. Many foreign agents and developers also advertise abroad, particularly in the publications listed in **Appendix A** and in expatriate magazines and newspapers in Greece and Cyprus. Most foreign agents have staff who speak English and other foreign languages, so don't be discouraged if you don't speak Greek.

Most agents offer after-sales services and will help you arrange legal advice, insurance, utilities, and interior decorators and builders. They may even offer a full management and rental service on behalf of non-resident owners. Note, however, that agents often receive commissions for referrals and therefore you may not receive independent advice.

Qualifications: Estate agents in Greece and Cyprus are regulated by law and must be professionally qualified and licensed. You should choose an agent who's a member of a professional association such as the Cyprus Real Estate Agents Association (CREAA), with which all bona fide agents must be registered. Members must possess a thorough knowledge of the law regarding immovable property, have extensive experience in selling real estate or be a university graduate in a relevant subject, possess an untarnished criminal and civic record, not be a bankrupt and have professional indemnity insurance for a minimum of CY£60,000. If you have a dispute with an estate agent, the CREAA will intercede on your behalf and, if necessary, will appoint a lawyer for you for a nominal fee. Ask to see an agent's registration number and have someone check it if you aren't convinced that it's genuine. You may also be afforded extra protection if the agent is a member of an international organisation, such as the European Federation of Estate Agents. **If you pay a deposit to an agent, you must ensure that it's deposited in a separate bonded account.**

Fees: There are no government controls on agents' fees in Greece and Cyprus, where an agent's commission is usually paid by the vendor and included in the purchase price. The commission charged by agents in Greece and Cyprus is usually between 2 and 5 per cent. Foreign agents located abroad often work with local agents and share the standard commission, so buyers usually pay no more by using them. However, check in advance whether this is the case and how much you're required to pay. When buying, also check whether you need to pay commission or any extras in addition to the sale price (apart from the normal fees and taxes associated with buying a property).

Viewing: If possible, you should decide where you want to live, what sort of property you want and your budget *before* visiting Greece or Cyprus. Obtain details of as many properties as possible in your chosen area and price range, and make a shortlist of those you wish to view. Usually the details provided by estate agents are sparse and few agents provide detailed descriptions of properties. Often there's no photograph; even when there is, it usually doesn't do a property justice. Note that there are no national property listings in Greece or Cyprus, where agents jealously guard their list of properties, although many work with overseas agents in areas popular with foreign buyers. Agents who advertise in foreign journals or who work closely with overseas agents usually provide coloured photographs and a full description, particularly for the more expensive properties. Agents vary enormously in their efficiency, enthusiasm and professionalism, and the best agents provide an abundance of information. If an agent shows little interest in finding out exactly what you want, you should go elsewhere. If you're using a foreign agent, confirm (and reconfirm) that a particular property is still for sale and the price, before travelling abroad to view it. Many estate agents have websites, so you can check what's on offer from the comfort of your home, although sites rarely show all properties for sale or the latest properties on their books.

Note that an agent may ask you to sign a document before showing you any properties, which is simply to protect his commission should you obtain details from another source or try to do a deal directly with the owner. You're usually shown properties personally by agents and won't be given the keys (especially to furnished properties) or be expected to deal with tenants or vendors directly. You should make an appointment with an agent rather than simply turn up and ask him to show you a property. If you make an appointment and cannot keep it, you should call and cancel it. If you happen to be on holiday, it's acceptable to drop in unannounced to have a look at what's on offer, but don't expect an agent to show you properties without an appointment. If you view properties during a holiday, it's best to do so at the beginning so that you can return later to inspect any you particularly like a second or third time. Note that local agents don't usually work during lunch hours and most are closed on Saturdays and Sundays.

You should try to view as many properties as possible during the time available, but allow sufficient time to view each property thoroughly, to travel between properties and take breaks for sustenance. Although it's important to see a sufficient number properties to form an accurate opinion of price and quality, however, don't see too many properties in one day, as it's easy to become confused over the merits of each property. If you're shown properties that don't meet your specifications, tell the agent immediately. You can also help the agent narrow the field by telling him exactly what's wrong with the properties you reject. It's sensible to make notes of both the good *and* bad features and take lots of photographs of the properties you like, so that you're able to compare them later at your leisure (but keep a record of which photos are of which house!). It's also wise to mark each property on a map so that you can return later on your own if you wish without getting lost (too often). The more a property appeals to you, the more you should look for faults and negative points – if you still like it after stressing the negative points, it must have special appeal.

Viewing Trips: Most agents and developers arrange viewing trips and provide inexpensive accommodation for prospective buyers and may even refund the cost if you buy a property. By all means take advantage of inspection flight offers, but don't allow yourself to be pressured into buying on a viewing trip. Always allow yourself sufficient time to view and compare properties offered by a number of agents and developers. A long weekend isn't enough time to have a good look around, unless you already know exactly what you want to buy and where, or are coming to view just a few properties.

INSPECTIONS & SURVEYS

When you've found a property that you like, you should make a close inspection of its condition. Obviously this will depend on whether it's an old house in need of complete restoration, a property that has been partly or totally modernised, or a modern home. One of the problems with a property that has been restored is that you don't know how well the job has been done, particularly if the owner did it himself. If work has been carried out by local builders, you should ask to see the bills.

Some simple checks you can do yourself include testing the electrical system, plumbing, mains water, hot water boiler and central heating. Don't take someone's word that these are functional, but check them for yourself. If a property doesn't have electricity or mains water, check the nearest connection point and the cost of extending the service to the property, as it can be *very* expensive in remote rural areas. If a property has a well or septic tank, you should also have them tested. An old property may show visible signs of damage and decay, such as bulging or cracked walls, rising damp, missing roof slates (you can check with binoculars) and rotten woodwork. Some areas are liable to flooding, storms and subsidence, and you should check an old property after a heavy rainfall, when any leaks should come to light. If you find or suspect problems, you should have a property checked by a builder or have a full structural survey carried out by a surveyor. You may also wish to have a property checked for termites and other infestations.

A local buyer wouldn't make an offer on an old property before at least having it checked by a builder, who will also be able to tell you whether the price is too high, given any work that needs to be done. However, it's unusual to have a survey on a property in Greece or Cyprus, particularly a property built in the last 10 or 20 years. Nevertheless, it isn't unusual to find serious faults with homes built in the '60s and '70s, many of which were built with inferior materials, and even relatively new buildings can have problems. **It's important to check who the developer or builder was, as a major company with a good reputation is unlikely to cut corners.**

If you're buying a detached villa, farmhouse or village house, especially one built on the side of a hill, it's *always* wise to have a survey carried out. Common problems in old buildings include rusting water pipes and leaky plumbing, inadequate sewage disposal, poor wiring, humidity and rising damp (no damp course), uneven flooring or no concrete base, collapsing façades, subsidence, and cracked internal and external walls. Some of these problems are even evident in developments less than five or ten years old. Generally, if you would have a survey done if you were buying a similar property in your home country, you should have one done in Greece or Cyprus.

You could ask the vendor to have a survey done at his expense, which, provided that it gives the property a clean bill of health, will help him sell it even if you decide not to buy. You can make a satisfactory survey a condition of a contract, although this isn't usual and a vendor may refuse or insist that you carry out a survey at your expense *before* signing the contract. **If a vendor refuses to allow you to do a survey before signing a contract, you should look elsewhere.** Some foreign lenders require a survey before approving a loan, although this usually consists of a perfunctory valuation to ensure that a property is worth the purchase price. You can employ a foreign surveyor in some areas, although you must ensure that he is experienced in the idiosyncrasies of local properties and that he has professional indemnity insurance covering Greece or Cyprus (which means you can happily sue him if he does a bad job!).

Always discuss with the surveyor exactly what will be included and, most importantly, what will be omitted from the survey (you may need to pay extra to include certain checks and tests). A full structural survey should include the condition of all buildings, particularly the foundations, roofs, walls and woodwork; plumbing, electricity and heating systems; and anything else you want inspected such as a swimming pool and its equipment, e.g. filter system or heating. A survey can be limited to a few items or even a single system only, such as the wiring or plumbing in an old house. You should receive a written report on the structural condition of a property, including anything that could become a problem in the future. Some surveyors will allow you to accompany them and provide a video film of their findings in addition to a written report.

Buying Land: Before buying a home on its own plot of land, you should walk the boundaries and check fences, driveways, roads, and the overhanging eaves of buildings that might be encroaching upon the property. If you're uncertain about the boundaries, you should have the land surveyed, which is sensible in any case when buying a property with a large plot of land. When buying a rural property, you may be able to negotiate the amount of land you want included in the purchase. If a property is part of a larger plot of land owned by the vendor or the boundaries must be redrawn, you will need to hire a surveyor to measure the land and draw up a new plan. You should also have a lawyer check the local municipal plans to find out what the land can be used for and whether there are any existing rights of way. When considering buying land next to the sea, make sure you will be allowed to build before you commit yourself to the purchase – permits are extremely difficult to obtain for plots next to the sea. If you're buying a property within 500m of the shoreline, you should be aware that different building regulations apply, which in many cases have strict specifications including roof shape, number of windows etc. Finally you should double-check that the plot is large enough to build on – many expatriates buy rural plots that are too small to build on.

CONVEYANCING

Conveyancing (or conveyance) is the legal term for processing the paperwork involved in buying and selling a property and transferring the deeds of ownership. The purchase procedure in Cyprus is based on the British legal system, where a solicitor must be engaged to draw up a contract and perform the conveyancing. In Greece, some aspects of conveyancing, such as drawing up the deeds and witnessing the signatures, can be performed only by a public notary. A notary represents the government and one of his main tasks is to ensure that state taxes are paid on the completion of a sale. **However, he doesn't verify or guarantee the accuracy of statements made in a contract or protect you against fraud**, so it's vital to employ a lawyer to carry out the following checks:

- Verifying that a property belongs to the vendor or that he has legal authority to sell it. Note that when there's more than one owner, which is often the case in Greece and Cyprus, all must agree to the sale. **If a property has no deeds or isn't registered, you must be extremely wary.** The final transfer of ownership cannot take place until a separate title deed has been issued, which can take as long as two years; it's therefore important to check how long the title deed will take to obtain before signing a contract. The lawyer should also verify that trees on rural properties belong to the owner.

- Making sure that there are no tenants. If there are, you must ensure that you will obtain vacant possession.

- Checking that there are no pre-emption rights over a property and that there are no plans to construct anything that would adversely affect the value, enjoyment or use of the property such as roads, railway lines, airports, shops, factories or any other developments.

- Checking that the boundaries and measurements in the deeds are accurate. Obtain a certificate from the property register containing an accurate physical description of the property and maps. When buying a property with a plot of land, the boundaries must be surveyed.

- Ensuring that building permits and planning permissions, e.g. building licence, water and electricity supply, sewage connection, are in order and are genuine, and that a property was built in accordance with the plans.

- Checking that there are no encumbrances or liens, e.g. mortgages or loans, against a property or any outstanding debts, such as local taxes (rates), community charges, water, electricity or telephone. Note that if you buy a property on which there's an outstanding loan or taxes, the lender or local authority has first claim on the property and has the right to take possession and sell it to repay the debt. All unpaid debts on a property are inherited by the buyer.

- Ensuring that proper title is obtained and arranging the necessary registration of ownership.

Many estate agents will carry out the above checks for you and pass the information to your lawyer, but it's still wise to have your lawyer double-check. The cost of conveyancing depends on whether you employ a foreign or local lawyer or both (it's generally cheaper to use a local lawyer). Lawyers' fees in Greece are usually between 1 and 2 per cent of the purchase price. In Cyprus, lawyer's fees are between CY£200 and 500 or 1 per cent of the purchase price up to CY£75,000. Before hiring a lawyer, compare the fees charged by a number of practices and obtain quotations in writing. Always check what's included in the fee and whether it's 'full and binding' or just an estimate (a low basic rate may be supplemented by much more expensive 'extras'). You should also employ a lawyer to check the purchase contract (see below) before signing it to ensure that it includes everything necessary, particularly any relevant conditional clauses.

Notary's Duties: In Greece, the sales contract is prepared by a public notary, who's responsible for ensuring that it's drawn up correctly and that the purchase price is paid to the vendor. He also certifies the identity of the parties, witnesses the signing of the deed, arranges for its registration (in the name of the new owner) in the local property register and collects any fees or taxes due. Note, however, that a notary represents the state and *doesn't* protect the interests of the buyer or the seller and will rarely point out possible pitfalls in a contract, proffer advice or volunteer any information (as, for example, an estate agent usually will). Don't expect a notary to speak English or any language other than Greek (although some do) or to explain the intricacies of Greek property law.

Anyone buying (or selling) property abroad shouldn't even think about doing so without taking expert, independent legal advice. You should certainly never sign anything or pay any money before obtaining legal advice. Your lawyer should also check that the notary does his job correctly, thus providing an extra safeguard. It isn't wise to use the vendor's lawyer, even if this would save you money, as he is primarily concerned with protecting the interests of the vendor and not the buyer. See also **Avoiding Problems** on page 120.

PURCHASE CONTRACTS

The first stage in buying a property in Greece or Cyprus is usually the signing of a preliminary contract, although it's possible to go to a notary in Greece and have him draw up the sales deed without having a prior contract. However, when you're paying a deposit (see below), it's necessary to have a contract drawn up. The purchase procedure in Cyprus is based on the British legal system, where a lawyer must be engaged to draw up the contract and perform the conveyancing. Contracts are subject to a clear title being obtained and any necessary government permits. Builders, developers and estate agents often have ready-made contracts that are drafted to protect their own interests; these be scrutinised by your lawyer. You should also instruct your lawyer to obtain the necessary permits and not leave it to an estate agent or developer. It's sometimes possible to sign an option or reservation agreement, where you pay a small deposit to secure a property for a period, e.g. 30 days, while waiting for funds to arrive from abroad. This deposit is usually lost if you back out of the purchase.

The origin of funds used to buy property in Greece must be declared to the Bank of Greece using an official import document. Similarly, foreign currency must be imported to pay for property in Cyprus and an Import of Foreign Currency certificate is required by the Land Registry office. You should open a local bank account (see page 79), through which all payments relating to the property purchase must take place (particularly if you're paying in stages). This will provide an accurate record of payments and show that they emanated from abroad. In Cyprus, an application to purchase a property must be made to the Council of Ministers and costs around CY£200, although it's only a formality and is due to be abolished for EU nationals.

Buying Off Plan: When buying an uncompleted property off plan, i.e. a property yet to be built or partly built, payment is made in stages. Stage payments vary considerably and may consist of the following: a 20 per cent deposit; 20 per cent on completion of the roof; 20 per cent on tiling the bathroom and kitchen (or when the door and window frames are installed); 20 per cent when the building is complete; 15 per cent when the exterior work is completed (such as the patio, pool and landscaping); the remaining 5 per cent may be withheld for six months for maintenance and as 'insurance' against defects (see below). If a property is already partly built, the builder may ask for a higher initial payment, depending on its stage of completion.

The contract contains: the timetable for the property's completion; stage payment dates; the completion date and penalties for non-completion; guarantees for building work; details of the builder's insurance policy (against non-completion); and a copy of the plans and drawings. The floor plan and technical specifications are signed by both parties to ensure that sizes and standard of construction are adhered to. The contract should also contain a clause allowing you to withhold around 5 per cent of the purchase price for six months in case the builder fails to correct any faults in the property. The completion of each stage should be certified in writing by your own architect or lawyer before payments are made. It's important to ensure that payments are made on time, or you could forfeit all previous payments and the property could be sold to another buyer. **Note that it's important that the builder or developer has an insurance policy (or 'termination' guarantee) to protect your investment in the event that he goes bust before completing the property and its infrastructure.** If he doesn't, you shouldn't buy from him!

Buying a New or Resale Property: When you sign the contract for a new or resale property or a plot of land you must usually pay a deposit (see below). If you're buying a resale or a new finished property (i.e. not off plan), you usually pay a deposit of 10 per cent when signing the contract (the percentage may be negotiable), the balance being paid on completion when the deed of sale is signed. **Note that before signing a contract, it's important to have it checked by a lawyer.** One of the main reasons is to safeguard your interests by including any necessary conditional clauses (see below) in the contract.

Deposits: It's usual to pay a 10 per cent deposit when buying a resale property, although it may be up to 30 per cent in Greece. Deposits are refundable under strict conditions only, notably relating to any conditional clauses such as failure to obtain a mortgage. A deposit can also be forfeited if you don't complete the purchase transaction within the period specified in the contract. If you withdraw from a sale after all the conditions have been met, you won't only lose your deposit, but may also be required to pay the estate agent's commission.

The contract can be cancelled by either party, the buyer forfeiting his deposit or the vendor paying the buyer double the deposit. However, in some cases, if one of the parties wishes to withdraw from the sale, the other party can demand that he goes through with it or that he receives compensation for damages. **Always make sure that you know exactly what the conditions are regarding the return or forfeit of a deposit.** Note that many estate agents don't have legal authority to hold money on behalf of their clients and that deposits should be kept only in a separate, bonded account. It isn't wise to make out cheques for deposits or other monies in the name of an estate agent.

Conditional Clauses: Contracts, whether for new or resale properties, usually contain a number of conditional clauses that must be met to ensure the validity of the contract. Conditions usually apply to events out of the control of either the vendor or buyer, although almost anything the buyer agrees with the vendor can be included in a contract. If any of the conditions aren't met, the contract can be suspended or declared null and void, and the deposit returned. However, if you fail to go through with a purchase and aren't covered by a clause in the contract, you will forfeit your deposit or could even be compelled to go through with a purchase. Note that if you're buying anything from the vendor such as carpets, curtains or furniture that's included in the purchase price, you should have them listed and attached as an addendum to the contract. Any fixtures and fittings present in a property when you view it (and agree to buy it) should still be there when you take possession, unless otherwise stated in the contract (see also **Completion** on page 151). You should discuss with your lawyer whether conditional clauses are necessary.

There are many possible conditional clauses concerning a range of subjects, including the following:

- being able to obtain a mortgage;
- obtaining planning permission, building permits and, in Cyprus, approval of the Council of Ministers – this can take a year or longer, although you can take possession of the property in the meantime and approval is usually automatic (and will soon be unnecessary for EU nationals);
- obtaining special permits from the local authorities, e.g. foreigners wishing to purchase property close to the Greek border require official permission;
- being unable to obtain a residence permit;

- confirmation of the land area being purchased with a property;
- plans to construct anything, e.g. roads, railways, etc, that would adversely affect your enjoyment or use of a property;
- pre-emption rights or restrictive covenants over a property such as rights of way;
- dependence on the sale of another property;
- dependence on a satisfactory building survey or inspection.

Inheritance & Capital Gains Tax: Before registering the title deed, you should carefully consider the tax and inheritance consequences for those in whose name the deed will be registered. Property can be registered in a single name; both names of a couple or joint buyers' names (only possible between a husband and wife in Cyprus), the name or names of children, giving the parents sole use during their lifetime, or in the name of a local or foreign company (see below). However you decide to buy a property, it should be done at the time of purchase, as it will be more expensive (or even impossible) to change it later. Discuss the matter with your lawyer before signing a contract. See also **Capital Gains Tax** on page 95 and **Inheritance Tax** on page 97.

Buying Through a Company: Properties in both Greece and Cyprus can be purchased in the name of a local or offshore company. Offshore companies used to purchase property in Greece have various financial advantages, as well as making a property easier to sell. If a property in Cyprus is purchased via an offshore company, exchange controls don't affect the sale of a property and full repatriation of funds is possible. In addition, no land registry fees are payable, which can add up to a large saving. Buying a property through a local limited company (which in turn could be owned by an offshore company) has some advantages, but is of little or no benefit to the average buyer. Before buying a property through a company, it's essential to obtain expert legal advice and weigh up the long-term advantages and disadvantages. See also **Avoiding Problems** on page 120 and **Conveyancing** on page 147.

COMPLETION

Completion (or closing) is the name for the signing of the final deed, the date of which is usually one or two months after signing the preliminary contract, as stated in the contract (although it may be 'moveable'). Completion involves the signing of the deed of sale transferring legal ownership of a property and the payment of the balance of the purchase price, plus other payments such as the notary's or lawyer's fees, taxes and duties (although these may be paid earlier or later). When the necessary documents relating to a purchase have been returned to the notary or lawyer handling the sale, he will contact you and request the balance of the purchase price less the deposit and, if applicable, the amount of a mortgage. He will also send you a bill for his fees and taxes. At the same time, the notary should provide a draft deed of sale (if he doesn't, you should request one), which should be complete and not contain any blank spaces to be completed later. If you don't understand the deed of sale, you should have it checked by your lawyer.

Final Checks: Property is sold subject to the condition that it's accepted in the state it's in at the time of completion, so you should be aware of anything that occurs between the signing of the preliminary contract and completion. Before signing the deed of sale, it's important to check that the property hasn't fallen down or been damaged in any way, e.g. by a storm, vandals or the previous owner. If you have a lawyer or are buying through an agent, he should accompany you on this visit. You should also do a final inventory immediately prior to completion (the previous owner should already have vacated the property) to ensure that the vendor hasn't absconded with anything that was included in the price. You should have an inventory of the fixtures and fittings and anything that was included in the contract or purchased separately, e.g. carpets, light fittings, curtains and kitchen appliances, and check that they're present and in good working order. This is particularly important if furniture and furnishings (and major appliances) were included in the price. You should also ensure that expensive items, such as kitchen appliances, haven't been substituted by inferior (possibly second-hand) items. Any fixtures and fittings (and garden plants and shrubs) present in a property when you viewed it should still be there when you take possession, unless otherwise stated in the contract.

If you find that anything is missing or damaged or isn't in working order, you should make a note and insist on immediate restitution, such as an appropriate reduction in the amount to be paid. In such cases it's normal for the notary or lawyer to delay the signing of the deed until the matter is settled, although an appropriate amount could be withheld from the vendor's proceeds to pay for repairs or replacements. **You should refuse to go through with the purchase if you aren't completely satisfied, as it will be difficult or impossible to obtain redress later.** If it isn't possible to complete the sale, you should consult your lawyer about your rights and the return of your deposit and any other funds already paid.

Signing: The final act of the sale is the signing of the deed of sale, which takes place in the notary's (Greece) or lawyer's (Cyprus) office. Before the deed of sale is signed, the notary or lawyer checks that the conditions contained in the contract have been met. It's normal for all parties to be present when the deed of sale is read, signed and witnessed by the notary, although either party can give someone a power of attorney to represent them. This is quite common among foreign buyers and sellers and can be arranged by your lawyer. If a couple buys a property in both their names, the wife can give the husband power of attorney (or vice versa). If a power of attorney cannot be arranged in Greece or Cyprus, it can be signed at a consulate in your home country, although this is more expensive than doing it abroad. The notary or lawyer reads through the deeds, and both the vendor and buyer (or their representatives) must sign it, indicating that they've understood and accept the terms of the document. If you don't understand Greek, you should take along an interpreter.

Payment: As stated under purchase contracts above, the origin of funds used to buy property in Greece must be declared to the Bank of Greece using an official import document. Similarly, foreign currency must be imported to pay for property in Cyprus, where an Import of Foreign Currency certificate is required by the Land Registry office. Proof that the funds have been imported must be produced at completion. The balance of the price (after the deposit and any mortgages are subtracted) must be paid by banker's draft or bank transfer. For most people the most convenient way is by banker's draft, which also means that you will have the payment in your possession (a bank cannot lose it!) and the notary can confirm it immediately. It also allows you to withhold payment if there's a last minute problem that cannot be resolved.

When the vendor and buyer are of the same foreign nationality, they can agree that the balance is paid in any currency and payment can also be made abroad. However, the deed of sale must state the sale price in local currency, as taxes are paid on this price. At the time of signing, both the vendor and buyer declare that payment has been made in the agreed foreign currency. In this case the payment should be held by an independent lawyer or solicitor in the vendor's or buyer's home country. After paying the money and receiving a receipt, the notary or lawyer will usually give you a copy of the deed showing that you're the new owner of the property. You will also receive the keys!

Registration: After the deed is signed, the original is lodged at the property registry office and the new owner's name is entered on the registry deed. It's important to send the signed deed to the property registry as soon as possible, although the actual registration may take some time. Only when the deed has been registered do you become the legal owner of the property.

RENOVATION & RESTORATION

Many old country or village homes purchased by foreigners in Greece and Cyprus are in need of total restoration, renovation or modernisation. Before buying a property requiring restoration, you should consider the alternatives. A relatively small extra sum spent on a purchase may represent better value than spending the money on building work. It's often cheaper to buy a restored or partly restored property than a ruin in need of total restoration, unless you're going to do most of the work yourself. The price of most restored properties doesn't reflect the cost and amount of work that went into them and many people who have restored a 'ruin' would never do it again and advise others against it. In general, the locals don't care for old homes and much prefer modern apartments and villas with all mod cons.

Inspections: It's vital to check a property for any obvious faults, particularly an old property. Most importantly, a building must have sound walls, without which it may be cheaper to erect a new building! Almost any other problem can be fixed or overcome (at a price). A sound roof that doesn't leak is desirable, as ensuring that a building is waterproof is the priority if funds are scarce. Don't believe a vendor or agent who tells you that a roof or anything else can be repaired or patched up, but obtain expert advice from a local builder. Sound roof timbers are also important as they can be expensive to replace. Old buildings often need a damp-proof course, timber treatment, new windows and doors, a new roof or extensive reroofing, a modern kitchen and bathroom, re-wiring and central heating. Electricity and mains water should already be connected, as they can be expensive to extend to a property in a remote area (this also applies to a telephone line). **If a house doesn't have electricity or mains water, it's important to check the cost of extending these services to it.** Many rural properties have a spring or well as their water supply, which is usually fine, but you should check the reliability of the water supply – wells can and do run dry! If you're seeking a waterside property, you should check the frequency of floods and, if commonplace, ensure that a building has been designed with floods in mind, e.g. with electrical installations above flood level and solid tiled floors.

Planning Permission & Building Permits: If modernisation of an old building involves making external alterations, such as building an extension or installing larger windows or new doorways, you will need planning permission from the local town hall. If you plan to do major restoration or building work, you should ensure that a conditional clause is included in the contract stating that the purchase is dependent on obtaining planning permission (copies of the applications must be sent to the notary or lawyer handling the sale). **Never start any building work before you have official permission.**

DIY or Builder: One of the first decisions you need to make regarding restoration or modernisation is whether to do all or most of the work yourself or have it done by professional builders or local artisans. A working knowledge of Greek is essential for DIY, especially the words associated with building materials and measurements (renovating a house in Greece will also greatly improve your ability to swear in Greek!). Note that when restoring a period property, it's important to have a sensitive approach to restoration. You should aim to retain as many of a building's original features as possible and stick to local building materials, reflecting the style of the property. When renovations and 'improvements' have been botched, there's often little that can be done except to start again from scratch. It's important not to over-modernise an old property, to the extent that much of its natural rustic charm and attraction is lost. Note that even if you intend to do most of the work yourself, you will still need to hire craftsmen for certain jobs. Bear in mind that it can be difficult to find good craftsmen, who are in high demand and short supply in some areas.

Finding a Builder: When looking for a builder, you should obtain recommendations from local people you can trust, e.g. neighbours and friends. Note that estate agents, lawyers and other professionals aren't always the best people to ask, as they may receive commissions. Always obtain references from previous customers. It may be better to use a local building consortium or contractor than a number of independent tradesmen, particularly if you won't be around to supervise them (although it will cost you a bit more). On the other hand, if you supervise the work yourself using local hand-picked craftsmen, you can save money and learn a great deal into the bargain.

Supervision: If you aren't on the spot and able to supervise work, you should hire a 'clerk of works' such as an architect to oversee it, particularly if it's a large job, or it can drag on for months (or years) or be left half-finished. This will add to the bill but is usually worthwhile. Be extremely careful whom you employ if you have work done in your absence, and ensure that your instructions are accurate in every detail. Always make certain that you understand exactly what has been agreed and, if necessary, get it in writing (with drawings). It isn't unknown for foreign owners to receive bills for work done in their absence that shouldn't have been done at all! **If you don't speak Greek, it's even more important to employ someone to oversee building work. Progressing on sign language and a few words of Greek is a recipe for disaster!** Being able to speak Cypriot Greek isn't so important, as most Cypriots speak English.

Quotations: Before buying a home abroad that needs restoration or modernisation, it's essential to obtain an accurate estimate of the work and costs involved. You should obtain written estimates from at least two builders before employing anyone. Note that for quotations to be accurate, you must detail exactly the work required (e.g. for electrical work this would include the number of lights, points and switches), and the quality of materials to be used. If you've only a vague idea of what you want, you will receive a vague and unreliable quotation. Make sure that a quotation includes everything you want done and that you fully understand it (if you don't, get it translated). You should fix a date for the start and completion of work and, if you can get a builder to agree to it, include a penalty for failing to finish on time. After signing a contract it's usual to pay a deposit, the amount of which depends on the size and cost of a job.

Cost: Building work such as electrical work, masonry and plumbing is costed by the square metre or metre. The cost of restoration depends on the type of work involved, the quality of materials used and the region. As a rough guide you should expect the cost of totally renovating an old 'habitable' building to be at least equal to its purchase price and possibly much more. How much you spend on restoring a property will depend on your purpose and the depth of your pockets. If you're restoring a property as an investment, it's easy to spend much more than you could ever hope to recoup when you sell it. On the other hand, if you're restoring a property as a holiday or permanent home, there's no limit to what you can do and how much money you can spend. Always keep an eye on your budget (which will inevitably be 25 per cent above or below your actual expenditure – usually below!) and don't be in too much of a hurry. Some people take many years to restore a holiday home, particularly when they're doing most of the work themselves. It isn't unusual for buyers to embark on a grandiose renovation scheme, only to run out of money before it's completed and be forced to sell at a loss.

Swimming Pools: It's common for foreign buyers to install a swimming pool at a detached home in Greece or Cyprus. If you're letting, this will greatly increase your rental prospects and the rent you can charge. Many self-catering holiday companies won't take on properties without a pool. There are many local swimming pool installation companies or you can buy and install one yourself. Above ground pools are the cheapest, but they're unsightly and recommended only for those who cannot afford anything better. A better option is a liner pool, which can be installed by anyone with basic DIY skills. A liner pool measuring 8 x 4 metres costs around €12,000/CY£8,000. A saline water option costs a bit more, but gives better quality water and offers lower maintenance costs. A concrete, fully-tiled pool of 8 x 4 metres costs from €12,000 to 17,500/CY£8,000 to 12,000 installed, including filtration and heating, and can be almost any shape. Note that you need planning permission to install a pool and should apply at least a few months in advance. Pools require regular maintenance and cleaning. If you have a holiday home or let a property, you will need to employ someone to maintain your pool (you may be able to get a local family to look after it in return for using it).

See also **Buying a Resale Home** on page 137, **Inspections & Surveys** on page 145, **Water** on page 162 and **Heating & Air-conditioning** on page 164.

MOVING HOUSE

After buying a home in Greece or Cyprus, it usually takes only a few weeks to have your belongings shipped from within continental Europe. From anywhere else it varies considerably, e.g. around four weeks from the east coast of America, six weeks from the west coast of America and the Far East, and around eight weeks from Australasia. Customs clearance is no longer necessary when shipping your household effects to Greece from another European Union (EU) country. However, when shipping your effects from a non-EU country to Greece or when shipping belongings to Cyprus from anywhere, you should enquire about customs formalities in advance. If you fail to follow the correct procedure, you can encounter problems and delays and may be erroneously charged duty or fined. The relevant forms to be completed may depend on whether your home will be your main residence or a second home. Removal companies usually take care of the paperwork and ensure that the correct documents are provided and properly completed (see **Customs** on page 176).

It's recommended to use a major shipping company with a good reputation. For international moves it's best to use a company that's a member of the International Federation of Furniture Removers (FIDI) or the Overseas Moving Network International (OMNI), with experience in Greece or Cyprus. Members of FIDI and OMNI usually subscribe to an advance payment scheme, which provides a guarantee whereby, if a member company fails to fulfil its commitments to a client, the removal is completed at the agreed cost by another company or your money is refunded. Some removal companies have local subsidiaries or affiliates, which may be more convenient if you encounter problems or need to make an insurance claim.

You should obtain at least three written quotations before choosing a company, as rates vary considerably. Removal companies should send a representative to provide a detailed quotation. Most companies will pack your belongings and provide packing cases and special containers, although this is naturally more expensive than packing them yourself. Ask a company how they pack fragile and valuable items, and whether the cost of packing cases, materials and insurance (see below) are included in a quotation. If you're doing your own packing, most shipping companies will provide packing crates and boxes. Shipments are charged by volume, e.g. the square metre in Europe and the square foot in the USA. You should expect to pay from €3,000 to 6,000/CY£2,000 to 4,000 to move the contents of a three to four-bedroom house within western Europe, e.g. from London to Athens or Nicosia. Note that you should obtain the maximum transit period in writing, otherwise you may have to wait months for delivery! .

Be sure to fully insure your belongings during removal with a well established insurance company. Don't insure with a shipping company that carries its own insurance, as it will usually fight every penny of a claim. Insurance premiums are usually 1 to 2 per cent of the declared value of your goods, depending on the type of cover chosen. It's prudent to make a photographic or video record of valuables for insurance purposes. Most insurance policies cover for 'all risks' on a replacement value basis. Note, however, that china, glass and other breakables can usually only be included in an all risks policy when they're packed by the removal company. Insurance usually covers total loss or loss of a particular crate only, rather than individual items (unless they were packed by the shipping company). If there are any breakages or damaged items, they should be noted and listed before you sign the delivery bill (although it's obviously impractical to check everything on delivery). If you need to make a claim, be sure to read the small print, as some companies require clients to make a claim within a few days, although seven is usual. Send a claim by registered mail. Some insurance companies apply an excess of around 1 per cent of the total shipment value when assessing claims. This means that if your shipment is valued at GB£20,000 and you make a claim for less than GB£200, you won't receive anything.

If you're unable to ship your belongings directly to Greece or Cyprus, most shipping companies will put them into storage and some offer a limited free-storage period prior to shipment, e.g. 14 days. **If you need to put your household effects into storage, it's important to have them fully insured, as warehouses have been known to burn down!** Make a complete list of everything to be moved and give a copy to the removal company. Don't include anything illegal, e.g. guns, bombs, drugs or pornography, with your belongings as customs checks can be rigorous and penalties severe. Provide the shipping company with *detailed* instructions how to find your home abroad from the nearest motorway or main road and a telephone number where you can be contacted. After considering the shipping costs, you may decide to ship only selected items of furniture and personal effects and buy new furniture locally. If you're taking pets with you, you may need to get your vet to tranquillise them, as many pets are frightened (even more than people) by the chaos and stress of moving house.

Bear in mind when moving home that everything that can go wrong often does, so allow plenty of time and try not to arrange your move to your new home on the same day as the previous owner is moving out. That's just asking for fate to intervene! **Last but not least, if your home abroad has poor or impossible access for a large truck you must inform the shipping company (the ground must also be firm enough to support a heavy vehicle).** Note that if your belongings need to be transferred to a smaller vehicle at the end of the road or carried a long distance or if large items of furniture need to be taken in through an upstairs window or via a balcony, you may need to pay extra. See also **Customs** on page 176 and the **Checklist** on page 179.

HOME SECURITY

When moving into a new home, it's often wise to replace the locks (or lock barrels) as soon as possible, as you will have no idea how many keys are in circulation for the existing locks. This is true even for new homes, as builders often give keys to sub-contractors. In any case, you should change the external lock barrels regularly, e.g. annually, particularly if you let a home. If they aren't already fitted, it's best to fit high security (double cylinder or dead bolt) locks. In areas with a high risk of theft, e.g. most resort areas and major cities, your insurance company may insist on extra security measures such as two locks on external doors, internal locking shutters, and security bars or metal grilles on windows and patio doors on ground, first and second floors of buildings. A policy may specify that all forms of protection on doors must be employed when a property is unoccupied.

You may wish to have a security alarm fitted, which is usually the best way to deter thieves and may also reduce your household insurance (see page 51 Ideally it should include all external doors and windows or have internal infra-red security beams. It may include a coded entry keypad (which can be frequently changed and is useful for clients if you let) and 24-hour monitoring. With some systems it's possible to monitor properties remotely via a computer from another country. With a monitored system, when a sensor detects an emergency, e.g. smoke or forced entry, or a panic button is pushed, a signal is sent automatically to a 24-hour monitoring station. The person on duty will telephone to check whether it's a genuine alarm and if he cannot contact you or someone gives the wrong code, a security guard will be sent to investigate.

You can deter thieves by ensuring that your house is well lit at night and not conspicuously unoccupied. External security 'motion detector' or PIR lights (that switch on automatically when someone approaches), random timed switches for internal lights, radios and TVs, dummy security cameras, and tapes that play barking dogs (etc.) triggered by a light or heat detector may all help deter burglars. In rural areas, it's common for owners to fit two or three locks on external doors, alarm systems, grilles on doors and windows, window locks, security shutters and a safe for valuables. The advantage of grilles is that they allow you to leave windows open without inviting criminals in (unless they're *very* slim). Note, however, that security grilles must be heavy duty, as the bars on cheap grilles can be prised apart. Many people also wrap a chain around their patio or balcony grilles and secure them with a padlock when a property is unoccupied (although it might not withstand bolt-cutters). You can fit UPVC (toughened clear plastic) security windows and doors, which can survive an attack with a sledge-hammer without damage, and external steel security blinds (which can be electrically operated), although these are expensive. A dog can be useful to deter intruders, although it should be kept inside where it cannot be given poisoned food. Irrespective of whether you actually have a dog, a warning sign showing an image of a fierce dog may act as a deterrent. You should have the front door of an apartment fitted with a spy-hole and chain so that you can check the identity of visitors before opening the door.

Holiday homes are particularly vulnerable to thieves, especially in rural areas, and are occasionally ransacked. No matter how secure your door and window locks, a thief can usually gain entry if he is sufficiently determined, often by smashing a window or even breaking in through the roof or by knocking a hole in a wall in a rural area! In isolated areas, thieves can strip a house bare at their leisure and an un-monitored alarm won't be a deterrent if there's no-one around to hear it. If you have a holiday home, you shouldn't leave anything of real value (monetary or sentimental) there and should have full insurance for your belongings (see page 53). One guaranteed way to protect a home when you're away is to employ a house-sitter to look after it. This can be done for short periods or for six months, e.g. during the winter, or longer if you have a holiday home. It isn't usually necessary to pay someone to house-sit for a period of six months or more, when you can usually find someone to do it in return for free accommodation. However, you must take care whom you engage and obtain references. **Remember, prevention is always better than cure, as stolen property is rarely recovered.**

An important aspect of home security is making sure that you have an early warning of a fire by installing smoke detectors, which should be tested periodically to ensure that the batteries aren't exhausted. You can also fit an electric-powered gas detector that activates an alarm when a gas leak is detected. When closing up a property for an extended period, e.g. over the winter, you should ensure that everything is switched off and that it's secure. If you vacate your home for a long period, you may also be obliged to notify a caretaker, landlord or insurance company, and to leave a key with a caretaker or landlord in case of emergencies. If you have a robbery, you should report it immediately to your local police station where you must make a statement. You will receive a copy, which is required by your insurance company if you make a claim.

There are many specialist home security companies in Greece and Cyprus who will inspect your home and offer free advice on security, although you should obtain at least two quotations before having any work done.

UTILITIES

Electricity

Electricity in Greece and Cyprus is provided by *Dimmossia Steria Ilektrismou* (DEH) and the Electricity Authority of Cyprus (EAC) respectively, both of which are monopolies, although the EAC is a non-profit making company. However, deregulation started in February 2001 in Greece, introducing some much-needed competition, which is obligatory under EU law.

Registration: Immediately after buying a property, you must sign a contract with the local electricity company. This usually entails a visit to the company's office. You need to take with you some identification, e.g. passport, your tax number in Greece and proof of rental or purchase of a property, e.g. your land registry number in Cyprus. The estate agent may arrange for the utilities to be transferred to your name or go with you to the electricity company's office (no charge should be made for this service). Make sure all previous bills have been paid and that the contract is put into your name from the day you take over, or you will be liable for debts left by the previous owner. If you're a non-resident owner, you should also give your foreign address in case there are any problems requiring your attention, such as a bank failing to pay the bills.

Power Supply: The electricity supply in Greece and Cyprus is 220–240 volts AC with a frequency of 50 Hertz (cycles). Power cuts are frequent in some areas of Greece (almost daily) and last from a few micro-seconds (just long enough to crash a computer) to a few hours. If you use a computer, it's sensible to fit an uninterrupted power supply (UPS) with a battery back-up, which allows you time to save your work and shut down your computer after a power failure. If you live in an area where cuts are frequent and rely on electricity for your livelihood, you may need to install a back-up generator. **Even more important than a battery back-up is a power surge protector for appliances such as TVs, computers and fax machines, without which you risk having equipment damaged or destroyed.** In remote rural areas of Greece you will need to install a generator if you want electricity, as there's no mains electricity, although some people make do with gas and oil lamps (and without television and other modern conveniences). Note that in some developments, water is provided by electric pump, so if your electricity supply fails, your water supply is also cut off.

Converters & Transformers: If you have electrical equipment rated at 110 volts AC (for example, from the USA) you will require a converter or a step-down transformer to convert the 220 volt supply. However, some electrical appliances are fitted with a 110/220-volt switch. Check for the switch, which may be inside the casing, and make sure it's switched to 220 volts *before* connecting it to the power supply.

Converters can be used for heating appliances, but transformers are required for motorised appliances. Total the wattage of the devices you intend to connect to a transformer and make sure that its power rating *exceeds* this sum.

Generally, small, high-wattage, electrical appliances, such as kettles, toasters, heaters, and irons need large transformers. Motors in large appliances such as cookers, refrigerators, washing machines, dryers and dishwashers will need replacing or fitting with a large transformer. In most cases it's simpler to buy new appliances locally, which are of good quality and reasonably priced. Note also that the dimensions of cookers, microwave ovens, refrigerators, washing machines, dryers and dishwashers purchased abroad may differ from those in Greece or Cyprus, so they may not fit into a local kitchen.

An additional problem with some electrical equipment is the frequency rating, which, in some countries, e.g. the USA, is designed to run at 60 Hertz (Hz) and not Europe's 50Hz. Electrical equipment *without* a motor is generally unaffected by the drop in frequency to 50Hz (except televisions). Equipment with a motor may run with a 20 per cent drop in speed, but automatic washing machines, cookers, electric clocks, record players and tape recorders must be converted from 60Hz to 50Hz. To find out, look at the label on the back of the equipment. If it says 50/60Hz, there shouldn't be a problem; if it says 60Hz, you can try it, **but first ensure that the voltage is correct as outlined above.** Bear in mind that the transformers and motors of electrical devices designed to run at 60Hz will run hotter at 50Hz, so make sure that apparatus has sufficient space around it for cooling.

Wiring Standards: Most modern properties, e.g. less than 20 years old, have good electrical installations. You should ensure that the electricity installations are in good condition well in advance of moving house, as it can take some time to get a new meter installed or to be reconnected.

Meters: All detached homes have their own electricity meters. Meters for apartment blocks or community properties may be installed in a basement or in a meter 'cupboard' under the stairs or outside a group of properties. You should have free access to your meter and should be able read it (some meters don't have a window to allow you to read the consumption).

Plugs & Fuses: Depending on the country you've come from, you will usually need new plugs or a lot of adapters. Greece uses two-pin plugs, with or without earth points, as in many other European countries, while Cyprus has British-style, flat three-pin plugs with an earth pin. Therefore imported British appliances can be used in Cyprus without adapters or new plugs. Plug adapters can be purchased in Greece or Cyprus, although it's wise to bring some adapters with you, plus extension cords and multi-plug extensions that can be fitted with local plugs. There's often a shortage of electric points in homes, with perhaps just one per room (including the kitchen), so multi-plug adapters may be essential. Small low-wattage electrical appliances such as table lamps, small TVs and computers, don't require an earth. However, plugs with an earth must always be used for high-wattage appliances such as fires, kettles, washing machines and refrigerators. Electrical appliances that are earthed have a three-core wire and must never be used with a two-pin plug without an earth socket. **Always make sure that a plug is correctly and securely wired, as bad wiring can be fatal.**

In modern properties, fuses are of the circuit breaker type. When there's a short circuit or the system has been overloaded, a circuit breaker is tripped and the power supply is cut. If your electricity fails, you should suspect a fuse of tripping off, particularly if you've just switched on an electrical appliance (usually you will hear the power switch off). Before reconnecting the power, switch off any high-power appliances such as a stove, washing machine or dishwasher. Make sure you know where the trip switches are located and keep a torch handy so you can find them in the dark.

Gas

Mains gas is available only in Athens; in other towns and rural areas in Greece you will need to use gas bottles. There's no mains gas in Cyprus. Bottled gas costs around €4.50/CY£3 for a 10kg bottle, which will last an average family around a month when used just for cooking. In rural areas, many people use as many gas appliances as possible, e.g. for cooking, hot water and heating. You can have a combined gas hot water and heating system (providing background heat) installed, which is relatively inexpensive as well as being cheap to run. Bear in mind that gas bottles are heavy and have a habit of running out at the most inconvenient times, so keep a spare bottle handy and make sure you know how to change them (get the previous owner or a neighbour to show you).

Water

Water, or rather the lack of it, is a major concern in Greece and Cyprus and the price paid for all those sunny days. Shortages are exacerbated by poor infrastructure (much is lost from leaking pipes), wastage due to poor irrigation methods, and the huge influx of visitors to resort areas where the local population swells five to tenfold during the summer tourist season (the hottest and driest period of the year). **As in all hot countries, water is a precious resource and not something simply to pour down the drain!** Contact the local town hall for information about the local water supply and to transfer bills to your name. Water is particularly expensive in Greece, where bills increase frequently.

Restrictions: During water shortages, local municipalities may restrict water consumption or cut off supplies altogether for days at a time. You can forget about watering the garden or washing your car unless you have a private water supply. If a water company needs to cut off your supply, e.g. to carry out maintenance work on pipes or installations, it will usually notify you in advance so that you can store water for cooking. In some areas, water shortages can create low water pressure, resulting in insufficient water to take a bath or shower and sometimes no water at all on the upper floors of apartment buildings. Note that in some developments, water is provided by electric pump and therefore if your electricity is cut off, so is your water supply. In communal developments, the tap to turn water on or off is usually located outside properties, so if your water goes off suddenly you should check that someone hasn't switched it off by mistake. In areas where water shortages are common, water tankers deliver to homes – some properties don't have a mains supply at all, but a storage tank that's filled periodically by a tanker.

Check the Supply: One of the most important tasks before buying a home abroad is to investigate the reliability of the local water supply (over a number of years) and the cost. Ask your prospective neighbours and other local residents for information. In most towns and cities, supplies are adequate, although there may be cuts in summer. In rural areas there are often severe shortages in summer unless you have your own well. Note that a well containing water in winter may be bone dry in summer and you may have no rights to extract water from a channel running alongside your land. Dowsing or divining (finding water by holding a piece of forked wood) is as accurate as anything devised by modern science (it has an 80 per cent success rate) and a good dowser can also estimate the water's yield and purity with 80 or 90 per cent accuracy. Before buying land without a water supply, engage an experienced dowser with a successful track record to check it.

Storage Tanks: If you have a detached house or villa, you can reduce your water costs by collecting and storing rainwater, and by having a storage tank installed. Tanks can be roof mounted or installed underground; the latter are cheaper and can be any size but require an electric pump. Check whether a property has a water storage tank or whether you can install one. Most modern properties have storage tanks and these are usually large enough to last a family of four around a week or even longer with careful use. It's also possible to use recycled water from baths, showers, kitchens and apparatus such as washing machines and dishwashers, to flush toilets or water a garden.

Hot Water: Water heating in apartments may be provided by a central heating source for the whole building, or apartments may have their own water heaters. Many holiday homes have quite small water boilers, which are inadequate for more than two people. If you install your own water heater, it should have a capacity of at least 75 litres (sufficient for two people). If you need to install a water heater (or fit a larger one), you should consider the merits of both electric and bottled gas heaters.

A 75l electric water boiler usually takes between 60 and 90 minutes to heat water to 40 degrees in winter. A gas flow-through water heater is more expensive to purchase and install than an electric water boiler but gives you unlimited hot water immediately whenever you want it and there are no standing charges. Make sure that a gas heater has a capacity of 10 to 16 litres per minute if you want it for a shower. Note that a gas water heater with a permanent flame may use up to 50 per cent more gas than one without one. A resident family with regular water consumption is better off with an electric heater operating on the night tariff, while non-residents using a property for short periods will find a self-igniting gas heater more economical. Solar energy can also be used to provide hot water (see page 164) and many modern homes have a combined solar/electric water heater.

Water Quality: Water is supposedly safe to drink in all urban areas, although it can be of poor quality (possibly brown or rust coloured), full of chemicals and taste awful. Many residents prefer to drink bottled water. In rural areas, water may be extracted from mountain springs and taste excellent, although the quality standards applied in cities are usually ignored and it may be of poor quality. Water in rural areas may also be contaminated by fertilisers and nitrates used in farming, and by salt water in some coastal areas. If you're in any doubt about the quality of your water, you should have it analysed. **Note that, although boiling water will kill any bacteria, it won't remove any toxic substances contained in it.** You can install filtering, cleansing and softening equipment to improve its quality or a water purification unit to provide drinking water. Note, however, that purification systems operating on the reverse osmosis system waste three times as much water as they produce. Obtain expert advice before installing a system, as not all are effective.

HEATING & AIR-CONDITIONING

If you're used to central heating and like a warm house in winter, you will probably want central heating in Greece or Cyprus during winter, even in the warmest areas. Central heating systems may be powered by oil, gas, electricity, solid fuel (usually wood) or even solar power – see below. Whatever form of heating you use, it's important to have good insulation, without which around half of the heat generated is lost through the walls and roof. Note that many homes, particularly older and cheaper properties but also new ones, don't have good insulation and builders don't always adhere to current regulations. In cities, apartment blocks may have a communal central heating system which provides heating for all apartments, the cost of which is divided among the tenants.

Oil & Solid Fuel Heating: Oil-fired central heating isn't common because of the high cost of oil and the problems associated with storage and delivery. In rural areas, many houses have open, wood-burning fireplaces and stoves, which may be combined with a central heating system.

Electric Heating: Electric heating isn't particularly common, as it's expensive and requires good insulation and a permanent system of ventilation. You should avoid totally electric heating in regions with a cold winter, as the bills can be astronomical, although night-storage heaters operating on a night tariff can be economical. Some stand-alone electric heaters are expensive to run and are best suited to holiday homes. An electric air-conditioning system (see below) with a heat pump provides cooling in summer and economical heating in winter.

Gas Heating: Stand-alone gas heaters using standard gas bottles are an inexpensive way of providing heating in areas with mild winters. Note that gas heaters must be used only in rooms with adequate ventilation and it can be dangerous to have too large a difference between indoor and outdoor temperatures. Gas poisoning due to faulty ventilation ducts for gas heaters, e.g. in bathrooms, isn't uncommon. It's possible to install a central heating system operating from standard gas bottles (Primus of Sweden is one of the leading manufacturers).

Solar Heating: The use of solar energy to provide hot water and heating (with a hot-air solar radiator) is relatively rare in Greece and Cyprus, although on the increase. The amount of energy provided by the sun each year is equivalent to eleven gas bottles per square metre – the sun provides around 8,000 times the world's present energy requirements annually! A solar power system can be used to supply all your energy needs, although it's usually combined with an electric or gas heating system, as it cannot usually be relied upon for year-round heating and hot water. Solar power can also be used to provide electricity in a remote rural home, where the cost of extending mains electricity is prohibitive, or to heat a swimming pool.

The main drawback is the high cost of installation, which varies considerably according to the region and how much energy you require. A 400-litre hot-water system costs around €3,000/CY£2,000 and must be installed by an expert. The advantages are no running costs, silent and maintenance-free operation, and no (or very small) electricity bills. A system should last 30 years (it's usually guaranteed for ten years) and can be uprated to provide additional power in the future. Advances in solar cell and battery technology are expected to dramatically increase the efficiency and reduce the cost of solar power, which is expected to become the main source of energy world-wide in the next century.

Air-conditioning: In summer, the temperature in Greece frequently exceeds 40°C (104°F) and it's often over 30°C (86°F) in Cyprus. Properties are built to withstand the heat, but you may wish to install air-conditioning. You can choose from a huge variety of air-conditioners: fixed or moveable; indoor or outdoor installation; high or low power. Expect to pay around €1,500/CY£1,000 for a unit sufficient to cool an average size room. An air-conditioning system with a heat pump and outside compressor provides cooling in summer and economical heating in winter. Many people fit ceiling fans for extra cooling in summer (costing from around €35/CY£25), which are standard fixtures in some new homes. Note that air-conditioning can have negative effects if you suffer from asthma or respiratory problems.

Humidifiers: Central heating dries the air and may cause your family to develop coughs and other ailments. Those who find dry air unpleasant can install humidifiers. These range from simple water containers hung from radiators to electric or battery-operated devices. Humidifiers that don't generate steam should be disinfected occasionally with a special liquid available from chemists (to prevent the build-up of bacteria).

PROPERTY INCOME

Many people planning to buy a holiday home in Greece or Cyprus are interested in owning a property that will provide them with an income, e.g. from letting, to cover the running costs and help with mortgage payments. Note, however, that foreign property owners aren't permitted to let their homes in Cyprus, although the rule isn't strictly enforced and many foreigners do. **In any case, you're highly unlikely to meet your mortgage payments and running costs from rental income.** Buyers who over-stretch their financial resources often find themselves on the rental treadmill, constantly struggling to raise sufficient income to cover their running costs and mortgage payments. In the early '90s many foreign homeowners lost their holiday homes after defaulting on their mortgage payments, often because rental income failed to meet expectations. Note that it's difficult to make a living providing holiday accommodation in most areas, as the season is too short and there's simply too much competition (the market is saturated in most regions). The good news is that the letting season can be up to 24 weeks or longer in the Greek islands and Cyprus, although the rental market isn't as well developed as in many other popular European holiday destinations, such as France and Spain. If you're buying as an investment, bear in mind that buying property abroad isn't usually a good investment compared with the return on income that can be achieved by investing elsewhere and **most experts recommend that you shouldn't purchase a home abroad if you need to rely heavily on rental income to pay for it.** On the other hand, letting a home for just a few weeks in the summer can recoup your running costs and pay for your holidays. See also **Renting** on page 127.

Taxation: Rental income earned by individuals (and companies) in Greece is subject to income tax and rental income must be declared annually. Rates in 2001 ranged from 5 to 42.5 per cent. Rental payments are also subject to stamp duty, calculated at 3.6 per cent and payable monthly. At present rental payments aren't subject to VAT. See **Income Tax** on page 86 for further information on tax liability.

Location & Facilities: If income from your Greek home is a high priority, you should buy a property with this in mind. To maximise rental income a property should be located as close as possible to the main attractions and/or a beach, be suitably furnished and professionally managed. A swimming pool is obligatory in most areas, as properties with pools are much easier to let than those without, unless a property is situated on a beach, lake or river. It's usually necessary to have a private pool with a single-family home, although a shared pool is adequate for an apartment or townhouse. You can charge a higher rent for a property with a private pool and it may be possible to extend the season by installing a heated or indoor pool. Some private letting agencies won't handle properties without a pool.

Rents: Rental rates vary considerably according to the season, the region, and the size and quality of a property. An average apartment or townhouse sleeping four to six in an average area can be let for between €300 and 600 per week, depending on the season, location and quality. At the other extreme, a luxury villa in a popular area with a pool and accommodation for 8 to 12 can be let for €1,500 to 3,000 per week in the high season. The high season includes the months of July and August and possibly the first two weeks of September. The mid-season usually comprises June, late September and October (and sometimes also the Easter and Christmas periods), when rents are around 25 per cent lower than in high season; the rest of the year is usually the low season, which may extend from October to May, when rates are usually up to 50 per cent lower than in high season. In winter, rents may drop as low as €75 to 150 per week for a two-bedroom apartment, although there may be a minimum let of around two months. Note that rates usually include linen, gas and electricity, although electricity and heating, e.g. gas bottles, are usually charged extra in winter.

Furnishings & Keys: If you let a property, don't fill it with expensive furnishings or valuable personal belongings. While theft is rare, items will eventually be damaged or broken. When furnishing a property that you plan to let, you should choose hard-wearing, dark coloured carpets, which won't show stains, and buy durable furniture and furnishings. Simple, inexpensive furniture is best in a modest home, as it will need to stand up to hard wear. Two-bedroom properties should have a settee in the living room that converts into a double bed and properties should generally be well equipped with cooking utensils, crockery and cutlery. It's also usual to provide bed linen and towels, and you may need a cot or high-chair for young children. Depending on the price and quality of a property, your guests may also expect central heating, a washing machine, a dishwasher, a microwave, covered parking, a barbecue and garden furniture. Some owners provide bicycles and badminton and table-tennis equipment. It isn't usual to have a telephone in rental homes, although you could install a pay phone or one that will receive incoming calls only.

You will need several sets of spare keys, as keys inevitably get lost at some time. If you employ a management company, its address should be on the key fob and *not* the address of the house. If you let a home yourself, you can use a 'key-finder' service, whereby lost keys can be returned to the key-finder company by anyone finding them. You should ensure that you get 'lost' keys returned, otherwise you may need to change the lock barrels (in any case it's sensible to change them annually if you let a home). You don't need to provide clients with keys to all external doors, only the front door (the others can be left inside). If you arrange your own letting, you can mail keys to clients in your home country; otherwise they can be collected from a local caretaker. It's also possible to install a key-pad entry system, the code of which can be changed after each let.

Although the law is on your side, you should be aware that if a tenant with a short-term rental contract refuses to leave, it can take months to have him evicted. Note also that if you receive rent and accept a lessee without protest, you're usually deemed to have entered into a contractual relationship, even if there's no written contract.

Letting Agents: If you're letting a second home, the most important decision is whether to let it yourself or use a letting agent (or agents). If you don't have much spare time, you're better off using an agent, who will take care of everything and save you the time and trouble of advertising and finding clients. An agent will charge commission of between 20 and 40 per cent of gross rental income, although some of this can be recouped through higher rents. If you want your property to appear in an agent's catalogue, you must contact him the summer before you wish to let it (the deadline is usually September). Note that, although self-catering holiday companies may fall over themselves to take on a luxury property in Greece or Cyprus, the top letting agents turn down most properties they're offered.

Most agents don't permit owners to use a property during the peak letting season (July and August) and may also restrict their use at other times. There are numerous self-catering holiday companies operating in Greece and Cyprus, and many local estate agents also act as letting agents for holiday and long-term lets. **Take care when selecting an agent, as it isn't unknown for them to go bust.** You should ensure that your income is kept in an escrow account and paid regularly or, even better, choose an agent with a bonding scheme who pays you the rent *before* the arrival of guests (some do). It's absolutely essential to employ a reliable and honest (preferably long-established) company, as anyone can set up a holiday letting agency and there are many 'cowboy' operators. Always ask a management company to substantiate rental income claims and occupancy rates by showing you examples of actual income received from other properties. Ask for the names of satisfied customers and check with them.

Other things to ask a letting agent include who they let to, where they advertise, whether they have contracts with holiday and travel companies, whether you're expected to contribute towards advertising and marketing costs, and whether you're free to let the property yourself and use it when you wish. The larger companies market homes via newspapers, magazines, overseas agents and direct mail and have representatives in a number of countries. Management contracts usually run for a year and should include arranging routine and emergency repairs, reading meters (if electricity is charged extra), general maintenance of house and garden, including lawn cutting and pool cleaning, arranging cleaning and linen changes between lets, advising guests on the use of equipment, and providing guests with information and assistance (24 hours a day in the case of emergencies). Agents may also provide someone to meet and greet clients, hand over keys and check that everything is in order.

The extent of the services provided will usually depend on whether a property is a basic apartment or a luxury villa costing €1,500 or more a week. A letting agent's representative should also make periodic checks when a property is empty to ensure that it's secure and that everything is in order. Note that when letting a property short-term, you must check that it's permitted under the community rules and you may also be required to notify your insurance company.

Doing Your Own Letting: Some owners prefer to let a property to family, friends, colleagues and acquaintances, which allows them more control (with luck the property will also be better looked after). In fact, the best way to get a high volume of lets is usually to do it yourself, although many owners use a letting agency in addition to doing their own marketing in their home country. If you wish to let a property yourself, there's a wide range of local and foreign newspapers and magazines in which you can advertise, e.g. *Dalton's Weekly* and newspapers such as the *Sunday Times* and *Sunday Telegraph* in Britain. Many of the English-language newspapers and magazines listed in **Appendix A** also include advertisements from property owners. You will need to experiment to find the best publications and days of the week or months to advertise.

There are also companies that produce directories of properties let directly by owners, e.g. Private Villas (☎ UK 01564-794011) in Britain, where you pay for the advertisement and handle bookings yourself. Regional tourist agencies can put you in touch with local letting agents. You can also advertise among friends and colleagues, in company and club magazines (which may even be free), and on notice boards in companies, stores and public places. The more marketing you do, the more income you're likely to earn. It also pays to work with other local people in the same business and send surplus guests to competitors (they will usually reciprocate). It isn't necessary to restrict your advertising to your local area or even your home country, as you can extend your marketing abroad (or advertise via the Internet). However, it's usually necessary to have a telephone answering machine and possibly a fax machine.

To get an idea of the rent you should charge, simply ring a few letting agencies and ask them what it would cost to rent a property such as yours at the time of year you plan to let it. They're likely to quote the highest rent you can charge. You should also check the advertisements in newspapers and magazines. Set a realistic rent, as there's usually a lot of competition. Add a returnable deposit, e.g. €150, as security against loss of keys and breakages. A deposit should be refundable up to six weeks before the booking, after which it's forfeited. It's normal to have a minimum two-week rental period in July and August. You will need a simple agreement form that includes the dates of arrival and departure and approximate times. Note that if you plan to let to non-English speaking clients, you may need to get your letting agreement translated into their language.

If you plan to let a home yourself, you will need to decide how to handle enquiries about flights and car rentals. It's easier to let clients make bookings themselves, but you should be able to offer advice and put them in touch with airlines, ferry companies, travel agents and car rental companies. You will also need to decide whether you want to let to smokers and whether to accept pets and young children – some people don't let to families with children under five owing to the risk of bed-wetting. It's usually best to provide linen (some agents provide a linen hire service), which is generally expected, and electricity is also usually included in the rental fee.

It's best to produce a coloured brochure containing external/internal pictures (or a single colour brochure with coloured photographs affixed to it, although this doesn't look professional), important details, the exact location, information about local attractions, details of how to get there (with a map), and the name, address and telephone number of your local caretaker or letting agent. You should enclose a stamped addressed envelope when sending out leaflets. It's necessary to make a home look as attractive as possible in a brochure without distortion of the facts or misrepresentation. Advertise honestly and don't over-sell your property.

Local Information: You should also provide an information pack in your home including: an explanation of how things work, e.g. heating and air-conditioning; security measures; what not to do; where to shop; recommended restaurants; local emergency numbers and health services such as doctors, hospitals and dentists; and where to find assistance such as a general repairman, plumber, electrician and pool maintenance company. If you allow young children and pets, you should make a point of emphasising any dangers, such as falling into the pool (which should, in any case, be protected). It's also beneficial to have a visitor's book where your clients can write their comments and recommendations. If you want to impress your guests, you may wish to arrange for fresh flowers, fruit, a good bottle of wine and a grocery pack to greet them on their arrival. It's little touches like this that ensure repeat business and recommendations. If you go 'the extra mile', it will pay off and you may even find after the first year or two that you rarely need to advertise. Many people return to the same property each year and you should do an annual mail-shot to previous clients and send them some brochures. **Word-of-mouth advertising is the cheapest and always the best.**

Caretaker: If you own a second home abroad, you will find it beneficial or even essential to employ a local caretaker, irrespective of whether you let it. You can have your caretaker prepare the house for your family and guests as well as looking after it when it isn't in use. If you have a holiday home abroad, it's wise to have your caretaker check it periodically, e.g. weekly, and give him the authority to carry out repairs. If you let a property yourself, your caretaker can arrange for (or do) cleaning, linen changes, maintenance and repairs, bill paying and gardening (you may need to employ a gardener as well). If you employ a caretaker or housekeeper you should expect to pay at least the minimum local hourly wage.

Increasing Rental Income: It's possible to increase rental income outside the high season by offering special interest or package holidays, which could be organised in conjunction with other local businesses in order to broaden a property's appeal and cater for larger parties. These may include activities such as golf, tennis, cycling or hiking, cooking, gastronomy and wine tasting, and arts and crafts such as painting, sculpture, photography and writing courses. You don't need to be an expert or conduct courses yourself, but can employ someone to do it for you.

Long-term Furnished Lets: To maximise low season rental income, you may decide to offer lets of one to six months, although you shouldn't expect to earn more than around €150 per week in most regions for a property sleeping four to six. The tenant usually pays for electricity and heating, which is essential if you want to let long-term in some areas.

Closing a Property for the Winter: Before closing a property for the winter, you should turn off the water at the mains (required by insurance companies) and drain pipes, remove fuses (except the one for a dehumidifier or air-conditioner if you leave it on while you're away), empty the food cupboards and the refrigerator/freezer, disconnect gas cylinders and empty dustbins. You should also leave the interior doors and a few small windows (with grilles or secure shutters) open to provide ventilation. Lock the doors and shutters, and secure anything of value against theft or leave it with a neighbour or friend. Check whether any essential work needs to be done before you leave and, if necessary, arrange for it to be done in your absence. Most importantly, leave a set of keys with a neighbour or have a caretaker check your home periodically.

SELLING A HOME

Although this book is primarily concerned with buying homes in Greece or Cyprus, you may wish to sell your home at some time in the future. Before offering your home for sale, you should investigate the property market. For example, unless you're forced to, you shouldn't think of selling during a property slump when prices are depressed. It may be wiser to let your home long-term and wait until the market has recovered. It's also unwise to sell in the early years after purchase, when you will probably make a loss (unless the property was an absolute bargain). Having decided to sell, your first decision will be whether to sell it yourself (or try) or use the services of an estate agent. Although the majority of resale properties are sold by estate agents, a large number of people sell their own homes. If you need to sell a property before buying a new one, this must be included as a conditional clause (see page 150) in the contract when buying a new home.

Price: It's important to bear in mind that property, like everything, has a market price, and the best way of ensuring a quick sale (or any sale) is to ask a realistic price. In the early to mid-'90s when prices plummeted and buyers dried up, many properties remained on the market for years largely because owners asked absurd prices. As in most countries, it's easier to sell a cheaper property, e.g. one priced below €75,000/CY£50,000, than an expensive property. However, there's also a strong and constant demand for villas priced between €150,000 and 300,000/CY£100,000 to 200,000, particularly if they're exceptionally attractive and in a popular area or a superb location.

If your home's fairly standard for the area, you can find out its value by comparing the prices of other homes on the market or those that have recently been sold. Most agents will provide a free appraisal of a home's value in the hope that you will sell it through them. However, don't believe everything they tell you, as they may over-price it simply to encourage you. You can also hire a professional valuer to determine the market value. You should be prepared to drop the price slightly, e.g. 5 or 10 per cent, and should set it accordingly, but shouldn't grossly over-price a home, which will deter buyers. Don't reject an offer out of hand unless it's ridiculously low, as you may be able to get a prospective buyer to raise his offer. When selling a second home, you may wish to include the furnishings (plus major appliances) in the sale, which is a common practice in resort areas when selling a relatively inexpensive second home with modest furnishings. You should add an appropriate amount to the price to cover the value of the furnishings; alternatively, you can use them as an inducement to a prospective buyer at a later stage, although this isn't normal practice.

Presentation: The secret to selling a home quickly lies in its presentation (assuming that it's competitively priced). First impressions (both exterior and interior) are vital when marketing a property and it's important to present it in its best light and make it as attractive as possible to potential buyers. It may pay to invest in new interior decoration, new carpets, exterior paint and landscaping. A few plants and flowers can do wonders. Note that when decorating a home for resale, it's important to be conservative and not do anything radical, such as installing a red or black bathroom suite or painting the walls purple. White is a good neutral colour for walls, woodwork and porcelain.

It may also pay you to do some modernisation such as installing a new kitchen or bathroom, as these are of vital importance (particularly kitchens) when selling a home. Note, however, that although modernisation may be necessary to sell an old home, you shouldn't overdo it, as it's easy to spend more than you could ever hope to recoup on the sale price. If you're using an agent, you can ask him what you should do (or need to do) to help sell your home. If a home is in poor repair, this must be reflected in the asking price and if major work is needed that you cannot afford, you should obtain a quotation (or two) and offer to knock this off the price.

Selling Your Own Home: While certainly not for everyone, selling your own home is a viable option for many people and is particularly recommended when you're selling an attractive home in a favourable market. It may allow you to offer it at a more appealing price, which could be an important factor if you're seeking a quick sale. How you market your home will depend on the type of property, the price, and the country or area from where you expect your buyer to come. For example, if your property isn't of a type and style or in an area that's desirable to local inhabitants, it's usually a waste of time advertising it in the local press.

Marketing: Marketing is the key to selling your home. The first step is to get a professional looking 'for sale' sign made (showing your telephone number) and erect it in the garden or place it in a window. Do some research into the best newspapers and magazines for advertising your property (see **Appendix A**), and place an advertisement in those that look most promising. You could also have a leaflet printed (with pictures) extolling the virtues of your property, which you could drop into local letter boxes or have distributed with a local newspaper (many people buy a new home in the vicinity of their present home). You may also need a printed fact sheet (if your home's vital statistics aren't included in the leaflet mentioned above) and could offer a 'reward', e.g. €750/CY£500, to anyone who finds you a buyer. Don't forget to market your home through local companies, schools and organisations, particularly if they have many foreign employees. Finally, it may help to provide information about local financing sources for potential buyers. With a bit of effort and practice you may even make a better job of marketing your home than an estate agent! Unless you're in a hurry to sell, set yourself a realistic time limit for success, after which you can try an agent. When selling a home yourself, you will need to draft a contract or engage a lawyer to do it for you.

Using An Agent: Most owners prefer to use the services of an agent or agents, either in Greece or Cyprus or their home country, e.g. when selling a second home. If you purchased the property through an agent, it's often wise to use the same agent when selling, as he will already be familiar with it and may still have the details on file. You should take particular care when selecting an agent, as they vary considerably in their professionalism, expertise and experience (the best way to investigate agents is by posing as a buyer). Note that many agents cover a relatively small area, so you should take care to choose one who regularly sells properties in your area and price range. If you own a property in an area popular with foreign buyers, it may be worthwhile using an overseas agent or advertising in foreign newspapers and magazines, such as the English-language publications listed in **Appendix A**.

Agents' Contracts: Before he can offer a property for sale, an agent must have a signed authorisation from the owner in the form of an exclusive or non-exclusive contract. An exclusive contract gives a single agent the right to sell a property, while a non-exclusive contract allows you to deal with any number of agents and to negotiate directly with potential buyers. Most people find that it's better to place a property with a number of agents under non-exclusive contracts. Exclusive contracts are rare and are for a limited period, e.g. three to six months. Choose an agent who regularly sells properties in your price range and enquire how the property will be marketed and who will pay the costs. See also **Estate Agents** on page 143.

Agents' Fees: When selling a property, the agent's commission is usually paid by the vendor and included in the purchase price. Fees vary from 2 to 5 per cent, according to the price of a property, and are lower with an exclusive contract than with a non-exclusive contract. Shop around for the best deal, as there's fierce competition among agents to sell good properties (many agents 'tout' for properties to sell by advertising in the expatriate press). **Note that if you sign a contract without reserving the right to find your own buyer, you must pay the agent's commission even if you sell your home yourself!** Make sure that you don't sign two or more exclusive contracts to sell your home – check the contract and make sure you understand what you're signing. Contracts state the agent's commission, what it includes, and most importantly, who must pay it. **Generally, you shouldn't pay any fees unless you require extra services and you should never pay the agent's commission before a sale is completed and you've been paid.**

Capital Gains Tax: If you're selling a second home in Cyprus, you may be liable for capital gains tax (see page 95). The first CY£50,000 profit is exempt, after which capital gains tax is payable at a flat rate of 20 per cent. **There's no capital gains tax on property in Greece.**

Warning: As when buying a home, you must be very careful who you deal with when selling a home. Make sure that you're paid with a certified banker's draft before signing over your property to a buyer; once the deed of sale has been signed, the property belongs to the buyer, whether you've been paid or not. **Be extremely careful if you plan to use an intermediary, as it isn't uncommon for a 'middle man' to disappear with the proceeds!** Never agree to accept part of the sale price 'under the table'; if the buyer refuses to pay the extra money, there's nothing you can do about it (at least legally). Sellers have been known to end up with no property *and* no money! All sales should be conducted through a lawyer.

5.

ARRIVAL & SETTLING IN

On arrival in Greece or Cyprus, your first task will be to negotiate immigration and customs. This presents few problems for most people, particularly European Union (EU) nationals. However, non-EU nationals visiting Cyprus for any purpose other than a holiday may require a visa (see page 18). Greece is a signatory to the Schengen agreement (named after a Luxembourg village on the Moselle River), which came into effect in 1994 and introduced an open-border policy between member countries. Other Schengen members include Austria, Belgium, France, Germany, Iceland, Italy, Luxembourg, the Netherlands, Portugal, Spain and Sweden. Under the agreement, immigration checks and passport controls take place when you first arrive in a member country, after which you can travel freely between member countries without further checks. Cyprus has associate member status of the EU and has applied to become a full member, which is expected to happen around 2003.

In addition to information about immigration and customs, this chapter also contains checklists of tasks to be completed before or soon after arrival in Greece or Cyprus and when moving house, plus suggestions for finding local help and information.

IMMIGRATION

When you arrive in Greece from a country that's a signatory to the Schengen agreement (see above), there are usually no immigration checks or passport controls, which take place when you first arrive in a Schengen member country. Officially, Greek immigration officials should check the passports of EU arrivals from non-Schengen countries (such as Britain and Ireland), although this doesn't always happen. If you're a non-EU national and arrive in Greece by air or sea from outside the EU, you must go through immigration for non-EU citizens. If you have a single-entry visa, it will be stamped by the immigration official. **If you require a visa to enter Greece or Cyprus and attempt to enter without one, you will be refused entry.** In any case, unless you're simply on holiday, it may be wise to ask for a stamp in your passport as confirmation of your date of entry into the country.

If you're a non-EU national coming to Greece or Cyprus to live, work or study, you may be asked to show documentary evidence. Immigration officials may also ask non-EU visitors to produce a return ticket and proof of accommodation, health insurance and financial resources, e.g. cash, travellers' cheques and credit cards. The onus is on visitors to show that they don't intend to breach the immigration laws – immigration officials aren't required to prove that you will breach the immigration laws and can refuse anyone entry simply on the grounds of suspicion. **Note that Greece will refuse entry to any foreigners, whatever their nationality, whose passport indicates that they've visited Northern Cyprus since November 1993.**

CUSTOMS

The Single European Act, which came into effect on 1st January 1993, created a single trading market and changed the rules regarding customs for EU nationals. The shipment of personal (household) effects to Greece from another EU country is no longer subject to customs formalities. EU nationals planning to take up permanent or temporary residence in Greece are permitted to import their furniture and personal effects free of duty or taxes, provided that they were purchased tax-paid within the EU or have been owned for at least six months. When moving to Greece or Cyprus, you should make a detailed inventory of your belongings (although it's unlikely that anyone will check your belongings) and provide the shipping company with a photocopy of your passport.

For further information about customs regulations, contact the Director of Customs, Ministry of Finance, 10 Karageorgi Servias Street, 10184 Athens (☎ 01-347 8706) or the Department of Customs and Excise, 29 Katsonis Street, Ay. Omoloyitae, 1440 Nicosia (☎ 03-865213).

Visitors

Visitors' belongings aren't subject to duty or VAT when they're visiting Greece or Cyprus for up to six months (182 days). This applies to the import of private cars (90 days in Cyprus), camping vehicles (including trailers or caravans), motorcycles, aircraft, boats and personal effects. Goods may be imported without formality, provided that their nature and quantity doesn't imply any commercial aim. All means of transport and personal effects imported duty-free mustn't be sold or given away and must be exported when a visitor leaves the country. If you cross into Greece by road you may drive slowly through the border post without stopping (unless requested to do so). However, any goods and pets that you're carrying mustn't be subject to any prohibitions or restrictions (see page 176). Customs officials may stop anyone for a spot check, e.g. for drugs or illegal immigrants.

If you arrive at a seaport by private boat, there are no particular customs formalities, although you must show the boat's registration papers on request. A vessel registered outside the EU may remain in Greece for a maximum of six months in any calendar year, after which it must be exported or imported (when duty and tax must be paid). Foreign-registered vehicles and boats mustn't be lent or rented to anyone while in Greece or Cyprus.

Residents

Greece: Non-EU nationals planning to take up permanent or temporary residence in Greece are permitted to import their furniture and personal effects free of duty or taxes, provided they've owned them for at least six months. An application form must be completed (available from Greek consulates), plus a detailed inventory of the items to be imported showing their estimated value in euros. All items to be imported should be included on the list, even if some are to be imported at a later date. These documents must be signed and presented to a Greek consulate with your passport. If you won't be present when your effects are cleared by customs in Greece, a photocopy of the principal pages of your passport is required.

If you use a shipping company to transport your belongings to Greece, the company will usually provide the necessary forms and take care of the paperwork. Always keep a copy of forms and communications with customs officials, both in Greece and in your previous country of residence. Note that if the paperwork isn't in order, your belongings may end up incarcerated in a customs storage depot for a number of months. If you personally import your belongings, you may need to employ a customs agent at the point of entry to clear them. You should have an official record of the export of valuables from any country, in case you wish to re-import them later.

Cyprus: Personal effects, household goods and furniture can be imported free of any taxes by immigrant retirees, including a car (retired couples are permitted to import two cars duty-free) under certain conditions. New items are subject to duty at various rates plus VAT at 10 per cent. Goods that you've owned for at least a year are exempt from duty provided that:

- they're for your own use;
- you haven't lived in Cyprus for more than 365 days in the last two years;
- you intend to settle permanently in Cyprus;
- you're present in Cyprus at the time the goods are imported.

To apply for an exemption from import duty, you must complete a *Customs Declaration* form (C102) and, if you're using an agent to clear your goods, an *Authority to Agent* form (C7).

A government levy, known as the temporary refugee levy (TRL), applies to all imported goods, whether new or used. The rate of 1.7 per cent is applied to the declared value or actual cost of new items and to a nominal value calculated by customs officials for used household goods and personal effects. (The insured or market value of used goods isn't taken into account.) You should expect to pay between CY£75 and 150 for a typical shipment. Some electrical items, including TVs, VCRs, washing machines, dryers, refrigerators and freezers, are liable to a separate charge, currently CY£5 per item.

Diplomatic personnel are exempt from duties and taxes, and the foreign employees of offshore companies may be permitted to import certain new items (excluding furniture, air conditioners, VCRs, cameras and carpets) free of duty and VAT, but TRL is still payable.

Prohibited & Restricted Goods

Certain goods are subject to special regulations, and in some cases their import and export is restricted or prohibited. This particularly applies to the following goods: animal products, plants, wild fauna and flora and products derived from them, live animals, medicines and medical products (except for prescribed drugs and medicines), firearms and ammunition, certain goods and technologies with a dual civil/military purpose, and works of art and collectibles. If you're unsure whether any goods you're importing fall into the above categories, you should check with the local customs authority.

Note that the import of illegal drugs (even small amounts) into Greece is a serious offence and offenders are liable to fines of up €300,000 and a prison sentence of between ten years and life!

FINDING HELP

One of the major problems facing new arrivals in Greece or Cyprus is how and where to obtain help with day-to-day problems, such as finding accommodation, schooling and insurance. This book will be a great help, but in addition to the information provided here you will need detailed *local* information. How successful you are at finding local help depends on the town or area where you live, e.g. residents of cities and resort areas are better served than those living in rural areas, your nationality, language proficiency, your employer (if you work) and your sex (women are usually better catered for than men through women's clubs).

There's an abundance of information available in Greece, but little in English and other foreign languages. There's much more information available in English in Cyprus. An additional problem is that much of the available information isn't intended for foreigners and their particular needs. You may find that your friends and colleagues can help, as they can often offer advice based on their own experiences and mistakes. **But take care!** Although they mean well, you're likely to receive as much false and conflicting information as accurate and helpful advice. (It may not be wrong but often won't apply to your situation or circumstances.)

Your town hall may be a good source of information, but you usually need to speak Greek (except in Cyprus) to benefit and may still be sent on a wild goose chase from department to department. A wealth of useful information is available in major cities and resort towns, where foreigners are generally well-served by English-speaking clubs and expatriate organisations. Contacts can also be found through many expatriate publications (see **Appendix A**), and many consulates provide their nationals with local information, including details of lawyers, translators, doctors, dentists, schools, and social and expatriate organisations.

CHECKLISTS

Before Arrival

The checklists on the following pages include tasks which you need (or may need) to complete before and after arrival in Greece or Cyprus and when moving your home permanently abroad.

● Check that your family's passports are valid.

● Obtain a visa, if necessary, for all members of your family (see page 18). Obviously this *must* be done *before* your arrival.

● Arrange health and travel insurance for your family (see pages 48 and 55). This is essential if you aren't covered by an international health insurance policy and won't be covered by local social security.

● If you don't already have one, it's prudent to obtain an international credit card or two, which will prove particularly useful abroad.

● Obtain an international driving licence, if necessary (see page 34).

- Open a local bank account (see page 79) and transfer funds. You can open an account with many Greek or Cypriot banks while abroad, although it's best done in person locally.
- Obtain some local currency before your arrival, which will save you having to queue to change money on arrival (and you will probably receive a better exchange rate).

If you plan to become a permanent resident you may also need to do the following:

- Arrange schooling for your children.
- Organise the shipment of your personal and household effects.
- Obtain as many credit references as possible, e.g. from banks, mortgage companies, credit card companies, credit agencies, companies with which you've had accounts, and from professionals such as lawyers and accountants. These will help you to establish a credit rating in Greece or Cyprus.

If you're planning to become a permanent resident, don't forget to take all your family's official documents with you. These may include birth certificates, driving licences, marriage certificate, divorce papers or death certificate (if a widow or widower), educational diplomas and professional certificates, employment references and curricula vitae, school records and student ID cards, medical and dental records, bank account and credit card details, insurance policies (plus no-claims records), and receipts for any valuables. You also need the documents necessary to obtain a residence permit plus certified copies, official translations and numerous passport-size photographs (students should take at least a dozen).

After Arrival

The following checklist contains tasks to be completed after arrival (if not done before):

- On arrival at the airport or port, have your visa cancelled and your passport stamped, as applicable.
- If you aren't taking a car with you, you may wish to rent (see page 127) or buy one locally. Note that it's difficult or impossible to get around in rural areas without a car.
- Open a cheque account (see page 79) at a local bank and give the details to any companies that you plan to pay by direct debit or standing order (such as utility and property management companies).
- Arrange whatever insurance is necessary such as health, car and household insurance.
- Contact offices and organisations to obtain local information (see page 179).
- Make courtesy calls on your neighbours and the local mayor within a few weeks of your arrival. This is particularly important in small villages and rural areas if you want to be accepted and become part of the local community.

If you plan to become a permanent resident, you will need to do the following within the next few weeks (if not done before your arrival):

- Apply for a residence permit.
- Apply for a social security card from your local social security office (in Cyprus, this applies only if you're working there).
- If necessary, apply for a local driving licence (see page 34).
- Find a local doctor and dentist.
- Arrange schooling for your children.

Moving House

When moving permanently to Greece or Cyprus there are many things to be considered and a 'million' people to be informed. Even if you plan to spend just a few months a year abroad, it may be necessary to inform a number of people and companies in your home country. The checklists below are designed to make the task easier and help prevent an ulcer or a nervous breakdown (provided you don't leave everything to the last minute). See also **Moving House** on page 156.

- If you live in rented accommodation, give your landlord adequate notice (check your contract).
- Arrange to sell or dispose of anything you aren't taking with you, e.g. house, car and furniture. If you're selling a home or business, you should obtain expert legal advice, as you may be able to save tax by establishing a trust or other legal vehicle. Note that if you own more than one property, you may have to pay capital gains tax on any profits from the sale of second and subsequent homes.
- Arrange shipment of your furniture and belongings by booking a shipping company well in advance (see page 156). Major international moving companies usually provide a wealth of information and can advise on a wide range of matters concerning an international relocation. Find out (from a local embassy or consulate) the exact procedure for shipping your belongings to Greece or Cyprus.
- If you're exporting a car, you will need to complete the relevant paperwork in your home country and re-register it locally after your arrival. Contact a local Greek or Cypriot embassy or consulate for information.
- Check whether you need an international driving licence or a translation of your national driving licence(s). Note that some foreigners are required to take a driving test before they can buy and register a car in Greece or Cyprus.
- Check whether you're entitled to a rebate on your road tax, car and other insurance. Obtain a letter from your motor insurance company stating your no-claims discount.
- Arrange inoculations and shipment for any pets you're taking with you (see page 60).
- You may qualify for a rebate on your tax and social security contributions. If you're leaving a country permanently and have been a member of a company or state pension scheme, you may be entitled to a refund or be able to continue

payments to qualify for a full (or larger) pension when you retire. Contact your company personnel office, local tax office or pension company for information.

- It's wise to arrange health, dental and optical check-ups for your family before leaving your home country. Obtain a copy of health records and a statement from your private health insurance company stating your present level of cover.

- Terminate any outstanding loan, lease or hire purchase contracts and pay all bills (allow plenty of time, as some companies are slow to respond).

- Return any library books and anything borrowed.

- Inform the following:
  - your employers, e.g. give notice or arrange leave of absence, or clients if you're self-employed;
  - your town hall or municipality (you may be entitled to a refund of your local property or income taxes);
  - the police, if it was necessary to register with them in your home country (or present country of residence);
  - your electricity, gas, water and telephone companies (contact companies well in advance, particularly if you need to have a deposit refunded);
  - your insurance companies (e.g. health, car, home contents and private pension), banks, post office (if you have a post office account), stockbroker and other financial institutions, credit card, charge card and hire purchase companies, lawyer and accountant, and local businesses where you have accounts;
  - your family doctor, dentist and other health practitioners (health records should be transferred to your new doctor and dentist abroad, if applicable);
  - your children's schools (try to give a term's notice and obtain a copy of any relevant school reports or records from your children's current schools);
  - all regular correspondents, social and sports clubs, professional and trade journals, friends and relatives (give them your new address and telephone number and arrange to have your mail redirected by the post office or a friend);
  - your local or national vehicle registration office if you have a driving licence or car, and return your car's registration plates if applicable.

- If you will be living abroad for an extended period (but not permanently), you may wish to give someone 'power of attorney' over your financial affairs in your home country so that he can act for you in your absence. This can be for a fixed or unlimited period and can be for a specific purpose only. **Note, however, that you should take expert legal advice before doing this!**

- Finally, allow plenty of time to get to the airport, register your luggage, and clear security and immigration.

Have a good journey!

APPENDICES

APPENDIX A: USEFUL ADDRESSES

Embassies

The lists below contain only embassies, which are located in the country capitals, but some countries also have consulates in other cities or resorts. These are listed in the Yellow Pages. Note that some countries have more than one office; therefore before writing or calling in person you should telephone to confirm that you have the correct office.

Greece

Embassies are located in Athens and its environs. The area code for Athens is 01 (not shown below).

Albania: 1 Karachristou Street, 115 21 Athens (☎ 723 4412).

Algeria: 14 Vas. Konstantinou Avenue, 116 35 Athens (☎ 726 4191–3).

Argentina: 59,Vas. Sofias Avenue, 115 21 Athens (☎ 722 4753, 722 4710).

Armenia: 159, Syngrou Avenue, 171 21 N. Smyrni (☎ 934 5727, 935 2187).

Australia: 37, D. Soutsou & 24, An. Tsocha Streets, 115 21 Athens (☎ 644 7303).

Austria: 26, Alexandras Avenue, 106 83 Athens (☎ 821 1036, 821 6800, 822 3067).

Bangladesh: 81, Akti Miaouli, 185 38 Piraeus (☎ 428 3315–7).

Belgium: 3 Sekeri Street, 106 71 Athens (☎ 361 7886–7, 360 7981).

Bolivia: 5 Korai Street, 146 71 Kastri (☎ 620 8324).

Brazil: 14 Filikis Eterias Square Kolonaki, 106 73 Athens (☎ 721 3039, 724 3444, 723 4450).

Bulgaria: 33A Stratigou Kalari Street, 154 52 P. Psychico (☎ 647 8105–8).

Cameroon: 180-182 Kifissias Avenue, 154 51 N. Psychico (☎ 672 4415).

Canada: 4 I. Genadiou Street, 115 21 Athens (☎ 725 4011).

Chad: 114 Alimou Street, 164 52 Argyroupoli (☎ 991 6523).

Chile: 25 Vass. Sofias Avenue, 106 74 Athens (☎ 725 2574).

China: 2A Krinon Street, 154 52 P. Psychico (☎ 672 3282).

Colombia: 3 Vrassida Street, 115 28 Athens (☎ 723 6848, 723 1420).

Costa Rica: 10 Gr. Lambraki Street, 166 74 Glyfada (☎ 968 0620–1).

Croatia: 4 Tzavela Street, 154 51 N. Psychico (☎ 677 7059, 677 7049, 677 7037).

Cuba: 5 Sofokleous Street, 152 37 Filothei (☎ 682 6638).

Cyprus: 16 Irodotou Street, 106 75 Athens (☎ 723 7883, 723 2727, 723 9377).

Czech Republic: 6 G. Seferis Street, 154 52 P. Psychico (☎ 671 3755, 671 9701, 672 5332).

Denmark: 11 Vas. Sofias Avenue, 106 71 Athens (☎ 360 8315).

Dominican Republic: 23 Evrou Street, 115 27 Athens (☎ 778 4381).

Ecuador: 6 Sotiros Street, 185 35 Piraeus (☎ 422 3800–4).

Egypt: 3 Vas. Sofias Avenue, 106 71 Athens (☎ 361 8612–3, 362 1905).

Finland: 1 Eratosthenous Street & Vas.Konstantinou Avenue, 116 35 Athens (☎ 701 1775, 751 4966, 751 9795).

France: 7 Vas. Sofias Avenue, 106 71 Athens (☎ 339 1000).

Gabon: 22 K. Paleologou Street, 104 38 Athens (☎ 523 6795).

Germany: 3 Karaoli Dimitriou Street, 106 75 Athens (☎ 728 5111).

Ghana: 367 Syngrou Avenue, 175 64 P. Faliro (☎ 938 0700).

Guatemala: 2 Karageorgi Servias Street, 105 62 Athens (☎ 323 8816).

Haiti: 5 Dimokritou Street, 106 71 Athens (☎ 361 0766).

Honduras: 122 Vas. Sophias Avenue, 115 26 Athens (☎ 778 2014).

Hong Kong: 13 Dimokratias Street, 151 27 Melissia (☎ 804 2896).

Hungary: 16 Kalvou Street, 154 52 P. Psychico (☎ 672 5337, 672 5994, 672 3753).

Iceland: 5 Paraschou Street, 154 52 P. Psychico (☎ 672 6154).

India: 3 Kleanthous Street, 106 74 Athens (☎ 721 6227, 721 6481).

Indonesia: 55 Papanastassiou Street, 154 52 P. Psychico (☎ 671 2737, 687 7991).

Iran: 16 Stratigou Kalari Street, 154 52 P. Psychico (☎ 647 1436, 647 1937, 647 9930).

Iraq: 4 Mazaraki Street, 154 52 P. Psychico (☎ 672 2330, 647 9690, 672 1566).

Ireland: 7 Vas. Konstantinou Avenue,106 74 Athens (☎ 723 2771–2, 723 8645).

Israel: 1 Marathonodromon Street, 154 52 P. Psychico (☎ 671 9530–1, 671 9773).

Italy: 2 Sekeri Street, 106 74 Athens (☎ 361 7260, 361 7263, 361 7273–5).

Ivory Coast: 13 Lykiou Street, 106 56 Athens (☎ 721 2375).

Japan: 2-4 Messogion Avenue, 115 27 Athens (☎ 775 8101–3).

Jordan: 30 P. Zervou Street, 154 10 P. Psychico (☎ 647 4161, 687 5618).

Korea (South): 1 Eratosthenous Street, 116 35 Athens (☎ 701 2122, 751 4328, 701 6997).

Kuwait: 27 Marathonodromon Street, 154 52 P. Psychico (☎ 647 3593–5).

Lebanon: 6 25th March Street, 154 52 P. Psychico (☎ 685 5873–4).

Liberia: 13 Vyronos Street, 154 52 P. Psychico (☎ 647 2120–2).

Luxembourg: 11-13 Skoufa Street, 106 73 Athens (☎ 364 3958, 364 0040).

Madagascar: 18 Dimitressa Street, Ilissia (☎ 724 2845).

Malaysia: 114 Alimou Street, 174 55 Argyroupolis (☎ 991 6523, 992 2774).

Maldives: 3-3A Kassandras Street, 185 33 Piraeus (☎ 422 4220–7).

Malta: 2 Efplias Street, 185 37 Piraeus (☎ 418 5715–6).

Mexico: 73A Diamantidou Street, 154 52 P. Psychico (☎ 647 5908, 647 0852, 647 2966).

Morocco: 14 Mousson Street, 154 52 P. Psychico (☎ 647 4209–10).

The Netherlands: 5-7 Vas. Konstantinou Avenue, 106 74 Athens (☎ 723 9701–4).

New Zealand: 24 Xenias Street, 115 28 Athens (☎ 771 0112).

Norway: 7 Vas. Konstantinou Avenue, 106 74 Athens (☎ 724 6173–4).

Pakistan: 6 Loukianou Street, 106 75 Athens (☎ 729 0214, 729 0122).

Panama: 42 Panepistimiou Street, 106 79 Athens (☎ 363 6121).

Paraguay: 2 Alopekis Street, 106 75 Athens (☎ 724 9511).

Peru: 105-107 Vas. Sofias Avenue, 115 21 Athens (☎ 641 1221, 641 1321).

Philippines: 26 Antheon Street, 154 52 P. Psychico (☎ 672 1837, 672 1883).

Poland: 22 Hrissanthemon Street, 154 52 P. Psychico (☎ 671 6917–8, 681 8394).

Portugal: 44 Karneadou Street, 106 76 Athens (☎ 729 0096, 729 0052, 724 5122).

Romania: 7 Emm. Benaki Street, 154 52 P. Psychico (☎ 671 8020, 671 8008).

Russia: 28 N Litra Street, 154 52 P Psychico (☎ 672 5235, 672 6130).

Saudi Arabia: 71 Marathonodromon Street, 154 52 P. Psychico (☎ 671 6911–3).

Slovakia: 4 Seferi Street, 154 52 P. Psychico (☎ 687 6757–8).

Slovenia: 10 Mavili Street, 154 52 P. Psychico (☎ 687 5683–5).

South Africa: 60 Kifissias Avenue, 151 25 Maroussi (☎ 680 6645).

Sudan: 44 Amalias Street, 105 58 Athens (☎ 331 3261–2).

Spain: 29 Vas. Sofias Avenue, 106 74 Athens (☎ 721 4885, 722 4242).

Sweden: 7 Vas. Konstantinou Avenue, 106 74 Athens (☎ 729 0421–4).

Switzerland: 2 Iassiou Street, 115 21 Athens (☎ 723 0364, 724 9208).

Syria: 61 Diamantidou Street, 154 52 P. Psychico (☎ 672 5577, 6725 575, 671 1604).

Taiwan: 57 Marathonodromon Street, 154 52 P. Psychico (☎ 687 6750).

Thailand: 23 Getou Street, 154 52 P. Psychico (☎ 671 7969, 671 0155).

Togo: 7 Filellinon Street, 105 57 Athens (☎ 323 0330).

Tunisia: 2 Antheon & Marathonodromon Street, 154 52 P. Psychico (☎ 671 7590, 6710 826, 674 9791).

Turkey: 8 Vas. Georgiou II St, 106 74 Athens (☎ 724 5915–7).

United Kingdom: 1 Ploutarhou Street, 106 75 Athens (☎ 723 6211).

United States of America: 91 Vas. Sofias Ave, 115 21 Athens (☎ 721 2951–9, 7218401).

Uruguay: 1c Likavitou Street, 106 72 Athens (☎ 360 2635, 361 3549).

Venezuela: 112 Vas. Sofias Avenue, 115 27 Athens (☎ 770 9962, 770 8769, 771 2709).

Yemen: 9 Patission Street, 104 31 Athens (☎ 522 0622, 524 5912).

Yugoslavia: 106 Vas, Sofias Avenue, 115 27 Athens (☎ 777 4355, 777 4344).

Zaire: 2 Ariadnis Street, 152 37 Filothei (☎ 687 6706).

Cyprus

Embassies are located in Nicosia (*Lefkosia*). The area code for Nicosia is 02 (not shown below).

Australia: Gonia Leoforou Stasinou & Annis Komninis 4, 2nd Floor, 1060 Nicosia (☎ 473001).

Bulgaria: Konstantinou Palaiologou 13, 2406 Egkomi, Nicosia (☎ 672486–7).

China: Archimidous 28, Egkomi, PO Box 24531,1300 Nicosia (☎ 352182).

Cuba: Giannaki Talioti 7, 2014 Strovolos, Nicosia (☎ 512332).

Czech Republic: Arsinois 48, Akropolis, PO Box 25202, 1307 Nicosia (☎ 421118).

Egypt: Leoforos Aigyptou 3, PO Box 21752, 1097 Nicosia (☎ 472626).

France: Ploutarchou 6, 2406 Egkomi, PO Box 21671, 1512 Nicosia (☎ 779910).

Germany: Nikitara 10, 1080 Nicosia, PO Box 21795, 1513 Nicosia (☎ 664362).

Greece: Leoforos Vyronos 8-10, PO Box 21799, 1513 Nicosia (☎ 441880/2, 511273).

Hungary: Prigkipissis Annis 13A, Agios Dometios, PO Box 24067, 1700 Nicosia (☎ 369074).

India: Indira Gkandi 3, Montparnasse Hill, Egkomi, PO Box 25544, 1310 Nicosia (☎ 351741, 351170).

Iran: Armenias 42, Akropolis, PO Box 28145, 2090 Nicosia (☎ 314459, 315896).

Israel: I. Grypari 4, PO Box 21049,1500 Nicosia (☎ 445195/6).

Italy: 25 Martiou 11, 2408 Egkomi, Nicosia (☎ 357635–6, 358112, 358258).

Lebanon: Vasilissis Olgas 1, 1101, Nicosia (☎ 774216).

Libya: Estias 14, PO Box 23669, 1685 Nicosia (☎ 317366, 317902–3).

Poland: Acharnon 11, 2027 Strovolos, Nicosia (☎ 427077).

Romania: Leoforos Tzon Kennedy 83, PO Box 22210, 1518 Nicosia (☎ 379303).

Russia: Gonia Agiou Prokopiou & Arch. Makariou III, Egkomi, PO Box 21845, 1514 Nicosia (☎ 774622).

Slovakia: Kalamatas 4, Akropolis, PO Box 21165, 1503 Nicosia (☎ 311683).

Switzerland: Themistokli Dervi 46, MEDCON Bldg., 6th floor, PO Box 20729, 663 Nicosia (☎ 766261).

Syria: Gonia Androkleous & Thoukydidou, PO Box 21819, 1513 Nicosia (☎ 474481–2).

United Kingdom: Alexandrou Palli, PO Box 21978, 1587 Nicosia (☎ 771131, 861100).

United States of America: Gonia Metochiou & Ploutarchou, Egkomi, 2406 Nicosia (☎ 776400, 776100).

Yugoslavia: Vasilissis Olgas 2, 1101 Nicosia (☎ 777511).

English-Language Newspapers & Magazines

Athens News, 3 Christou Lada, 10237 Athens (☎ 01-333 3555, 💻 http://athens news.dolnet.gr). Daily newspaper.

Cyprus Magazine, PO Box 45Y, London W1 45Y, UK. Bi-monthly magazine.

Cyprus Daily/Weekly, PO Box 21144, 1502 Nicosia, Cyprus (☎ 02-672074/670412, 💻 www.cynews.com).

Homes Overseas, Blendon Communications, 46 Oxford Street, London W1N 9FJ, UK (☎ 020-7636 6050, 💻 www.homesoverseas.co.uk). Bi-monthly property magazine.

Greek Gazette, 55 Westbourne Grove, London W2, UK (☎ 020-7727 1121).

Greek Tourist News, 39 Halandriou Street, Paradissos, 15125 Marousi, Athens (☎ 01-689 9400). Monthly tourist newspaper.

Greek Weekly News, 15 Averof, Polutechniou, 10433 Athens (☎ 01-825 0848).

International Homes, 3 St Johns Court, Moulsham Street, Chelmsford, Essex CM2 0JD, UK (☎ 01245-358877, 💻 www.internationalhomes.com). Bi-monthly magazine.

Resident Abroad, Subscriptions Department, PO Box 387, Haywards Heath RH16 3GS, UK (☎ 01444-445520). Monthly expatriate magazine.

World of Property, 1 Commercial Road, Eastbourne, East Sussex BN21 3XQ, UK (☎ 01323-726040, ✉ outbounduk@aol.com). Quarterly property magazine.

Miscellaenous

Greece

Automobile Association & Touring Club of Greece (ELPA), Athens Tower, 204 Messogion Avenue, 1527 Athens (☎ 01-779 1615).

British Hellenic Chamber of Commerce, 25 Vas Sofias Avenue, 10674 Athens (☎ 01-721 0493).

Director of Customs, Ministry of Finance, 10 Karageorgi Servias Street, 10184 Athens (☎ 01-347 8706).

Federation of Greek Industries, 5 Xenofontos Street, 10557 Athens (☎ 01-323 7325).

Federation of Overseas Property Developers, Agents and Consultants (FOPDAC), PO Box 3524, London NW5 1DQ, UK (☎ 020-8744 2362).

Greek Embassy, 2221 Massachusetts Ave., NW, Washington, DC 20008, USA (☎ 0202-939 5800).

Greek Embassy, 1A Holland Park, London W11 3TP, UK (☎ 020-7221 6467).

International Chamber of Commerce, 27 Kaningos Street, 10682 Athens (☎ 01-361 0879).

IKA, International Relations Office, IKA, Tmima Diethon Scheseon, 178 Kifissias Avenue, 15321 Athens (☎ 01-647 1140).

Ministry of Finance, Ypourgio Ikonomikon, Tmima Diethon Scheseon, 2-4 Sina Street, 10184 Athens (☎ 01-360 4825).

Ministry of Foreign Affairs, 1 Akadimias, 10671 Athens (☎ 01-361 0581).

Ministry of Labour, Ypourgio Ergassias, Tmima Diethon Scheseon, 40 Piraeus Street, 10182 Athens (☎ 01-522 9140/523 3111),

National Tourist Office of Greece, 4 Conduit Street, London W1R 0DJ, UK (☎ 020-7734 5997).

National Tourist Office of Greece, 645 Fifth Avenue, Olympic Tower, New York, NY 10022, USA (☎ 0212-4215777).

Cyprus

Central Bank of Cyprus, International Business Department, 80 Kennedy Avenue, PO Box 25529, 1395 Nicosia, Cyprus (☎ 02-394225, 🖥 www.centralbank.gov.cy, ✉ idoe@centralbank.gov.cy).

Centre for Overseas Retirement Studies, PO Box 3293, P. Lordos Centre, 1st Floor, Block B, Byron Street, Limassol, Cyprus (☎ 05-354371)

Cyprus Chamber of Commerce and Industry, PO Box 21455, 1509 Nicosia (☎ 02-669500).

Cyprus Embassy, 22110 R St., NW, Washington, DC 20008, USA (☎ 0202-462-5772).

Cyprus High Commission, 93 Park Street, London W1Y 4ET, UK (☎ 020-7499 8272).

Cyprus Real Estate Agents Association, PO Box 1455, Nicosia (☎ 02-449500).

Cyprus Tourist Office, 17 Hanover Street, London W1R 0AA, UK (☎ 020-7569 8800, ✉ ctolon@ctlon.demon.co.uk).

Cyprus Tourism Organisation, PO Box 24535, 1390 Nicosia (☎ 02-337715, 🖥 www.cyprustourism.org).

Cyprus Tourism Organization, 13 East 40th Street, New York, NY 10016, USA (☎ 0212-683-5280, ✉ gocyprus@aol.com).

Cyprus Trade Centre, 29 Princes Street, London W1R 7RG, UK (☎ UK 020-7629 6288).

Cyprus Trade Center, 13 East 40th Street, New York, NY 10016, USA (☎ 0212-213 9100).

Department of Customs and Excise, 29 Katsonis Street, Ay. Omoloyitae, 1440 Nicosia (☎ 02-865213).

Inland Revenue Department, Vyantiou – Argyrokastrou Streets, Strovolos, 1472 Nicosia (☎ 02-306807).

Migration Department, Dem. Severis Avenue, 1447 Nicosia (☎ 02-804533).

Ministry of Commerce, Industry and Tourism, 2A Araouzos Street, 1421 Nicosia (☎ 02-300805).

North Cyprus Tourist Office Representative, 29 Bedford Square, London WC1B 3EG, UK (☎ 020-7631 1920).

APPENDIX B: FURTHER READING

The books listed below are just a small selection of the many written for visitors to Greece and Cyprus. Note that some titles may be out of print, but may still be obtainable from book shops and libraries. Books prefixed with an asterisk (*) are recommended by the author.

Greece

General Tourist Guides

*AA Baedeker Greece (AA Publishing)

AA Essential Greece, Mike Gerrard (AA Publishing)

*Blue Guide: Greece, Robin Barber (A&C Black)

*Crete: The Rough Guide, John Fisher & Geoff Garvey (Rough Guides)

*DK Travel Guides: Greece, Athens & The Mainland (Dorling Kindersley)

*Eperon's Guide to the Greek Islands, Arthur Eperon (Pan)

Fodor's Greece (Fodor's)

*Frommers Greece (Macmillan Travel)

*Greek Island Hopping, Frewin Poffley (Thomas Cook)

*Greek Islands: The Rough Guide, Mark Ellingham & Others (Rough Guides)

*Greece: Off the Beaten Track, Marc Dubin (Moorland)

*Greece: The Rough Guide, Mark Ellingham, Mar Dubin & Others (Rough Guides)

*Insight Guide Crete (APA Publications)

*Insight Guide Greece (APA Publications)

Let's Go Greece & Turkey including Cyprus (Pan)

*Lonely Planet: Greece, David Willet, Rosemary Hall & Others (Lonely Planet)

Nelles Guide: Greece (Nelles Guides)

*The Rough Guide to Corfu, John Gill (Penguin)

*The Rough Guide to Rhodes, the Dodecanese & the East Aegean, Marc Dubin (Penguin)

A Visit to Greece, Peter & Connie Roop (Heinemann)

Visitors Guide to Athens & Peloponnese, Brian & Eileen Anderson (Moorland)

*Which Guide to Greece & The Greek Islands (Penguin)

Travel Literature

*Ebdon's Odyssey, John Ebdon

The Greek Islands, Lawrence Durrell (Penguin)

*An Island Apart, Sarah Wheeler (Abacus)

A Literary Companion to Travel in Greece, Richard Stoneman (OUP)

*My Family and Other Animlas, Gerald Durrell (Penguin)

The Olive Grove: Travels in Greece, Katherine Kizilos (Lonely Planet)

Reflections on a Marine Venus, Lawrence Durrell (Penguin)

*Stars Over Paxos, John Gill (Pavilion)

Travels in the Morea, Nikos Kazantzakis

Under Mount Ida: A Journey into Crete, Oliver Birch (Ashford)

*The Unwritten Places, Tim Salmon (Lycabettus)

Miscellaneous

Architecture of the World: Greece (Herron Books)

A Concise History of Greece, Richard Clogg (Cambridge UP)

**Buying a Home Abroad, David Hampshire (Survival Books)

The Foods of Greece, Aglaia Kremezi & Martin Brigdale (Stewart, Tabori & Chang)

Greece by Rail, Zana Katsikis (Bradt)

*Modern Greece: A Short History, C. M. Woodhouse (Faber & Faber)

*The Most Beautiful Villages of Greece and the Greek Islands, Mark Ottway & Hugh Palmer (Thames & Hudson)

The Mountains of Greece: A Walkers' Guide, Tim Salmon (Cicerone)

Pocket Menu Reader Greece (Langenscheidt)

*A Traveller's History of Greece, Timothy Boatswain & Colin Nicholson (Windrush)

*Trekking in Greece, Marc S. Dubin (Lonely Planet)

Wild Flowers of Greece, George Sfikas (Efstathiadís)

*The Wines of Greece, Miles Lambert-Gócs (Faber & Faber)

Cyprus

General Tourist Guides

*AA Baedeker Cyprus (AA Publishing)

AA Essential Cyprus, Robert Blumer (AA Publishing)

AA Explorer Cyprus, George McDonald (AA Publishing)

Berlitz Pocket Guide to Cyprus (Berlitz)

*Blue Guide: Cyprus, Bernard McDonagh & Ian Robertson (A&C Black)

Cyprus, Barnaby Rogerson (Cadogan)

Cyprus (Nelles Guides)

*Cyprus: The Rough Guide, Marc Dubin (Rough Guides)
Globetrotter Travel Guide to Cyprus, Paul Harcourt Davies (New Holland)
*Insight Guide Cyprus (APA Publications)
Landmark Visitors Guide: Northern Cyprus, K. Gursoy & L. Smith (Landmark)
*Lonely Planet: Cyprus, Paul Hellander (Lonely Planet)
*North Cyprus, Diana Darke (Bradt)
*Northern Cyprus, John & Margaret Goulding (Windrush Press)
Thomas Cook Traveller Cyprus (AA Publishing)
Visitors Guide to Cyprus, Fiona Bulmer (Moorland)

Miscellaneous

*Bitter Lemons of Cyprus, Lawrence Durrell (Faber)
Cyprus in Colour, Georges Kyriakou (KP Kyraikou)
The Cyprus Conspiracy, Brendan O'Malley & Ian Craig (IB Tauris)
Cyprus and its People, Vangelis Calotychos (Westview Press)
*Cyprus: Ethnic Conflict and International Politics, Joseph S. Joseph (Macmillan)
Cyprus: Divided Island (World in Conflict), Tom & Thomas Streissguth (Lerner)
*The Cyprus Revolt, Nancy Cranshaw
The European Union and Cyprus, Christopher Brewin (Eothen Press)
The Flora of Cyprus, R.D. Meikle (Bentham-Moxon Trust)
The Floral Charm of Cyprus, Sinclair (Interworld)
Footprints in Cyprus, Sir David Hunt (Trigraph)
*Journey into Cyprus, Colin Thubron (Penguin)
Nature of Cyprus, Christos Georgiades
Plant Checklist for Cyprus, Lance Chilton (Merengo)
The Republic of Cyprus, Kypros Chrysostomides (Martus Nijhoff)
Taste of Cyprus, G. Davies (Interworld)
Traditional Greek Cooking from Cyprus and Beyond, Julia & Xenia Chrysanthou (Olivetree)
*Walking in Cyprus, Donald Brown (Cicerone)
Walks in Western Cyprus, Lance Chilton (Marengo)
*Wines of Cyprus, Giovanni Mariti (Nicolas Books)

APPENDIX C: WEIGHTS & MEASURES

Greece and Cyprus use the metric system of measurement. Nationals of a few countries (including the Americans and British) who are more familiar with the imperial system of measurement will find the tables on the following pages useful. Some comparisons shown are only approximate, but are close enough for most everyday uses. In addition to the variety of measurement systems used, clothes sizes often vary considerably with the manufacturer (as we all know only too well). Try all clothes on before buying and don't be afraid to return something if, when you try it on at home, you decide it doesn't fit (most shops will exchange goods or give a refund).

Women's Clothes

Continental	34	36	38	40	42	44	46	48	50	52
UK	8	10	12	14	16	18	20	22	24	26
USA	6	8	10	12	14	16	18	20	22	24

Pullovers

	Women's						Men's					
Continental	40	42	44	46	48	50	44	46	48	50	52	54
UK	34	36	38	40	42	44	34	36	38	40	42	44
USA	34	36	38	40	42	44	sm	medium	large			xl

Note: sm = small, xl = extra large

Men's Shirts

Continental	36	37	38	39	40	41	42	43	44	46
UK/USA	14	14	15	15	16	16	17	17	18	-

Men's Underwear

Continental	5	6	7	8	9	10
UK	34	36	38	40	42	44
USA	small	medium		large	extra large	

Children's Clothes

Continental	92	104	116	128	140	152
UK	16/18	20/22	24/26	28/30	32/34	36/38
USA	2	4	6	8	10	12

Children's Shoes

Continental	18	19	20	21	22	23	24	25	26	27	28	29	30	31	32
UK/USA	2	3	4	4	5	6	7	7	8	9	10	11	11	12	13

Continental	33	34	35	36	37	38
UK/USA	1	2	2	3	4	5

Shoes (Women's and Men's)

Continental	35	35	36	37	37	38	39	39	40	40	41	42	42	43	44	44
UK		2	3	3	4	4	5	5	6	6	7	7	8	8	9	9	10
USA			4	4	5	5	6	6	7	7	8	8	9	9	10	10	11	11

Weight

Avoirdupois	Metric	Metric	Avoirdupois
1 oz	28.35 g	1 g	0.035 oz
1 pound*	454 g	100 g	3.5 oz
1 cwt	50.8 kg	250 g	9 oz
1 ton	1,016 kg	500g	18 oz
1 tonne	2,205 pounds	1 kg	2.2 pounds

* A metric 'pound' is 500g, g = gramme, kg = kilogramme

Length

British/US	Metric	Metric	British/US
1 inch	2.54 cm	1 cm	0.39 inch
1 foot	30.48 cm	1 m	3 feet 3.25 inches
1 yard	91.44 cm	1 km	0.62 mile
1 mile	1.6 km	8 km	5 miles

Note: cm = centimetre, m = metre, km = kilometre

Capacity

Imperial	Metric	Metric	Imperial
1 pint (USA)	0.47 litre	1 litre	1.76 UK pints
1 pint (UK)	0.57 litre	1 litre	0.26 US gallons
1 gallon (USA)	3.78 litre	1 litre	0.22 UK gallon
1 gallon (UK)	4.54 litre	1 litre	35.21 fluid oz

Square Measure

British/US	Metric	Metric	British/US
1 square inch	0.45 sq. cm	1 sq. cm	0.15 sq. inches
1 square foot	0.09 sq.m	1 sq. m	10.76 sq. feet
1 square yard	0.84 sq. m	1 sq. m	1. 2 sq. yards
1 acre	0.4 hectares	1 hectare	2.47 acres
1 square mile	259 hectares	1 sq. km	0.39 sq. mile

Temperature

° Celsius	° Fahrenheit	
0	32	freezing point of water
5	41	
10	50	
15	59	
20	68	
25	77	
30	86	
35	95	
40	104	

Note: The boiling point of water is 100°C / 212°F.

Oven Temperature

Gas	Electric	
	°F	°C
-	225–250	110–120
1	275	140
2	300	150
3	325	160
4	350	180
5	375	190
6	400	200
7	425	220
8	450	230
9	475	240

For a quick conversion, the Celsius temperature is approximately half the Fahrenheit temperature.

Temperature Conversion

Celsius to Fahrenheit: multiply by 9, divide by 5 and add 32.
Fahrenheit to Celsius: subtract 32, multiply by 5 and divide by 9.

Body Temperature

Normal body temperature (if you're alive and well) is 98.4° Fahrenheit, which equals 37° Celsius.

APPENDIX D: MAPS

The map of Cyprus below shows the regions of Cyprus and major cities. The map of Greece opposite shows the regions of Greece (listed below). A map of the eastern Mediterranean is shown on page 6.

Attica (including Athens)

Central Greece (Stereá Ellhada and Thessaly)

Crete

Cyclades Islands

Dodecanese Islands

Epirus and the West

Evia and the Sporades

Ionian Islands

North-eastern Aegean Islands

Northern Greece (Macedonia and Thrace)

Peloponnese

Saronic Gulf Islands

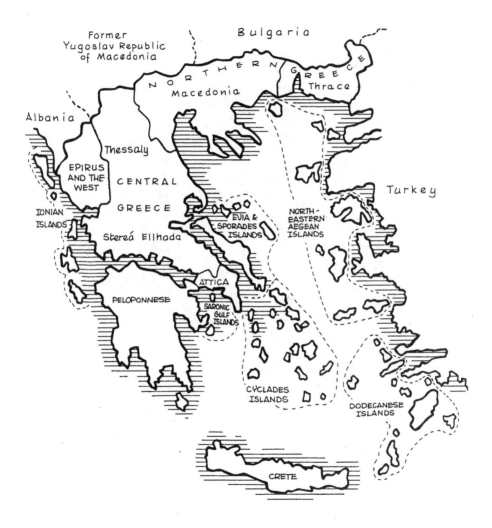

INDEX

SUGGESTIONS

Please write to us with any comments or suggestions you have regarding the content of this book (preferably complimentary!). We are particularly interested in proposals for improvements that can be included in future editions. For example, did you find any important subjects were omitted or weren't covered in sufficient detail? What difficulties or obstacles have you encountered which aren't covered here? What other subjects would you like to see included?

If your suggestions are used in the next edition of *Buying a Home in Greece and Cyprus*, you will receive a free copy of the Survival Book of your choice as a token of our appreciation.

NAME: _____

ADDRESS: _____

_____

_____

Send to: Survival Books, PO Box 146, Wetherby, West Yorks. LS23 6XZ, United Kingdom.

My suggestions are as follows (please use additional pages if necessary):

BUYING A HOME ABROAD

Buying a Home Abroad is essential reading for anyone planning to purchase property in Ireland and is designed to guide you through the jungle and make it a pleasant and enjoyable experience. Most importantly, it is packed with vital information to help you avoid the sort of disasters that can turn your dream home into a nightmare! Topics covered include:

- Avoiding Problems
- Choosing the Region
- Finding the Right Home & Location
- Estate Agents
- Finance, Mortgages & Taxes
- Home Security
- Utilities, Heating & Air-conditioning
- Moving House & Settling In
- Renting & Letting
- Permits & Visas
- Travelling & Communications
- Health & Insurance
- Renting a Car & Driving
- Retirement & Starting & Business
- And Much, Much More!

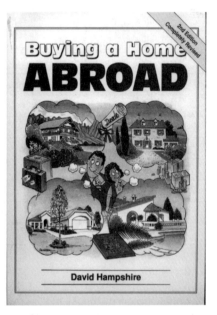

Buying a Home Abroad is the most comprehensive and up-to-date source of information available about buying property abroad. Whether you want a detached house, townhouse or apartment, a holiday or a permanent home, this book will help make your dreams come true.

Buy this book and save yourself time, trouble and money!

Order your copies today by phone, fax, mail or e-mail from: Survival Books, PO Box 146, Wetherby, West Yorks. LS23 6XZ, United Kingdom (☎/🖨 +44 (0)1937-843523, ✉ orders@ survivalbooks.net, 💻 www.survivalbooks.net).

ORDER FORM – ALIEN'S / BUYING A HOME SERIES

Qty.	Title	Price (incl. p&p)*			Total
		UK	Europe	World	
	The Alien's Guide to America	Autumn 2001			
	The Alien's Guide to Britain	£5.95	£6.95	£8.45	
	The Alien's Guide to France	£5.95	£6.95	£8.45	
	Buying a Home Abroad	£13.45	£14.95	£16.95	
	Buying a Home in Britain	£13.45	£14.95	£16.95	
	Buying a Home in Florida	£13.45	£14.95	£16.95	
	Buying a Home in France	£13.45	£14.95	£16.95	
	Buying a Home in Greece & Cyprus	£13.45	£14.95	£16.95	
	Buying a Home in Ireland	£13.45	£14.95	£16.95	
	Buying a Home in Italy	£13.45	£14.95	£16.95	
	Buying a Home in Portugal	£13.45	£14.95	£16.95	
	Buying a Home in Spain	£13.45	£14.95	£16.95	
	Rioja and its Wines	£13.45	£14.95	£16.95	
	The Wines of Spain	£14.45	£15.95	£17.95	
				Total	

Order your copies today by phone, fax, mail or e-mail from: Survival Books, PO Box 146, Wetherby, West Yorks. LS23 6XZ, UUK (☎/▤ +44 (0)1937-843523, ✉ orders@survivalbooks.net, 🖳 www.survivalbooks.net). If you aren't entirely satisfied, simply return them to us within 14 days for a full and unconditional refund.

Cheque enclosed/please charge my Delta/Mastercard/Switch/Visa* card

Card No. _ _ _ _ _ _ _ _ _ _ _ _ _ _ _ _

Expiry date_____ **Issue number (Switch only)** _____

Signature _____ **Tel. No.** _____

NAME _____

ADDRESS _____

_____

_____

* Delete as applicable (price includes postage – airmail for Europe/world).

LIVING AND WORKING IN AMERICA

Living and Working in America is essential reading for anyone planning to spend some time there including holiday-home owners, retirees, visitors, business people, migrants, students and even extraterrestrials! It's packed with over 500 pages of important and useful information designed to help you **avoid costly mistakes and save both time and money.** Topics covered include how to:

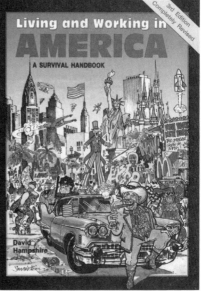

- find a job with a good salary & conditions
- obtain a residence permit
- avoid and overcome problems
- find your dream home
- get the best education for your family
- make the best use of public transport
- endure motoring in America
- obtain the best health treatment
- stretch your dollars further
- make the most of your leisure time
- enjoy the American sporting life
- find the best shopping bargains
- insure yourself against most eventualities
- use post office and telephone services
- do numerous other things not listed above

Living and Working in America is the most comprehensive and up-to-date source of practical information available about everyday life in America. It isn't, however, a boring text book, but an interesting and entertaining guide written in a highly readable style.

Buy this book and discover what it's *really* like to live and work in America.

Order your copies today by phone, fax, mail or e-mail from: Survival Books, PO Box 146, Wetherby, West Yorks. LS23 6XZ, United Kingdom (☎/▤ +44-1937-843523, ✉ orders@survival books.net, ▣ www.survivalbooks.net).

ORDER FORM – LIVING & WORKING SERIES

Qty.	Title	Price (incl. p&p)*			Total
		UK	Europe	World	
	Living & Working Abroad	£14.95	£16.95	£20.45	
	Living & Working in America	£14.95	£16.95	£20.45	
	Living & Working in Australia	£14.95	£16.95	£20.45	
	Living & Working in Britain	£14.95	£16.95	£20.45	
	Living & Working in Canada	£14.95	£16.95	£20.45	
	Living & Working in France	£14.95	£16.95	£20.45	
	Living & Working in Germany	£14.95	£16.95	£20.45	
	Living & Working in Holland, Belgium & Luxembourg	£14.95	£16.95	£20.45	
	Living & Working in Ireland	£14.95	£16.95	£20.45	
	Living & Working in Italy	£14.95	£16.95	£20.45	
	Living & Working in London	£11.45	£12.95	£14.95	
	Living & Working in New Zealand	£14.95	£16.95	£20.45	
	Living & Working in Spain	£14.95	£16.95	£20.45	
	Living & Working in Switzerland	£14.95	£16.95	£20.45	
				Total	

Order your copies today by phone, fax, mail or e-mail from: Survival Books, PO Box 146, Wetherby, West Yorks. LS23 6XZ, UK (☎/▤ +44 (0)1937-843523, ✉ orders@survivalbooks.net, ▣ www.survivalbooks.net). If you aren't entirely satisfied, simply return them to us within 14 days for a full and unconditional refund.

Cheque enclosed/please charge my Delta/Mastercard/Switch/Visa* card

Card No. _ _ _ _ _ _ _ _ _ _ _ _ _ _ _ _

Expiry date_____ **Issue number (Switch only)** _____

Signature _____ **Tel. No.** _____

NAME _____

ADDRESS _____

_____

_____

* Delete as applicable (price includes postage – airmail for Europe/world).